Jaber F. Gubrium
David R. Buckholdt

Toward Maturity

Jossey-Bass Publishers

San Francisco • Washington • London • 1977

TOWARD MATURITY
The Social Processing of Human Development
by Jaber F. Gubrium and David R. Buckholdt

JACKET DESIGN BY WILLI BAUM

FIRST EDITION

Code 7711

The Jossey-Bass
Behavioral Science Series

THE AUTHORS

Jaber F. Gubrium is associate professor of sociology, Marquette University. He received the Ph.D. in sociology from Wayne State University in 1970. Gubrium has done extensive research on the social organization of patient care in a nursing home, which resulted in his recent book *Living and Dying at Murray Manor.*

David R. Buckholdt is associate professor of sociology, Marquette University. He received the Ph.D. in sociology in 1969 from Washington University. Together with Robert Hamblin and others, he has conducted studies on the social contexts of learning in public schools. He is a co-author of *The Humanization Processes.*

Gubrium and Buckholdt are currently studying the practice of professional decision making in a residential treatment center for emotionally disturbed children.

*For Aline, Erika, Michael, and Mark, who,
in their own way, are wise to the
world and its schemes*

Preface

The aim of this book is to present a radically new approach to what is conventionally called "human development." It is a sociology of life change that treats matters such as life stages, growth, and maturity as a kind of ordinary language that people use to organize the meaning of their lives over time.

The common practice of human scientists is to take the existence of development or the life cycle for granted. They view it as a stagelike, unfolding process with a beginning, a middle, and an end. An early period (childhood or adolescence) precedes a middle one (middle age), which in turn is replaced by a late period (old age). In this view, the crucial problems are, first, to identify the characteristics of persons in the various stages and, second, to locate the mechanisms that either facilitate or hinder movement from one stage to another.

An alternative approach, the one we take here, is unconventional in that we do not assume that life inherently cycles in some ordered or progressive fashion. Rather, the important questions for us are what ideas are held about the advance of life, how do people use these ideas to construct and control each other's lives in terms of time, and how do they come to think and talk about movement from one stage of life to another. The "truths" about life change become what people believe and say about it and how these beliefs and such talk accomplish human development—lifework—rather than the conventional notion of a relatively inflexible and inevitable stage-like developmental process. For example, coming of age is a matter of who convinces whom that someone is now "really mature," for all practical purposes.

Age-related expectations are created by members of society as they interact with one another on varied occasions. They share ideas about what is real and what is false, practical theories about age and behavior in relation to themselves and others. As a collection of people who deal with each other in the affairs of everyday life, they talk about growth, age, maturity, regression, and the like. The meaning of age is presented and negotiated from moment to moment as people participate in sometimes elusive but serious conversation. Through statements like "act your age," "look how grown-up he is," and "you're too old for that kind of work," people invoke life-course expectations and thus make age. When they are convincing, a life may seem to cycle. When they are not, a life seems problematic until a proper definition of age is secured.

We are, of course, giving the terms *life stage, growth, maturity,* and the like very general connotations. This stems from our view that such terms do not specify particular and well-defined features of the life course but, rather, are ways of describing any behavior that people judge to be relevant to life change. Such terms are the very stuff of the practical rhetoric that people present to each other as they go about the business of making sense of growth and change in their lives.

Life change occurs in multiple settings. In one situation a person may be convincingly old and in another, deliberately young. In a matter of moments, life not only changes, but changes in an unconventional order! Moreover, the appropriate age-definition of self in a situation is not simply given. In any circumstance, the question, "How old or mature am I, or are you, or are we?" must be resolved before meaningful dealings can begin. Only then do members carry on what they believe is their proper business.

By saying that chronological time does not provide an automatic or universal criterion for age and maturity, we do not mean to suggest that life and human development are a thicket of wide-awake, calculated negotiations for those involved in it. Actually, for the most part, the business of settling age is considered to be rather trivial by its participants. The rub comes, for them, when the "trivial" becomes overtly problematic. For example, when an elderly person pursues sexual pleasures or when the young child demands freedom to make choices or to pursue personal interests, it becomes painfully but only fleetingly, and certainly not ontologically, obvious what the life cycle is—but only at that time, in that place.

This book, then, presents ways that participants in the age-related affairs of everyday life accomplish what in a very general sense is maturity and immaturity. A new approach to the life cycle is needed. It is time we ceased to take human development for granted. After all, who is it other than us—all of us—who accomplish change in human lives?

Chapter One contrasts our approach to life change with seven conventional approaches (behavioral, psychoanalytic, cognitive, covert personality, symbolic interactionist, functional, and psychocultural). We briefly introduce our social phenomenological view of life in explaining why we categorize these as conventional. Our purpose here is to set the background for the development of the theme of life change as a matter of social negotiation and accomplishment.

Chapter Two turns, first, to the assumptions that underlie a social phenomenological approach to life change. Second, like any new conception that significantly diverges from ongoing approaches to a subject, social phenomenology has a number of terms with special connotations. We note some important ones (*member, accomplishing, practical rationality, glossing, background expectancies*) and discuss their meanings. This provides a working vocabulary for subsequent chapters in which we address select concrete issues of life change, ranging from the way people "predict" growth to how they reconstruct biography (or the life course).

Chapter Three is concerned with people's deliberations about whether they are on or off a normal life course. The main question here is how do people accomplish or not accomplish normal life change, for themselves, with others, and for others.

We use people's *time-orientation* in accomplishing life change to organize the next three chapters. On occasion, people speak of life and life change in terms of what they might become at some future time. They talk of predicting the course of life or a select stream of it such as success in school. This is the topic of Chapter Four, which we have entitled "Predicting Growth." At times, people are concerned with present readiness for change. They consider whether or not someone is ready, mature, or competent enough to be treated as a member of the next stage in human development. They virtually talk themselves into or out of maturity. This is the topic of Chapter Five, "Negotiating Competence." In Chapter Six—"Reconstructing Biography"—we focus on people as they take a past orientation to life change. The question here is how do people invoke or revoke reinterpretations of how they have come to live as they do, and what sorts of contingencies affect success or failure in this.

Finally, in Chapter Seven, we briefly address three general issues that concern the kind of human science that is implied by taking a point of view like our own toward life change.

Acknowledgments

We are grateful to Albert Jache, Dean of the Graduate School, and the Committee on Research, Marquette University, for the continued support they provided to the authors while researching and writing this book. A number of colleagues, friends, and students helped us to develop our ideas. Special thanks go to Daniel Ferritor, William Henry, John O'Neill, Anselm Strauss, and Norbert Wiley for their comments and incisive criticisms. We also thank Shelley Buckholdt for her able and expeditious assistance and Suzanne Gubrium for caustic optimism.

Milwaukee, Wisconsin   Jaber F. Gubrium
February 1977   David R. Buckholdt

Contents

Toward Maturity

*The Social Processing
of Human Development*

Chapter One

Some Conventional Approaches to Life Change

Concern with patterns of personal life change is certainly not new. The idea, its dimensions, and uses are probably as old as self-conscious human life itself. Both ancient historical documents and the recorded oral history of existing preliterate peoples show evidence of thought about it. Human living is considered to have a temporal character in that, in some manner, it changes from birth to death.

The theme of change in human living is, of course, quite general. Beyond this, it has been embellished and provided with any number of variations from one society or group to another. Birth and death may be considered merely the visible endpoints of an earthly lifetime beyond which it is assumed there are

1

other forms of pre- and post-living existence. Or birth and death might simply be treated as the tragic bounds of earthly hell. The birth-to-death portion of life has assumed different characteristics. In some cases, it is believed to have a linear course, growing progressively either negative or positive as one approaches death. In other cases, it is thought to be more nearly curvilinear and to cycle, proceeding from some fairly well delineated point, digressing from it, and eventually returning to its place of origin. Regardless of variation, the general theme is change over a lifetime.

The theme of change in life over time and variations on that theme usually refer to what happens to most people, not merely to a single individual. Life is encountered as a series of changes, changes that are expected normally to present themselves in the lives of all individuals who constitute the people whose lives flow in that fashion.

Aside from not being new, concern with life change is socially widespread. It is part of both lay and academic interest in patterns of change in personal living. In any group of people who live a common way of life, there are likely to be thoughts and behavior that reflect themes of general, expected changes in living for its members. Among academics who claim to be concerned with patterns of change in human living, there has been an abundance of thinking about themes of life change and their variations. The difference between lay and academic interest is not that one is greater than the other, but rather that lay concern tends to be part and parcel of thoughts and actions related to the practical problems of life change, while academic concern typically is believed to focus either on the thoughts and actions of laypersons concerning matters of life change or on more general social or maturational forces that may affect life change but may be only dimly recognized by laypersons. The thoughts of laypersons are contained in ideas and attitudes while the thoughts of academics come in more formal models and theories.

Out of the widespread historical and intellectual range of concern with life change, we shall address ourselves only to a narrow portion in this book. First of all, we shall not focus primarily on the history or anthropology of life change. Philippe Ariès (1962, 1974), for one, has admirably dealt with the history of childhood and death in the Western world while a number of anthropologists have used conceptions of the life cycle to organize ethnographic materials (Benedict, 1934; DuBois, 1944; Kiefer, 1974; Kluckhohn and Murray, 1948; M. Mead, 1928, 1930). Second, this is not the report of a survey of popular conceptions of the life cycle or of the comparative value that laypersons place on varied portions of it. A fairly large literature on popular conceptions and evaluations of the life cycle and its alleged stages exists and continues to grow, among others, at the hands of social gerontologists investigating current and changing attitudes toward age and aging (see Riley and Foner, 1968, chap. 14). Rather, we are concerned with a radical alternative to current conventional thinking about life change.

A number of approaches to life change exist in the human sciences. Some are more directly aimed at life change than others. Among these are many subvarieties. Perhaps the most explicit approaches can be found in psychology. Less explicit are approaches or models suggested by life course-related theorizing in sociology and psychological anthropology. The psychologists stress patterning and continuity in life change through the use of such terms as *development, growth,* and *maturation.* Sociologists and anthropologists, on the other hand, are more likely to speak of the subjective problems of structured continuity or discontinuity in socialization and the life course. Some approaches to life change limit their concern with life to the overt activity of a subject while others define life to be a matter of language and its subjective meaning for one or more persons. In some approaches, change as such is treated as more basic than its patterns. In others, certain specified patterns of change are treated as basic, normal forms around which other patterns "deviate."

Our aim both concerns and grows out of these conventional approaches to life change. This book lays the groundwork for a new, social phenomenological approach to it. This involves at least two tasks. First, it is important to take note of how a social phenomenological approach generally differs from more conventional treatments. We shall take this up in this chapter.

Second, in this and the remaining chapters, we shall elaborate the problematic and the varied dimensions of the new approach.

It should be emphasized that ours is not simply *the* phenomenological approach to life change. Like other intellectual traditions, phenomenology has its internal variations. Although all its forms, in one way or another, suspend belief in or deliberately doubt the reality of what are believed to be hard, constraining, influencing, socializing, or inherent life worlds separate from their members, some are more or less social than others. The work of Alfred Schutz (1962; 1964; 1967), in developing the social and phenomenological implications of Max Weber's (1947) theory of action, set the foundation for what might be called social phenomenology. Social phenomenology also has come to have its own variations. Some go by that name; others imply it: existential sociology (Manning, 1973); ethnomethodology (Garfinkel, 1967; Turner, 1974); phenomenological sociology (Psathas, 1973), and humanistic sociology (P. L. Berger, 1963). Our approach to life change is informed by each of these. At times, it is phenomenological in that it documents the subjective meaning of life presented in individual or collective expressions. At other times, it is ethnomethodological in that it is concerned with the methods by which people constitute what are collectively meaningless objects and events into what comes to be accepted as intersubjectively (socially) meaningful.

The Meaning of Conventional

We have referred to the collection of current approaches to life change in the human sciences as "conventional." This is not meant to be pejorative. Rather, we believe that, although these approaches have certain important differences, they are similar in one critical respect: In one sense or another, their views of life change are based on conventional (popular) beliefs about the positive reality of life change—life change, its sources, and its consequences are believed to be *things* separate from the subjects who experience them. The ways in which the several approaches develop this belief are what distinguish them, but the fact that they all accept it distinguishes them from social phenomenology. Let us briefly elaborate the difference between conventional and social phenomenological approaches.

In doing their work, conventional human scientists deal with two worlds of meaning. One is their own, as scientists, as it relates to the subjects of their research. This world is an analytic one. It includes assumptions about the nature of the subject, schemes by which to order and possibly explain behavior, and accepted rules of proof. The other world of meaning is that of their subjects as it relates to the research interests of the scientists. This is the empirical world. It may include things ranging from individuals' motives, personal investments, and self-images to their social statuses, norms that constrain them, and their institutional context. The relevant dimensions of the empirical world depend on the particular approach to it taken by the scientist.

These two worlds of meaning meet in many places as part of scientific research. For example, the two cross in the credence that their respective members (scientific researchers and subjects) give to objects and events in each other's worlds. At this point, we are not concerned with the credence that subjects give to objects and events in the analytic world of scientists, albeit this is not a matter currently being taken lightly in the human sciences. For example, it is the subject of debate about the "demand characteristics" of experimental subjects and "social desirability" effects (Phillips, 1973) in surveys composed of wide-awake, face-to-face interviews. Subjects remedy their behavior to conform to what they believe is proper in research situations (see Gubrium, 1976). Rather, we limit our comments to the credence that human scientists *analytically* give to objects and events in the subjects' world. It is an analytic difference in such credence that distinguishes conventional and phenomenological approaches to life change.

We are giving the term *world of everyday life* a special meaning. Egon Bittner (1973, pp. 119-120) put it this way:

> It is important to emphasize that the term 'world of everyday life' refers to a zone of reality that is not limited, as the term might be mistakenly taken to imply, to the ordinary,

routine, broadly common aspects of existence from which the
rare, the celebrated, the dramatic have been excluded. The feature that defines the world of everyday life is not its familiar-
ity—familiar though it surely is!—but that it is the zone in
which '*my* life takes place,' the zone in which '*my* presence is
actually located.' There exist certain other 'realities' (finite
provinces of meaning), as we all know, but '*this one is my
home*' . . . It is impossible to overestimate the *centrality of the
subject* for the phenomenal constitution of the world of everyday life.

In the world of everyday life, people think about and act as if
such entities as maturity, normal living, jobs, prestige, institutions, and social class were real things. It is evident in their talk
when they speak of "now being of age to do this or that,"
"what people would think," "the constraints of my job," "the
prestige of the rich," "institutional demands," or "what a difference money makes." When the human scientist considers
such entities, he may choose to treat them as realistically as his
subjects do or set aside his belief in them as things separate
from subjects. This is a reasonable choice since as we look at
and listen to people act and speak about their lives and what
they consider to be life's realities, two contradictory things
seem equally apparent. On the one hand, we "know" that people themselves speak of the realities of things such as social
norms, maturity, motives, prestige, and social class. They believe that such things affect their lives and they act accordingly.
As a matter of fact, human scientists, as plain people, behave
likewise. However, on the other hand, when we search people's
lives in order to find and "touch" the things which they speak
of and sometimes agonize over, we seem unable to locate the
things save for the references that people make to them as they
speak of such things. Faced with this paradox, we are forced
either to accept realities like the above ones as people do and
give them scientific status as such, or to set aside our belief in
them as things separate from people's sense of and reference to
them. Conventional human science treats at least some of them
in the same way that subjects do. Social phenomenology suspends belief in (brackets) their existence as things real and separate from people's language and actions.

For example, in the first instance, we might research the impact on worker stress of the differential norms of membership in traditional, extended families and highly mobile occupations. In the second instance, we might research the sense that workers make of what they speak of as stress as they refer to expert or commonsense knowledge of institutions, this sense varying according to what is accepted as knowledge in particular situations.

The approach taken is important in that it affects the way a human scientist does his work. In accepting the conventional (popular) reality of such entities as maturity, jobs, prestige, institutions, and class, the conventional human scientist makes propositions about their possible effects on people. He then may proceed to measure the empirical relations between those entities he considers theoretically significant, with appropriate adjustments for extraneous effects. Depending on his findings, he concludes that he has reason to believe that such entities are related in one way or another, for example, that social class affects one's personal values or that it affects the speed at which one's life cycles over such stages as socialization, accomplishment, and disengagement in any sphere of living. Conventional social science uses popular language and popular conceptions of life's realities to construct its own conceptual schemes and arguments; it then attempts to validate them in a popular world (see Filmer and others, 1972).

Social phenomenological research differs radically from the conventional approach. It makes no propositions about the possible effects of such entities as maturity, jobs, prestige, institutions, and class on people, for it sets aside belief in them (brackets them) as things separate from what people sense and say. It does not prejudge the reality of their existence in the world of everyday life. Rather, the important question is how do members of the world of everyday life collectively negotiate, come to accept, and settle on such "entities" as real, independent of themselves, and somehow subject to their fate? To negotiate is to tacitly and collectively entertain, interpret, and evaluate any number of practical "theories" of entities in order to deal with them as things—negotiation is the practical politics of everyday life. On some occasions, it is particularly visible, as in plea bargaining, psychotherapeutic engagement, and scientific criticism; on other occasions, it is fleeting and subtle, as in casual banter about the alleged decline in the morality of today's youth. The reality of entities is a product of people's treatments of their existence. Of central concern are the social processes by which people come to have a sense of maturity, social class, public opinion, social order, normality, and the like. These processes are best observed in people's talk of and about such "things." Maturity, for example, is a way of speaking about whether one has arrived at some point in life or come of age. As a matter of fact, documenting the situated emergence of such talk makes visible the processes by which all of these allegedly extrasubjective conventions are collectively realized by people as "things."

Our primary attitude toward the world is much like the state of mind of someone who looks at the world as containing members of situations, their practical sociological problems, and their ordinary talk. Social order, being continually problematic for members, emerges out of members' successes or failures in completing their collectively situated business. The references of their talk, for members, are serious and well-known things (serious argument, serious humor, serious sarcasm, serious frivolity about this thing or that). It is belief in the references of this seriousness—such as the things we listed above—that social phenomenologists set aside, treating them as problematic, asking the general question of how it is that people, in common, come to treat the entities of, and order in, their lives as real from one occasion to another.

Our point of view differs radically from that of a psychoanalyst, for example, in the appreciation and examination of how persons respond to change in their lives and how they proceed through life stages. For us, change, stages, and development have no existence save what people make of them in talk and deed. The important questions are not how people *respond to* life change or *proceed through* stages, but how they negotiate and generate the reality and meaning of change, stages, and development; how they come to have a sense of them as things separate from themselves (contrast Durkheim, 1950); and how they subsequently respond to them as real things. The very order that conventional human scientists take for granted—in this case, life stages—social phenomenology makes problematic.

Some Conventional Approaches to Life Change

We have suggested above the sense in which approaches to life change are considered conventional. Let us expand this discussion in relation to seven kinds of conventional treatment: behavioral, psychoanalytic, cognitive, covert personality, symbolic interactionist, functional, and psychocultural. These conventional approaches cut across disciplinary lines. Some are contained within the traditional bounds of psychology (behavioral, cognitive, covert personality), others within sociology (symbolic interactionist, functional). The psychoanalytic approach could be categorized as either psychiatric or psychological. The psychocultural approach may be included among the disciplines of anthropology and psychiatry. Each of the approaches has varied both in the problems with which it has concerned itself and in its empirical breadth. For example, psychoanalysis grew from a discipline concerned mainly with the affective dynamics of the psyche to become one that, among some practitioners, deals mainly with ego processes. Behaviorists have varied in the extent to which they have been concerned with learning as a common feature of all behaving creatures or only with human learning with its symbolic features. Each approach has its pioneers, elaborators, or revisionists. Among these are: Pavlov, Watson, Hull, Miller, Skinner, and Bandura (behavioral); Freud and Erikson (psychoanalytic); Piaget, Loevinger, and Kohlberg (cognitive); Neugarten and Gutmann (covert personality); George Herbert Mead, Cooley, Blumer, Becker, Strauss, and Rose (symbolic interactionist); Durkheim, Parsons, and Merton (functional); and Kardiner, Benedict, and Margaret Mead (psychocultural).

We have listed seven conventional approaches and quite a few names. This serves merely to locate the approaches. We shall deal only with the bare-bones flavor of each, thus not outlining a detailed history of thinking about life change and development as each sees them but, rather, emphasizing their conventional features and features that distinguish one approach from another. As we shall see, some conventional treatments, in some ways, come close to a social phenomenological approach while in other ways are quite distinct from it.

Behavioral Approach. The behavioral approach has been poorly named by its advocates. The approach cannot be defined simply in terms of an exclusive concern with visible or observable behavior. Certainly, some behaviorists have eschewed the products of mind as inappropriate subject matter for scientific study. For them, only outward, visible behavior can be studied objectively. Other behaviorists, however, have expanded the empirical referents of *behavior* to include symbolic activity, such as modeling (Bandura, 1969).

What has come to distinguish the behavioral from other approaches, however, is not so much its empirical focus, for, to be sure, other approaches also are concerned with such symbolic activity as modeling. Rather, its critical distinguishing feature is the kind of treatment that behaviorists give to these and other empirical referents. Behavior to the behaviorists is any activity, directly visible or otherwise, that can be treated as objective and predictably reactive to various kinds of stimuli, which, in turn, may also be behavior. There is no need to limit the empirical content of stimuli. It may include anything that objectively and predictably can affect the activity of those who behave.

The empirical world of the behavioral approach is considered to have two prime components: behaving entities or respondents and stimulating objects or stimuli. The first, whatever its species, exists as a real entity to be changed or not, while the second is taken to be a real source of change or stability. The empirical world is considered to have a certain kind of logic. This has been given a variety of names, the two most famous of which are conditioning and reinforcement. This logic links response and stimulus.

Given this treatment of behavior, what sense do behaviorists make of life change or of a life course or cycle? Although from a behavioral point of view it is unnecessary to limit our answer to human behavior, we shall do so nonetheless, since our comparisons in this chapter deal with treatments of human life change.

Given human beings who over time respond to a variety of objects and events (stimuli) in their daily lives, they come to be virtual *products* of reinforcement contingencies. When the contingent, reinforcing properties of objects and events are patterned (not randomly occurring) over the lifetime of individuals, there is some course to life. Life progresses in a linear fashion if reinforcement contingencies continually produce new behavior patterns that never repeat established patterns. Life cycles, on the other hand, if reinforcement contingencies create conditions that existed previously. When reinforcement contingencies are not well patterned, ensuing lives are without course or cycle, though not necessarily without change. Other variations may also occur, depending on the reinforcement schedule of a person or group of people.

Behaviorists make no claims about the reality of a life course or cycle separate from the reinforcement contingencies that affect living. Life may or may not cycle. There is no stipulation that life should do either, since cycling or being on course is theoretically rather trivial. It may, however, be a vivid empirical by-product of the relation between behavior and the variety of positive and negative stimuli affecting it.

Although from a behavioral viewpoint, the business of whether a life course or cycle exists is trivial, this evaluation does not extend to life change. As a matter of fact, the issue of change or modification (to use a familiar term) is foremost in the minds of behaviorists. Life change is considered to be more general than the life course or life cycle. As will be shown later, some conventional approaches partially reverse this so that certain forms of life change become special (often deviant) instances of "normal" life cycling.

Because behaviorists insist on using such concepts and terms as *response, stimulus, reinforcement,* and *modification,* they are often accused of systematically eliminating the possibility for human beings of "making their own lives." The usual accusation is that behaviorists eliminate human freedom, treating human beings like machines. Such accusations have not

rarely come from more so-called humanistic psychological quar-
ters. Ironically, however, in a sense, the behavioral insistence on
limiting patterning in human lives to a contingent and amoral
feature of the empirical world maximizes the possibility of
human freedom. It is as if behaviorists were saying, "Change,
yes, and any way you would have it." Strangely, the insistence
on basic or "normal" life patterning in some form (whether a
course, a cycle, a number of stages, or whatever) precludes the
possibility of human beings normally "making their lives"
otherwise—even before we try to understand them *in vivo*.

Psychoanalytic Approach. The psychoanalytic approach
is dramatically different from the behavioral one. Although it
certainly is concerned with change in individual lives over time,
it goes beyond this and specifies basic, normal patterning in
such change. There is nothing in the behavioral approach that,
in principle, necessitates delineating between normal and abnormal change. Rather, change to behaviorists is a predictive outcome of variations in reinforcement contingencies and sched-
ules. All change is taken as given, with no judgments made
about its normality.

In the behavioral approach, we have seen that the source
of change is located in reinforcement contingencies. Individuals
do not change themselves, except for variations in sensitivity to
stimuli, which complicate the behavioral paradigm by providing
for feedback effects. Psychoanalytic theorists, however, find
that the sources of change vary over the normal lifetime of the
person, initially being located in inherent psychobiological
growth and subsequently becoming a product of the meaningful
relations between dynamic components of the psyche.

The newborn human being is assumed to be a biological
entity with structurally undifferentiated psychological energy.
He lives and does very little that is noticeably patterned except
the activity that is associated with a satiated or unsatiated state
of biological needs. When he is biologically unsatiated, the
neonate is active until satisfaction of his "demands"—which he
presumably experiences as pleasurable.

Not much can be said about the psychic state that exists in
this newborn, other than that it appears to be closely tied to the
infant's biological apparatus and that its principal mode of oper-

ation seems to be the attainment of pleasure and avoidance of pain—a kind of psychobiologically gratifying (psychosexual) entity. Freud named this original entity and mechanism an "it" (id)—rather appropriate, it seems, for something that is minded and yet not consciously known to itself.

Given the bond between infant psychology and human biology, changes in the one are affected by changes in the other. What the infant becomes over time, psychologically, is a function of changes in the psychosexual importance of his body. This importance is considered to be sequentially patterned such that, at or about certain chronological ages, different areas (zones) of the body provide the focal point of psychosexual development. As the child grows bodily, his psychic apparatus develops. Since the one is usually sequential, so is the other.

The psychosexual emergence of body zones occurs in the following sequence: oral, anal, and finally phallic. Psychosexual development is at first focused around oral and anal gratification. When the infant realizes that gratification is contingent on the affairs of a world other than his immediate body, the original psychosexual apparatus is partially transformed into an entity that deals with contingencies external to itself. Part of the id becomes rational and, being so, is immediately also reflective and aware of itself. Thus, biological growth spawns the growth of consciousness.

At this point, human life has made one major change. The behaving apparatus has been transformed from a rather simple gratifying entity to one that includes the capacity to rationally act upon itself and its world. The transformation is biologically rooted and emerges over time.

Subsequently, objects of pleasure shift from those that satisfy bodily needs, such as food and elimination, to those that serve the ends of a genitally activated (phallic) need for sexual possession. Freud assumes that when the activated genital involved is a penis, normal possession for the child most readily involves his mother. When a vagina is involved, the father is desired. Certainly, Freud was not unaware of the variety of other possible familial sources of sexual gratification, but, in the Freudian approach, these are categorized as abnormal.

With the "classic" completion of these early stages of development, a mind emerges. It is fully structured and ready to deal with the world, potentially able to become one of its normal adult members.

From here on, there are certainly other stages. Erik Erikson's (1950) eight stages, ranging over the life span, are an example. Their development is believed now to be sufficiently independent of the body to allow for more purely psychological treatment. Although bodily factors are taken to be potentially critical, psychoanalysts do not turn to the body as such in analysis but, rather, to the meanings of the body and the early or present developmental issues that these meanings pose for the person. Thus, analysis is not a biological but, rather, an ego involvement with the person.

From a psychoanalytic viewpoint, life changes take two important routes. One course of development is a product of the normal resolution of gratification problems at various psychobiological stages. The other includes courses of development that emerge out of abnormal resolutions. Not only does life change for everyone, but it also has its appropriate course. Life changes that deviate from a normal course are pathological.

The psychoanalytic treatment of life change is more structured than that of the behavioral approach. Besides change, the psychoanalytic approach delineates normal direction. This value judgment limits human freedom much more than the behaviorists do. In effect, what the psychoanalysts are virtually saying is, "Change, yes, but properly only my way."

The psychoanalytic approach treats the following conventional notions as real: life change, the life course, stages, and normal development. Psychoanalysts investigate and theorize about how people *respond to* change, how they *proceed through* stages, and how they resolve or do not resolve psychosexual issues in normal or abnormal development.

Because the classic psychoanalytic approach considers the psychic apparatus as such to be a product of the psychosexual contingencies of early biological growth, further development is treated, in principle, as epiphenomenal. Whatever happens in early life to the growth of the psyche affects all further development. The course of human life is largely set in the earliest years of living. From then on, it basically emerges—sometimes normally, sometimes not.

Cognitive Approach. Jean Piaget is a central figure of the cognitive approach to life change. His approach focuses on intelligence, as he refers to it. There are two central questions of development here: Are there different, basic forms of thinking (intelligence) about the world, its objects, and events? Are these sequentially part of human development? Answers to these questions have certain affinities with both the behavioral and psychoanalytic approaches to life change.

Piaget has been concerned chiefly with cognitive changes in children, although he has considered and delineated the structures of children's intelligence in their own right, elaborating them as epistemological systems. Piaget's research with children involves careful observation and attention to their behavior and their verbal descriptions of objects and events. He makes his observations in a variety of "casual" experiments. His experiments focus on the sense that children of various ages make of commonplace circumstances they face or are faced with.

Piaget is interested in how children define the bounds of objects, the relations between them, and their relations to other objects. For example, in one famous experiment, water is poured from a short, squat beaker into a tall, thin one in front of a child. The child is then asked which beaker has more water in it. The young child (about two to about seven years) claims that they differ in quantity, sometimes saying the tall one has more and sometimes the short one, depending on whether he has centered his attention on the relative height or breadth of the beakers. The older child (about seven to about eleven years), however, says that they have equal amounts of water. In another experiment (the three-mountain problem), a child is seated at one side of a four-sided table around which there are four chairs. On the table are three cones, one of which is larger than the other two. The experimenter places a doll in one of the chairs and asks the child to draw the mountains (cones) as the doll sees them. The young child cannot draw them from the doll's perspective but portrays the cones as he himself sees them. The older child can systematically represent on paper the perspective of the doll when it is seated in any of the positions around the table.

From these and other experiments, Piaget concludes that there is a developmental aspect to cognition. The young child (post-sensori-motor) conceives of the world as a container of objects without an operational logic. A quantity of water that changes shape is a different amount. Everyone's three mountains are the same as his own. It is inferred that these kinds of "mistakes" could only occur if thought were not readily detachable from its personal viewpoint (decenterable). It is as if the young child thinks about objects and events in front of him without being able to think about his own thoughts. This cognition is called preoperational.

The older child sees as well as notices the transformation in a constant amount of water. He also shows evidence of being able to consider and report the doll's perspective in positions other than his own. The ability to do so is a matter of re-cognition, namely, he separates viewpoints from his immediate perspective. The older child perceives and reports on objects and events in front of him as well as considers what his own thoughts would be in a different relation to concrete objects and events. This cognition is called concrete operational.

The oldest child (about twelve and older) enters still another cognitive stage. Now his attention to and consideration of objects and events are not limited to their concrete presence. The child is increasingly capable of abstract reasoning. His thinking is more hypothetical than before so that he now considers alternative strategies of action in relation to hypothetical objects and events. In effect, he is now capable of theoretically (formally) addressing his world.

To the extent that the cognitive approach treats early life changes in intelligence as stagelike, it has affinities with the psychoanalytic approach. Stages by definition are ordered, so that one comes before another but not the reverse. The cognitive approach takes stages of intelligence to be sequentially ordered in childhood.

Movement from stage to stage in the psychoanalytic approach is a psychosexual process. Development is urged on, as it were, by the growing and changing biological sensitivities of the child. Movement from one stage of intelligence to another in the cognitive approach is more a matter of experience, both physical and social. In this respect, it has affinities with the behavioral approach to life change.

Piaget conceives of development as a process of equilibrium occurring between the child and his environment. The process is two-sided. On the one hand, there is assimilation. This is part of the equilibrating process in which new objects and events are integrated into a cognitive scheme, be it preoperational, concrete, or formal. On the other hand, there is accommodation. This part of the process is cognitively adjustive. As a result of encounters with new objects and events, the child may "see through and to" a new level of cognitive growth.

New experiences of all sorts challenge the child. By dealing with them (either through assimilation or accommodation), he settles his cognitive affairs (equilibrates) with their challenges. When challenged, perhaps the easiest kind of settlement is to assimilate. Although the child may be momentarily annoyed by its perversity, he accepts the challenge and works it into his existing mode of thinking about the world. This process may be somewhat forced. With other experiences and an increasing number of challenges, assimilation becomes a trying tactic. The child is likely to begin seeing the world as having another, more general perspective. When it becomes his own, he is said to have accommodated, having moved on to another mode of intelligence.

The process of cognitive change is somewhat closer to the behavioral conception of change than to the psychoanalytic conception. First of all, both cognitive and behavioral approaches emphasize experience as the catalyst of change. One calls the process equilibration; the other calls it learning. (Of course, there are differences, too; for example, the cognitive approach treats the subject as more active in the process than does the behavioral approach.) Second, in some sense, both new experiences in relation to a scheme of intelligence and new experience resulting from novel reinforcers operate (that is, lead to change or stability) like simple economies. New experiences are not accommodated, on the one hand, nor do they reinforce, on the other, unless on balance they are sufficiently annoying or enticing to warrant investment in new cognition or behavior.

The equilibration argument for cognitive growth is reminiscent of Thomas Kuhn's (1962) theory of scientific revolutions. The kind of revolutions of which Kuhn speaks are basic theoretical ones. He refers to these basic theories as paradigms. They are basic in that they are the logical and operational outcomes of accepting some as opposed to other assumptions about the universe (see also Gouldner, 1970, and Friedrichs, 1970).

According to Kuhn, most scientific activity occurs as normal science. In normal science, a paradigm (theory and method) from which the empirical world is examined remains fixed. Data are generated and given meaning by the paradigm (compare *assimilation*). This continues to occur even though some findings (anomalies) tend to challenge the existing paradigm's assumptions about the natural world. When challenges become too expensive (unresolvable) to assimilate, a crisis occurs. Science moves to accommodate anomalies by raising the question of whether or not there is a more economical way to deal with the world. This is the beginning of scientific revolution and imminent paradigm shift (compare *accommodation*).

Kuhn's argument is a rather felicitous one in that, like a "good" scientist, he is a respecter of the ultimate sanctity of the empirical world. He underemphasizes the sociopolitical relations between scientists themselves, whose "schools" and academic interests may be at stake in so-called scientific revolutions and thereby be a critical factor in their success or failure. (Kuhn attempts to give these sociopolitical factors greater weight in a 1969 Postscript to his original essay by referring to the "community structure" of science.) The same underemphasis of sociopolitical factors is a feature of Piaget's theory of equilibration. Like Kuhn, he ignores the contingencies of social interaction between the child and others as they might affect the way in which the child's experience is considered to be appropriately encountered, thus making him feel comfortable or annoyed with the way he sees and reports things. Piaget does not systematically investigate whether there are social circumstances that are more likely to "accommodate" one form of intelligence or another, thereby possibly making for oscillation rather than development in everyday cognition.

From a cognitive point of view, the status of pattern in change is similar to the status it has in the psychoanalytic approach. At certain approximate chronological ages, children are likely to be *at* a certain stage of intelligence. They are considered to move *from* one *to* another. Thus, it is theoretically reasonable to investigate the impact that a certain kind of intelligence has on performance in casual experiments. Types of intelligence, cognitive stages, and their developmental sequence are real entities, separable from performance.

Covert Personality Approach. Another approach to life change that conceives of it as having a fairly distinct course is one recently elaborated by Neugarten, Gutmann, and others (see Neugarten, 1968, chaps. 6, 10, 14, 17, and 49). They distinguish between two levels of personality dynamics. Covert processes are not considered to be immediately in awareness and do not directly enter into the performance of social acts. These may be measured indirectly through the use of projective techniques. Gutmann uses Thematic Apperception Test (TAT) cards and tell-a-story techniques in a variety of cultural contexts from the Maya to the Druze (Gutmann, 1967 and 1976). Overt processes are conscious to the person and are the ways that the person expresses himself in daily life.

These researchers have found that covert personality processes have a life course. There are three fairly distinct stages, which typify the covert life of persons in early, middle, and late adulthood. These are called mastery styles. They represent the ways persons, over their lifetime, unwittingly conceive of and deal with themselves in relation to the outer world. The first stage is one of active mastery. Here, the person emphasizes the controlling force of self over the outer world. The second stage is passive mastery. In this stage, the person comes to terms with himself in relation to his world through active accommodation. The third stage, which is typical of elderly adults, is magical mastery. Here, the person regresses to imaginary, noninstrumental kinds of accommodation with his world.

Development from one stage to the next is not based on early psychosexual change as it is in the psychoanalytic approach. Nor is change a matter of the equilibrating contingencies of experience in the way that Piaget conceives of cognitive growth. Rather, shifts in mastery styles are assumed to be intrinsic properties of getting older.

Since the developing stages of covert personality are intrinsic properties of aging, they are considered to be universal. Projective studies have been conducted in a variety of cultures from seminomadic to urban/industrial. Data are interpreted to show that the three postulated covert mastery styles vary with age across cultures. This relationship exists despite differences in activeness or prestige associated with the kinds of roles persons play over time.

The developmental course and its stages of mastery, as described by covert personality theorists, are not matters of human choice. They are, rather, intrinsic to aging and independent of personal control. Persons are said to go *through* these natural stages as they grow older. Covert mastery styles, in turn, serve as explanations for the kinds of persons that people come to be from early to late adulthood.

Symbolic Interactionist Approach. With symbolic interactionism we encounter an approach to life change that does not traditionally fall within or near the disciplinary bounds of psychology. It has been and continues to be typically a sociological concern, perhaps primarily because interactionists treat as meaningless any minded entity save that which is socially sensible.

Take the business of mental illness. Of the approaches we have discussed already, only the psychoanalytic theoretically deals with it, by distinguishing between the normal and abnormal. In their work, psychoanalytic (and psychiatric) clinicians look for personal symptoms of abnormality, diagnose them, and finally prescribe or undertake a plan of treatment. Behaviorists, by contrast, cannot *theoretically* distinguish between mental illness and health. However, in practice, they put learning principles to work in modifying publicly delineated "bad habits" (the practical, behavioral analogue of mental illness or personal pathology) in the service of agencies that desire such an approach. The cognitive and covert personality approaches, likewise, make little or no theoretical distinction between mental health and illness.

Consider the difference that an interactionist's social definition criterion makes in his treatment of mental illness compared to how it is psychoanalytically conceptualized. Although there may be mentally aberrant forms of behavior in the world, they are not socially significant until someone is labeled as aberrant. Socially significant mental illness is considered to be a product of successful social definition and social enforcement.

Given the interactionist treatment of meaning in human behavior, a whole range of developmental issues becomes meaningless. Life change, for instance, is understandable only as a product of others' definitions of it. Likewise, what is normal in the course of personal change over a lifetime is meaningless except as it is socially defined.

It is not impossible to have a well-patterned course of life or life cycle in this approach. In fact, symbolic interactionists allow for the existence of any number of natural, normal, abnormal, or pathological life courses. This is a matter of *others'* definitions or constructions of the long-term behavior in question.

So far, our comments have emphasized the socially shaping side of the interactionist approach to life change. This sort of emphasis brings it close to the behaviorists' treatment of life change except that behaviorists do not limit their concern with shaping to acting, social others as such in the subject's everyday world but, rather, see social others and things as potential modifiers of behavior through planned intervention.

There is another, equally important, side to the symbolic interactionist approach, namely, the subject's side. He is conceived as actively involved in searching his social world (others) for interpretation of his actions. Except for those meanings found in others' responses (meaningful gestures, language, and the like) to his actions, a person's behavior is meaningless to himself. The self is conceived as an entity that is constantly searching and testing the social waters for significant direction.

This activeness and reflectivity theoretically eschew a simple, socially shaping view of life change; they provide for deliberate human error, any number of social emergents, and a variety of changes and reconstructions all in the very same life.

At base, then, symbolic interactionism is a dualistic approach to life change. On the one hand, it postulates a striving, meaning-seeking self that looks toward others for definition and direction. This is the more psychological side of the approach, albeit a distinctly social psychological side. On the other hand, it postulates worlds of meaning that vary in their structuredness. Some are quite fleeting and could be thought of as elementary collective behavior (compare Blumer, 1969). Others are quite well crystallized and routine. Patterns of routine action are called roles when they refer to single actors, and institutions when they involve a plurality of roles.

How do symbolic interactionists make sense of the order in the course of lives? They do this in two ways. One is related to the self and its activity in the world of daily living. The other is related to the way the self becomes socially structured.

Becker (1960, 1964) relates empirical order in the course of living to the situational adjustments and commitments of the self. Because the self is, dialectically, both a socially defined and an active entity, as it moves from social situation to social situation, it produces a multifaceted awareness of the meanings of its action. In one situation, it may be mirrored as one entity, while in another it may reflect something rather different. As symbolic interactionists might put it: I see "me" like this in one situation and "me" like that in another.

In the process of gaining knowledge of and dealing with itself from one situation to another, the self (or I) "invests" itself. For example, as a by-product of being billed as a brand new Ph.D. ready to be launched into the academic and intellectual world, a person is likely to invest in the accouterments of such a role. He may cultivate academic friendships, which may replace his predoctoral ones. Or he may settle down in "respectable" academic housing, rather than graduate student, communal living. These are side-bets or investments that he makes as part of the value he places (given that he does) on his academic position. The gradual, often unwitting accumulation of side-investments generates what appears to be personal consistency by a certain circle of others significantly involved in them.

The consistency that is a by-product of personal social investments leads to order over a lifetime. Out of life changes that are generated by situational adjustments emerges a life course or career. A career, like symbolic interactionism, is a two-sided affair. It is both active (or self-imposed) and passive (or socially defined). Personal side-betting emphasizes the former.

Order in life change, as we have suggested, is also a product of social structuredness. Some areas of social life are more structured than others. Entry into some career lines may entail a rigid life course. This is perhaps most evident in careers that are integral parts of bureaucratic institutions. In such cases of life change, structured side-bets capture the process of life patterning better than self-investment (Becker and Strauss, 1956).

Strauss (1959) speaks of structured life patterning as "coaching." The idea is akin to socializing agent. In the process of building a career, a person submits himself to a variety of agents (either persons or teams) who, in effect, coach him (guide him) toward some socially appropriate capacity and presence. Coaches throttle their expectations of the person's behavior so as to allow for the reasonable mistakes of a novice while encouraging the backslider to live up to his own professed goals. The business of coaching is rather delicate, for again, like symbolic interactionism itself, it treads the uneasy line between the self-autonomy of the person being socialized, on the one hand, and social definition, on the other.

Rose (1965a, 1965b) distinguishes another kind of social structuring that orders life change. This he calls subcultures of age. Subcultures are fairly well insulated ways of living, maintained within some wider cultural context. A gang or a social class might be thought of as a subculture existing within, for example, American or British society. Rose suggests that the social meaning of age may be tied to the changing age subcultures that people enter as they grow older. Thus, what is otherwise thought of as a life cycle may be a matter of lifelong adjustments in self-definitions that progress with age, for most people, along a well-patterned sequence of ways of living.

From a symbolic interactionist point of view, it is proper to speak of a person as *entering upon* certain situations, committing himself *to* one situated definition of self rather than another, and having *a* career. In theory, symbolic interactionists emphasize the process by which life change becomes structured, assuming there is some meaningful condition of life toward which "becoming" is oriented, but which is constructed through others.

Functional Approach. Sociological functionalism, especially Parsons' (1951) brand, differs from the symbolic interactionist approach to life change in that its conceptual apparatus is not basically two-sided, giving separate but equal credence to self and society. Rather, its language is limited to concepts that refer to value-integrated social systems and their parts. Its focus, consequently, is not on how the self manages to work through the web of social life, but on how the web (as a dynamic, functioning system of parts) happens to shape people into socially functioning components.

When functionalists describe and study socialization, they speak of and report on a different world of data than do symbolic interactionists. Functional socialization provides for no personal autonomy or reciprocity between self and society (Gouldner, 1959b). Self is passive, social systemic stuff. It is often spoken of in terms of the actor, but its properties are more aptly connoted by the term *role player*.

From a strict functional point of view, socialization is a process of life change in which presocial (either primary, in which human beings learn the rudiments of social life, or secondary, in which they learn how to play roles in select areas of life) human beings learn to *internalize* social expectations, both evaluative and behavioral. All well-socialized life change is a matter of the proper, personal internalization and expression of social values.

In one respect, the functional approach to life change is similar to the psychoanalytic. Both define what proper life change is. Both are expressly normative theories of living. What to psychoanalysts is either normal or psychopathological, to the functionalist is either functional or dysfunctional. Psychoanalysts have tended to concentrate on psychopathology while functionalists seem more eager to describe the social intricacies of functioning social systems.

To the extent it is believed that social system viability necessitates proper patterning in personal life change, a life course or cycle normatively exists for human beings growing older in it (compare Cumming, 1963, and Cumming and Henry, 1961). A properly socializing course of life is ultimately a functional prerequisite to system viability. From a functional viewpoint, personal life change occurs as an integral part of the socially defined course of life. Persons are considered to be growing old "gracefully" only when they are functionally doing so. That, theoretically, is the only way. Any other reality is, in a strict functional sense, meaningless (see Dahrendorf, 1959, chap. 5).

The functional conception of socialization poses certain explanatory problems when the empirical world seemingly presents a range of socialization patterns from socially ideal (functional) to socially inappropriate (dysfunctional). A strict conceptualization of a value-integrated social system as such would not allow for such variations. One functional recourse, however, is to suggest that such variations in socialization are products of extrasocial systemic factors. Variations are explained, for example, at a different level of human living such as a psychological one. In this situation, anything other than functional life changes is the result of a personal quirk. The rub comes, however, when it theoretically follows from this that personal quirks should be distributed randomly throughout a social system, and, in fact, they are not. For example, it would be impossible to deal with data suggesting that life changes are structured along class lines since this implication would contradict the value base assumed to integrate social systems (Lockwood, 1967).

Thus, the life change envisioned by functionalists is very special. As far as particular social systems as such are concerned, life change encompasses little human variation—indeed, only that believed to be variation on the commonly accepted mode of human growth. Since viable social systems are depicted as value-integrated, life change within them is rational and ideal in the sense that it is not portrayed as being socially inconsistent, socially conflictive, or socially emergent.

Psychocultural Approach.   In the 1920s and 1930s, many disciplines were influenced by psychoanalytic notions. Among them was anthropology. Out of this influence emerged anthropological interest in culture and personality, which we call a psychocultural approach to life change.

The general working hypothesis of studies in culture and personality is that there is an intimate relationship between what human beings come to be in any society and the way of life of its people. Variations on the hypothesis are, to a great extent, influenced by whether emphasis is placed on "coming to be" or "way of life" as primary in the relationship. An extreme example of the former is represented by the psychological reductionism of Roheim (1950). Roheim considers the psychosexual conditions of early life described by Freud to be human universals, culture being an expression of these conditions. As LeVine (1973) summarizes Roheim's emphasis, "Culture patterns are, for the most part, seen as expressions of motives, emotional constellations, and preoccupations that are panhuman; the emphasis is more on universal themes and symbols than on variation along psychosocial dimensions" (p. 50). Studies on "cultural character" (M. Mead, 1928, 1930, 1935, 1954; Benedict, 1934, 1938) emphasize the "way of life" variable. They suggest that "in every culture a typical personality is transmitted to the young which more or less corresponds to the dominant configuration of that culture" (Singer, 1961, p. 49).

Between these two extremes stands Kardiner (1939, 1945) who, with Linton (1936, 1945), developed the view that personality mediates two aspects of culture: primary institutions, comprised of environmental and child-rearing constraints on the development of personality, and secondary institutions, consisting of symbolic expression such as religion and art. It is Kardiner's belief that "basic personality structure" actively integrates various aspects of culture but is not causally related to culture. Whiting and Child (1953) hold a similar view of the relation between culture and personality except that they treat their versions of the two aspects of culture (the "maintenance system" and child-rearing, on the one hand, and the "projective system," on the other) as causally related, with personality articulating the two. Whiting and Child apply correlational methods to ethnographic data from the Human Relations Area Files in order to validate hypotheses about the relation between child-rearing and adult behaviors.

The foregoing views of the relation between culture and personality are representative of three large categories of varying positions. Indeed, LeVine (1973) adds two other categories: anti-culture-personality views perhaps best represented by White (1949), and two-system views such as those of Inkeles and Levinson (1954) and Spiro (1961). Since the latter either do not allow for the separate existence of culture and personality or eschew their interdependence, it is dubious to treat them as psychocultural approaches at all.

Notwithstanding its varied emphases, the psychocultural approach to life change separates and treats as real both personality and culture. Persons may be *reflected products of* cultural configurations, cultural configurations may be *rooted in* the psychobiological contingencies of early life, or persons may *articulate* varied aspects *of* culture.

In the variety of approaches to life change we have discussed, differences exist in the significance of life patterning. The behavioral approach represents one extreme where, in principle, no definite patterning is basic to life change. The other extreme may be represented by the covert personality approach where a definite pattern in the growth of mastery styles is said to exist and is claimed to be a universal feature of covert personality development. The psychocultural approach to life change falls between these extremes in its conception of patterning. It speaks of definite patterning, but usually within cultural bounds. Life change may have a typical course in one society but a different one in another.

The Contrast with Social Phenomenology

Now that we have some idea of how seven important conventional approaches treat life change, let us summarize the way they generally differ from what we described as our social phenomenological approach. Although the difference from social phenomenology varies in content from one approach to another, their common a priori acceptance of extrasubjective realities is what essentially contrasts them with our point of view.

Each conventional approach takes for granted the reality of some extrasubjective entity in the world of everyday life. The behavioral approach accepts the reality of whatever is considered to be profitable or costly in people's worlds and treats such things as having predictable effects on them. The psychoanalytic approach assumes some mode of psychobiological growth through which people normally develop, and contrasts it with abnormal forms. The cognitive approach considers certain ways of thinking to be sequentially ordered and to be the changing means by which persons experience their world as they grow older. The covert personality approach defines certain inherent styles of inner experience that serve to organize people's sense of mastery in the world as they age. The symbolic interactionist approach takes for granted varied worlds of meaning and focuses its attention either on how people seek others for self-meaning or on the consequences of how others in such worlds serve to shape the self. The functional approach treats what human beings come to be as persons largely as an artifact of the operating (functioning) needs of social systems, be they societies, institutions, or families. Finally, the psychocultural approach considers the ways of life (culture) that collectively organize living to be intimately related to how individual growth is organized, some of its adherents suggesting that social life grows out of, and some suggesting that it is replicated in, early socialization.

The contrast between social phenomenology and symbolic interactionism needs to be more explicit since there has been recent controversy over how essentially similar or different the two approaches actually are (see Part Four of Douglas, 1970). Consider how each treats deviance as a type of life change.

Symbolic interactionists take traditional categories of deviance for granted (Warren and Johnson, 1973). For the most part, they choose to investigate the personal and organizational outcomes of deviance among those labeled deviant by others. They focus their attention on the process of becoming deviant, through others' definitions, and its consequences for the way deviants deal with varied problems of living (how deviants "make out" in one way or another). Their aim is to understand how this is done (N. J. Davis, 1975).

Howard Becker (1963), for example, has spoken of what it means to become an "outsider" like a marijuana user and the effort such a status entails in dealing with a straight world. Laud Humphreys (1970) has documented the way that male homosexuals organize the sexual portion of their lives in relation to the rest of it as well as in relation to others who consider their sexual activity repugnant. These symbolic interactionists present an image of persons who, save for their status as deviants, experience the same problems of living as anyone else, the difference between deviants and nondeviants being a matter of accomplished definition. Life changes such as becoming a marijuana user or a sexual deviant are investigated as active (self-seeking) or passive (socially shaping) artifacts of others' constructions.

Symbolic interactionists tend to see the construction process in a different way from social phenomenologists, though both are interested in and see construction in human behavior. Phenomenologists tend to follow Edmund Husserl in starting with the self or selves, while the symbolic interactionists tend to follow George Herbert Mead in starting with the other.

The contrast with social phenomenology is that symbolic interactionists accept the reality of others' definitions (for example, bad labels) rather than treating definition as problematic for everyone (all selves, or members of situations), investigating the problem in its own right.[1] To treat the construction

[1] Although Herbert Blumer's (1969) programmatic statements on the symbolic interactionist treatment of social life may easily be read as social phenomenological, symbolic interactionist research has not generally heeded him.

of human behavior as an artifact of others' definitions, as the symbolic interactionists do, siphons the construction process through a predetermined reality. What is documented by symbolic interactionists seems to be the working residue of others' definitions. How definitions are collectively realized as such is not of central concern to them; however, it is of central concern to us.

To focus on the definitional processes occurring between members of situations does not primarily entail an examination of what it means to be or become "acceptably" deviant. Rather, it centers attention on the ways that people come to settle on (accept as real, for all practical purposes) some status, deviant or not, for specific individuals. This means that the practical politics or negotiation that goes on between people about who or what is deviant or not (or anything else for that matter) is center stage.

Note that in focusing on the negotiation of someone's status, no a priori assumption is made about whether the subject of negotiation is indeed deviant. Rather, deviance is treated as one among any number of arguments that negotiators may invoke to explain what they believe is the nature of someone's actions. As Garfinkel (1956) states: "The work of the denunciation effects the recasting of the objective character of the perceived other: the other person becomes in the eyes of his condemners literally a different and new person. It is not that the new attributes are added to the old 'nucleus.' He is not changed, he is reconstituted. The former identity, at best, receives the accent of mere appearance . . . the former identity stands as accidental; the new identity is the 'basic reality.' What he is now is what, 'after all,' he was all along" (pp. 421-422). The problem for negotiators and the problematic for social phenomenologists is that no one knows what the "real" status of the subject is until some negotiator's argument has been collectively settled upon for the practical purposes of the business at hand. With a collective settlement emerges social order, the latter being as precarious as the former.

What conventionally are considered instances of life change toward or away from deviance, from a social phenomenological viewpoint are treated as life changes equal to any other form of change. No form of life change is more basic than any other form, nor is any form necessarily sequentially prior to any other. Life change itself, as we shall see throughout the following chapters, is problematic for people on any number of occasions when it arises as a question to be settled.

To date, social phenomenological research has focused mainly on negotiation occurring in formally organized settings, as most of our examples in the following chapters will reflect. However, negotiation processes are not necessarily limited to such settings. Indeed, negotiation is the means by which all social entities are accomplished, whether in formally organized settings or not.

Chapter Two

The Reality
of Life Change

In Chapter One, we discussed what a social phenomenological approach to life change is not. It is not conventional in that, in the construction and elaboration of its own ideas, it sets aside, or suspends, belief in the reality of such popular conventions as cycles, stages, development, maturity, and social structure. Although we briefly introduced a social phenomenological view of life in commenting on the meaning of *conventional,* we did not elaborate its assumptions and chief conceptions. Rather, our purpose was to set the background for a contrast with the theme of life change as a matter of social negotiation and construction.

In this chapter, we turn first to the assumptions that underlie a social phenomenological approach to life change. Second, like any new development that significantly diverges from ongoing approaches to a subject, social phenomenology has generated a number of concepts with special connotations. We shall note some important ones and discuss their meanings. This should provide a working vocabulary for use in subsequent chapters where we address a selection of issues in life change, ranging from the way people "predict" growth to how they reconstruct biography (or the life course).

Assumptions

Gouldner (1970) speaks of "domain assumptions" (or simply "assumptions") and so shall we when we refer to the underlying, often tacit ideas about the nature of that which we talk and think of when we undertake a particular science of behavior. Assumptions do not rest on evidence and are not subject to empirical verification. Rather, they are unproven beginnings that state, explicitly or implicitly, what is accepted by a scientist as given in the empirical world. To Kuhn (1962), they are basic beliefs that distinguish one scientific paradigm from another, those aspects of science which are not problematic for scientists as they go about their "normal" scientific work. Indeed, serious "scientific" interest in them is the hallmark of crisis and revolution in science, according to Kuhn.

Assumptions exist at many levels of scientific work. For example, it is basically a matter of faith (assumption) that an empirical world exists that is independent of the scientist and, thus, available for the verification of hypotheses. At a less general level are those assumptions that underpin theories of particular phenomena, for instance, assumptions about life change that differentiate a behavioral from a symbolic interactionist view. What assumptions underlie a social phenomenological view of life change?

Bracketing the Social World. First of all, life change is taken to be socially problematic. For example, no a priori distinction is made between what people call normal sexuality versus perversion, save their own use of the difference on the varied occasions when the distinction becomes collectively problematic for them. We assume that people are simply all plain people, notwithstanding what they may demean or honor among themselves. This conception of human behavior is quite different, for instance, from the psychoanalytic and functional approaches, which take for granted the social roles and statuses that people assign to each other.

Taking human living to be without inherent social meaning is what social phenomenologists mean when they say that they "bracket" it. *Bracketing* suggests, like its mathematical usage, to set aside—at least temporarily—so as to get on with the task at hand. The task is to understand how subjects themselves collectively make what they come to be as persons, which includes a wide range of socially constituted things from personality types, syndromes, regressions, and patients to adjusted or unadjusted members of society, role-players, and enculturated individuals.

Let us be more specific about the meaning of *bracketing*. In bracketing the social world, we temporarily assume that all that exists in the world of human living are members who are able to speak its ordinary languages and, thereby, seriously refer to its conventional objects as real, to-be-dealt-with things. Everything else in the world is treated as social fiction. Using this frame of reference, when members refer to such things as a "stage" of life that they have or have not reached, we treat the stages as features of their talk—not some place or entity at which they have arrived or may arrive. What members consider to be their talk *about* life and living, we treat as talk *of* them.

Consider a family whose members are negotiating (deliberating, arguing, yelling, making exceptions, crying, pleading, explaining, and so forth) whether or not Johnny "really" is mature enough to take his girl camping unchaperoned, everyone knowing that his father once boasted that he did as much with most of the girls in town at Johnny's age and, what's more, "made it" with each one. In bracketing this social scene, we approach it without prejudging who or what is mature. We take maturity to have no absolute or concrete existence that allows us to judge members' estimate of it. Rather, we treat maturity as a practical outcome of the work done by members on those occasions when they present it as a topic for discussion or negotiation. Albeit each member of the family may speak of his or her own sense of maturity, our attention is on how some sense of maturity comes to be constructed and taken as collectively real. This collective reality must be negotiated out of each separate understanding of the term as it is believed to characterize Johnny. Negotiation is the process by which this intersubjective understanding emerges. Johnny's maturity is, then, in reality, whatever it is constituted as being on each occasion it is considered.

We are not suggesting that the world is made up of wide-awake schemers. Far from it. In fact, what appears so strange is that people who actively work to construct the meaning of life states in practice emphatically deny the work. For the most part, they are unaware of their tacit "scheming" as such (use of practical theories such as maturity and growth). Rather, with all well-intentioned assurance, they admit, help, deny, or dissuade themselves and each other to and from any number of seemingly real stages, positions, levels of maturity, roles, and life courses.

From our perspective, social life is treated as organizing or disorganizing but never as organized or disorganized. It is in continuous process of being made by its members. Everyday life is an anarchic world. It has no standard structure. Whatever is real about the social world is located in the talk and work that members do to constitute it. They may or may not talk and work themselves into being mature or immature or adolescent or senescent or an awesome number of other things.

Having bracketed belief in conventional notions of life change, what do we make of members of situations who believe in its reality, whose attitudes are naturally attuned to it? Assuming the existence of a world of members, the answer is that this reality is nothing else than members' *sense* of it. Being mature, for instance, is a matter of the sense of maturity that people come to have about someone or about themselves on relevant occasions when maturity is of concern. Members come to know the sense of their own and others' maturity by talking about it. When talk is validated collectively, they or others feel and become mature, for all practical purposes. When it is not, maturity is at issue. As talk flows, so does maturity. For example, should Johnny's father succeed in convincing his family that what he did in his youth was "just different" or "an exception," then for all practical purposes, Johnny is presently immature.

A Constructed World. This brings us to our second assumption. Whatever is considered to be human living and life change —whether being mature, becoming insane, being socialized, being rehabilitated, or becoming aged—basically is constituted by people, from moment to moment, in order reasonably to get on with what they consider to be the business at hand. It is virtually invented or reinvented for each occasion. People, for the most part, take the reality of the business before them for granted, as just a matter of everyday life. We are opening this reality to question and are attempting, in this book, to delineate some resulting features of doing so.

Having peopled the world exclusively with members, we shall assume that whatever it is that they consider real is constructed by them as they go about the business of daily living. When they cease to talk of some "thing" (such as maturity, authority, dependence, and stages), it is nonexistent in practice. When their talk commonly objectifies some "thing," they treat it as real and respond to it as such.

Berger and Kellner (1970) describe marriage in a manner similar to the way we are considering life change. They conceive of the reality of marriage and its relation to the outside world as a matter of conversation. In the daily affairs of living with each other, those who are about to be or are married, along with marriage-relevant associates, talk about the relationship. In order to converse, conversationalists address each other so as to get on with the talk at hand, rather than dwell on talk itself. In so doing, they unwittingly come to use a common language in referring to various features of the relationship, as well as to make sense of things that are happening in the environment such as work relations and relations with neighbors. Each round of talk subsequently validates the content and referent of every previous round. For example, when a presiding official suddenly addresses a couple before him as husband and wife, others present then have a way of speaking about and to the two as a unit. When they do so, they contribute to the reality of the marriage.

Moreover, everyday events now become interpreted as they relate to this couple rather than to the separate individuals; events come to have a new meaning and reality. Both the married couple and others cast their references to, and actions toward, the marriage and varied events in a different manner than they had previously. This change, of course, is not an instantaneous one; it takes work. In time, for all concerned with it, the marriage comes to be something talked about. It comes to be a *thing* that is referred to, toward which people have sentiments, and that may be said to have changed, petrified, disintegrated, or have this or that merit in varied situations. It is some *thing*, judged, valued, mourned, celebrated, or whatever. The point is that it emerges and is transformed into an entity through conversation.

In assuming that people make their worlds, we are addressing the question of order in human living. A number of answers to this question have been proposed. Functionalists, for example, treat order as founded on collectively recognized and shared values that motivate individuals to act as socially responsible persons. Behaviorists conceive of order as a matter of habit, contingent on a profit principle. Habits (or order) continue undisturbed as long as returns on behavior investments do not diminish below some motivating point. Our own consideration of order suggests that it is a matter of the work that goes into negotiation. Therefore, order is a continuously precarious thing guided by the tacit scheming that people do in relation to each other.

Practical Procedures. This brings us to our third and final assumption. The way to gain an understanding of how life change occurs is to systematically document the practical procedures by which all people (laypersons and human scientists) make sense of and accomplish its existence in talk and deed. Both lay and scientific concerns with life change are practical. The entire social phenomenological approach to human living might be said to grow out of the distinction between seriously investigating how people make sense of life, on the one hand, and taking it for granted on the other.

The difference between seriously investigating the way

(practical procedures) members of everyday life make sense of life and taking it for granted is what Schutz (1953) had in mind when he distinguished between having a scientific and having a natural attitude toward everyday life. The data of everyday life look entirely different—and the difference appears strange indeed—when perceived while holding one attitude as opposed to the other. Consider our earlier example about Johnny's maturity. We might treat the family scene in two different ways. We can consider the issue of which its members speak (maturity) with the same natural seriousness that they do, asking whether or not Johnny is indeed mature enough. Or, suspending belief in the existence of maturity as a concrete stage or state of life, we can treat the scene as an arena of competing practical theories of maturity in order to describe how its reality arises out of negotiations of family members. In the first treatment, use by family members of theories (interpretations, explanations, disclaimers, exceptions, and the like) for deciding whether or not Johnny is mature enough to "make it as a man" are judged on whether or not they are reasonable or accurate decisions and conclusions, given his "real" status. In the second treatment, such judgments are impossible since we look for Johnny's maturity in the practical procedures themselves, in the negotiation process. The process of negotiation is a fleeting prophecy of his maturity. The contrast between the two treatments of Johnny's maturity is as strange as the feeling portrayed in the film *Dracula* by those actors who, at one moment, "know" that they are speaking with the real, living Count Dracula before them but, in the next moment, realize that no image of him is reflected in a distant mirror.

The Profundity of Documenting Practical Procedures

The social phenomenological investigation of how members "make sense" of and thereby *make* everyday life is, first and foremost, a matter of attitude. The methodology is simple and yet profound. It is simple in the sense that social phenomenological research basically requires only a certain attitude toward data. The rest is largely a technical matter of looking at,

listening to, recording, and explicating what people do as they
go about their everyday lives.

It is profound in two ways. First, it is rather difficult to
achieve and maintain (compare Castaneda, 1968, 1971, 1972).
Second, as in "looking at" the absence of Count Dracula's reflected image, the world has a radically different appearance
than it is popularly assumed to have.

The difficulty in achieving and maintaining the attitude
arises out of the perceptual and cognitive conventionality that
characterizes people's reports to themselves and others about
what goes on in their everyday affairs. Indeed, to be strict about
it, to describe *the* world prevents attention to the practice of
doing so. People are simply in the habit of describing the world
in conventional terms. For instance, when someone says that he
prays or exhibits prayerfulness or reports that he prayed or will
pray, the conventional datum at issue is the possible fact of
praying, at some time and in some place. A number of typical
questions may arise about the state of this datum, such as
whether or not a reported intention to pray is behaviorly (actively) accurate or predictive of prayer. But, conventionally,
prayer as a *state* of data is always at issue, not the practical existence of prayerful *data*. Conventional difficulties with data—of
prayer or something else—arise out of whether reports about (or
measures of) data are accurate depictions of the existence of
some *thing* that someone did or did not do.

Taking a social phenomenological attitude toward prayer
leads one to consider how it is achieved—that is, how whatever is
done in its name comes to be convincingly or unconvincingly
referred to as prayer. It necessitates documenting the talk and
deed that relevant members of prayerful circumstance exhibit
to make prayerful circumstance. Merely investigating whether
or not prayer occurred (in the fashion that one might survey
records for mortality statistics or mental patients' charts for
their diagnoses) takes the *fact* of prayer (or death and diagnoses) for granted. The "fact" of prayer lies in its accomplishment, how people come to see and think of it as fact.

What we are suggesting, methodologically, is that we
should avoid treating so-called "facts" as things. This is rather

difficult when the empirical world has been described, to most
laypersons and scientists for most of their lives and careers, as
hard and real, as a world of factual things. Even the language we
use to speak of facts attests to such experiences. Facts are said
to be "hard," "positive," and the ultimate proof that one can
be "shown." The social phenomenology of fact itself is much
the same as the social phenomenology of marriage as we briefly
discussed it above. Talk about facts and the questions and issues
that arise in relation to them assumes that its spokesmen's
world contains facts. As Berger and Kellner (1970) might suggest, scientists converse themselves into the reality of a factual,
empirical world.

Refusal to take facts for granted is likely to be rather irritating to laypersons and human scientists alike. Garfinkel
(1967) has shown this to be true among laypersons in a variety
of experiments conducted on their everyday talk about
"things." Though not reported by Garfinkel, consider the following example. An experimenter may be bid welcome by his
friend, upon entering the latter's home. The experimenter then
asks, "What do you mean, 'welcome'?" This surprises the friend,
who was prepared to gloss over the expression as merely being
an appropriate greeting (to gloss over is to take the meaning of
something for granted by not attending to it in a wide-awake,
analytic fashion). The friend is far from interested in the meaning of such an expression. It is a background feature of the entrance of someone into his home for a visit, the latter being the
"real" business at hand. The friend answers, "What the hell do
you think I mean? I said, 'Welcome.' Come in! Greetings!" The
experimenter persists, "How should I come in?" This uncivil
nit-picking may quickly become exasperating to the subject of
the experiment, resulting in disgust or a change in circumstance
altogether, such as the friend's sarcastic indulgence of the experimenter in what the former considers to be a temporary and
silly game. Persistence in the experiment involves the danger of
"going too far," which means that what seemed trivial has not
been taken for granted and glossed over, thereby unsettling the
emerging social order of a situation. The friend's willingness to
gloss over the practical meaning of *welcome* and the process by

which one enters a home is indexical to the occasion; that is, the gloss depends on the occasion. On this occasion, the meaning of *welcome* and the process of entry are considered to be obvious. The occasion makes it tacitly reasonable not to attend to such matters.

Conventional human scientists are likely to react in a similar fashion when their everyday talk about "things" (scientific facts) is challenged and not glossed over by associates or other persons. They are the same as laypersons in this sense. The scientist's treatment of facts as real is situationally bound (indexical) in that their practical obviousness as facts depends on occasions whose members take them for granted as such. For example, a scientist who, in presenting data before an interested audience, concludes that there is a relationship between suicide and social class (such as social class affecting suicide) is likely to be annoyed by the suggestion that suicide statistics (and thereby the "facts" of suicide) are *made* by those people who directly or indirectly record them. Suppose that those persons who are officially responsible for deciding the cause of deaths themselves believe that the likelihood of suicide varies with social class. In a circumstance in which people, such as these officials and others, take the belief for granted, might not the *belief* serve as an obvious reason for officials to constitute deaths accordingly? (Compare Douglas, 1967.) Such a possibility implies that, indeed, things such as facts of death may not be what they seem. Furthermore, it challenges the conventional human scientist to investigate something he takes for granted, namely, that there is an obvious thing called "suicide." This is doubly annoying in that taking it seriously entails assuming a radically different attitude toward "fact": The constitution of fact should be documented instead of facts simply being collected and analyzed. This, to say the least, is as provocative and irritating to the conventional human scientist as the experiment was to the friend. Questioning the facticity of suicide data is likely to lead to the same ending as in the experiment: felt annoyance and, with persistence, accusations of scientific incivility; or indulgence, acknowledgement of the problem, and a final gloss in someone's suggestion that "yes, that's interesting—

but let's get on with the presentation." The same, of course, would be true of a persistent suggestion to a social phenomenological researcher that he reflect upon and open to serious question his bracketing of the social world.

We mentioned that there are at least two ways in which taking a social phenomenological attitude in the investigation and analysis of life change is profound. The first is a procedural profundity, a radical shift in how one views "things." The second is a more substantive profundity. Suddenly, life change has a completely different meaning than it had when considered from a conventional point of view. The very moment a social phenomenological attitude becomes a working part of scientific research, "things" are not what they seem to be in conventional worlds of everyday life.

From a conventional point of view, "things" have substance. For example, when life is said to change, this suggests that from some point in time to another, an aspect of the "thing" called life has undergone some objective transformation. From a social phenomenological point of view, change is not conceived as such. Its only referent is the sense that members have of it. As we noted earlier, this sense of things has its most obvious expression in people's talk. Thus, when people begin to suggest that change has taken place in themselves or others, they talk about it; change has rhetorical existence.

In our earlier example concerning Johnny, we find his maturity being bandied about by members of the family. His father, for instance, suggests that Johnny is "not really ready for that sort of thing" since Johnny is only sixteen. Johnny, in turn, invokes the developmental chronology that he once heard his father boast of, concluding that maturity occurs at sixteen. His father responds with a "theory" that human sexual maturity has an historical feature by citing, "We grew up faster in those days." His son then begins to present other "evidence" of his maturity, this time implying that "actually" he is far ahead of his father at the same age, for as Johnny points out, "Look at all the things I've done that you said a lot of times you never even thought of doing till after you married Ma." Their practical reasoning continues to flow and so also, in practice, does

Johnny's maturity. Gradually, the children leave the scene.
Mother and father are alone. She brings up the maturity question again, asking her husband whether he "really" stopped to
think about what he said. She continues, gently reminding him
of what she believes were inconsistencies in his argument, glossing over her son's attempt to stack his own case. Her husband
reconsiders for a while, then begins to question the wisdom of
his statements to his son in view of his boasts about himself and
the "obvious" evidence of his son's self-reliance. What seemed
so clear-cut earlier, perhaps now seems to have been muddled.
He concludes that he will speak with his son about it later, hint-
ing that his son might be old enough at that.

The "substance" of people's worlds appears strange indeed
when it is considered to be a matter of occasioned talk and
meaningful gesture. There is a profound difference between
treating such entities as maturity, growth, and the life course as
part and parcel of the world in which people find themselves,
on the one hand, and as constituent aspects of their references
to it on the other. When we look at the world from the latter
point of view, for example, on the varied occasions when people
claim to be referencing the same things, what is thought to be
solid reasoning throughout takes as many forms as its backgrounds.

Documenting Practical Procedures

Before we go to the next section of this chapter, let us
briefly elaborate the technical meaning of the last assumption
we discussed. We noted two senses in which taking a social phenomenological attitude is a radical (profound) departure from a
conventional research attitude. Now, what does it mean, technically, to document members' procedures for making sense of
and accomplishing everyday life in talk and deed?

Whatever it might be that is conventionally considered fact
or data—be it mortality statistics, early life graphs indicating the
chronological ages at which children reach varied behavioral
stages, or the sections of patients' charts that presumably trace
their symptomatic progress toward or away from some category

of mental health or illness—a social phenomenological attitude toward conventional data necessitates a documentation of the ways they are used by those involved in constituting fact or data. To document means to make visible or take note of by writing down or portraying those deeds (talk and gesture) that members of fact-making situations do to enable themselves to treat the products of their activities as things (or facts). Documentation, then, necessitates being on the scene and explicating members' practices when facts are "dealt with" by them.

Consider some hypothetical records of geriatric patients. They contain varied bits of information about patients' ongoing behavior in a nursing home. One kind of data recorded in them is patients' behavioral progress toward some stage of mental competence. The record may be relatively explicit about the ideal course of such change. For example, it may indicate, in serial form, that they are codable as either "completely "senile," "unrealistic," "disoriented," "temporarily confused," "showing evidence of being alert," or, finally, "realistic."

Conventionally, we might raise any number of research questions about the social or personal outcomes of being at one stage or another. We might hypothesize, for instance, that the staff's behavior toward the patient shifts from authoritarian to something closer to peer equality as the patient moves from one stage to another on his way toward "realism." Patients' records then may be utilized to gather data about patient progress and these cross-tabulated with data on staff behavior.

Our concern with such entities as staff behavior and patients' stages of realism differs radically from this. For instance, there are the questions of how patients come to be spoken of (or recorded) as being at one stage or another, how the staff proceeds to exhibit one form of behavior or another on varied occasions, and what everyone involved (patients and staff) does or does not do to construct a relationship between stages and behavior.

The questions require documentation of several kinds of events. A number of events might be "made visible" as documents of how patients come to be recorded as being at a stage.

In order to reach a decision about the proper stage, a recorder presumably evaluates a patient's behavior for clues to his current mental competence. The researcher may document how recorders come to treat certain behavioral evidence of competence as clues to competence, on the one hand, and what other "clues" they gloss over, on the other—on the specific occasions such work is done. He then may document how recorders decide on what clues fit the precoded stages available on record. This involves making visible a range of practical procedures that staff members engage in, from interpreting the definition of stages in relation to the particular case at hand to invoking or revoking certain available clues as "really" relevant or irrelevant "when you think about it." Cutting across all this are recorders' "theories" about what it might mean for themselves or the patient or other staff members (recall staff attitudes in the hypothesis about attitudes and competence) if certain evidence is considered a sign of mental competence, or what it might mean if a stage for one patient is conceived in one way and for another patient is thought of differently. One staff member among those who are in the process of deciding the mental competence of a certain patient may speak of how "ideally, we should treat realistic patients like we treat any normal adult" (that is, as equals). It may have been suggested by another staff member that "the patient is now really quite alert." Then another adds, "I'm not about to treat *her* [the patient being considered] like *my* equal after she reported us last week." A few staff members sympathize with this. This leads into a discussion of how the patient may not, "after all," be as mentally competent as was first suggested. Extensive evidence is presented for the new image of the patient, while evidence for the patient's mental competence is discounted as not having been "really accurate in the first place." In practice, this conversation is accepted as quite reasonable. Whether or not a patient's life has changed is not just a matter of comparing indicators of change over time and examining this comparison against the patient's relations with staff members, for what we have just described suggests that the "factors" (staff behavior and patient realism) in the preceding hypothesis work to constitute themselves as factors.

The documentation of such events and others like them is the technical outcome of assuming a social phenomenological attitude toward everyday life, be it the everyday world of donning one's clothes or the everyday world of evaluating mental competence. It is an attitude that methodologically necessitates showing how members' practical procedures constitute existing and reportable objects and events in the world. In the preceding example, it involves showing how those involved construct stages out of the rhetoric of their business together, business that they take for granted and report to be that of diagnosing and recording mental competence.

Some Social Phenomenological Concepts

In discussing the foregoing assumptions, we defined a few terms, such as *glossing* and *indexicality,* which have been used by some social phenomenologists to describe features of people's negotiations. We also spoke of *members* and *accomplishing* (social construction), assuming an intuitive understanding of the terms. Let us be more explicit about the meaning of these two concepts. We shall also describe the sense in which we take *rationality* to be a feature of people's conduct.

Member. What conception of people does the term *member* express? Let us refer back to the various conventional approaches to life change discussed in Chapter One. Each approach, like the present one, names behaving entities. For example, behaviorists refer to behaving entities as subjects or respondents, and not as actors. This seems reasonable given their concern with the subject's capacities. Symbolic interactionists speak of selves and others and not usually of individuals or mere role-players. Functionalists refer to systems of roles and their players and not merely of individuals.

Our use of the term *member*—just plain people[1]—connotes

---

[1] It should be noted, however, that in their everyday wide-awake business together, people consider and speak of themselves as anything but

a sense of the world as comprising those who, in the course of their action, belong together at times and at other times not. It implies that, in their behavior, people take into account the practical meaning of belonging somewhere, at some time, in what they do and say there. As we mentioned elsewhere, their expressions index their membership in certain practical situations. Being members of some meaningful occasion, people speak a common ordinary language that references the same taken-for-granted realities; they take the same natural attitude toward things. To be a member of a collection of people gathered somewhere for some purpose is to proceed, together with other members, to use the same tacit rules and understandings (for example, glossing practices) to "put on" that place (see Cicourel, 1970b; Garfinkel, 1967).

The sense in which we are using the term *member* takes belonging to be a practical feature of being together as people. For a member to belong does not mean that he exists in a world constituted by others before or as he enters it (which is how a symbolic interactionist would treat belonging). Rather, when we speak of a member belonging somewhere at some time, we mean that, at least for the time being, he is in the business of speaking with other members in such a way that they are making meaningful sense of that very place, of its objects and its events.

Perhaps an example would help to distinguish between belonging in a social phenomenological sense and what the same term would signify from a symbolic interactionist point of view (see Denzin, 1969, for an opposite view). Take a behavior therapy situation.[2] It is conventionally composed of at least two categories of people: therapists and patients. What goes on there

---

plain as they refer to what they take for granted to be such real things as their expertise, their credentials, their positions, known and obvious facts or theories of this or that, the natural order of things, and so on.

[2] There is a sense in which we, in explaining the difference between social phenomenological and symbolic interactionist belonging, must fall prey to a nonphenomenological beginning. We must refer to some meaningful situation, such as therapy, before we can talk of how it is constituted by its members.

presumably is an episode in the application of certain therapeutic procedures to patients in attempts to change or rehabili-
tate their behavior.

From one sort of symbolic interactionist point of view, to
belong to such a situation would mean to sense the meaning of
being there and to manage oneself through its given events to
emerge in such a way as to appear to have done therapy while
preserving one's self-integrity. As we mentioned in Chapter One,
there are two sides to this sense of belonging. One side is the
entity that belongs, which might be called a self. The second
side is the others in the therapy situation, whose definitions are
treated as meaningfully given and separate from the self. A
symbolic interactionist might trace the varied nuances of the
process by which selves who belong to a therapy situation
manage to complete or not complete tasks to their own and
others' satisfaction. For example, data about how some people
don the facial expressions of "disoriented patients" and how
they feel about the need to do such things might be collected.

From a social phenomenological point of view, the primary, although tacit, concern of members is to make sense of
the situation itself and its roles. This is accomplished before and
during the actions that people as actors express and manage in
the role of patient or therapist. As far as the therapy situation is
concerned, then, therapy must be begun (constituted) before
one can manage himself through it; that is, as members, people
must constitute therapy as the situation at hand (note that therapy, like any other situation, is not taken by the social phenomenologist to be something separate from people, to which
people respond, although people take for granted that it is
so). Procedurally, the talk and gestures that constitute the circumstance at hand as a therapy situation would be documented.

When a member (speaking as a therapist) in the midst of
therapy implores another member (speaking as a patient) to
"behave and act right or we'll never finish this" or sarcastically
asks the latter whether he thinks that "this is just a game or
something," the speaking member has temporarily suspended
the normative rules of therapy in order to negotiate and possibly reconstitute the situation in a side sequence (see Jefferson,

1972) to his ongoing stream of talk and gesture as a therapist. The same may be done by a member who otherwise speaks like a patient in need of therapy. He may lean over (which is taken to signify a shift in realities) and engage in a side conversation with the therapist about himself as a patient and the therapist as a therapist—all of this before the next therapeutic episode occurs. For instance, in an aside, our erstwhile patient-in-need-of-therapy may inform the therapist that, "as a friend" or "just for your benefit" (in our terms, as a type of co-member of the place at hand), he would suggest that she (as a therapist) change her attitude toward the patients or "they won't go along with her anymore." There may be some negotiation between co-members of the aside as to the "proper" meaning of being a patient and therapist in therapy before the aside is closed and therapy, as another occasion, is reconstituted.

People construct asides and tacitly use them whenever anything in ongoing interaction needs clarification. People take the existence of asides for granted, but do not notice their work within, or in the production of, asides as such. Serious investigation of members in side and other such sequences of behavior makes visible how members constitute the meaning of their behavior—or as social phenomenologists sometimes say, accomplish or construct their worlds.

Accomplishing Life. We are primarily concerned with the *work* that people, as members of occasions, do to "realize" various things and events so that the very same people can get on with the business they believe to be at hand. Actors' performances in roles are of secondary concern, mostly as far as they are often the "thing" to which members refer when they converse about who or what people are, or "properly" should be, at the moment.

In order for any behavioral display to be treated by people collectively as something meaningful, it must be provided with meaning. This takes work. For example, returning to our therapy situation, it is by no means self-evident, to all the people involved, when therapy has begun or when it resumes after an aside. They must provide each other with clues to such shifts. To people, such clues are trivial features of their behavior since, in their usual natural attitude toward the affairs at hand (such as therapy), they do not bother to take notice of the work they do to provide clues. What is relevant to them, at the moment, is therapy, "of course." This very triviality, indeed, allows actors to seriously attend to the business at hand. It allows them, for example, to talk about therapy as something real (à la Durkheim), which they might judge as having been done poorly, well, unjustly, fairly, or what have you.

What to people is so trivial as to be unnoticed (and, if pointed out, likely to bring forth a response of "So what?" or, if pressed, an annoyed form of the same question which is likely to be "What the hell does this have to do with what we're talking *about?*" [our emphasis]) is from our point of view anything but trivial. Indeed, "trivial" asides, mundane talk, and seen but unnoticed gestures tacitly signify to people what they, as actors, are performing at the moment, what role each is playing, and whether or not they are ready for a pause in their activity. "Trivial" talk and deed are the very basis of the life scenes that actors play, from therapy to sarcastic social banter.

When we say that life is *tacitly* accomplished by people, we are implying that they are not wide-awake to the work they do, as work, in the process of constituting their existence. Rather, they attend to its referenced reality. They act as if life, indeed, had an existence separate from themselves. This means, for instance, that accomplishments such as mental illness, maturity, stages, senility, sarcasm, authority, dependence, and any number of other "obvious" features of daily living are "things" that people make by responding *to,* talking *of,* growing *through,* and so forth. The critical question, for us, is *how* life as a real thing is accomplished. That is the sense in which we use the term *accomplish.*

Practical Rationality. When human scientists speak of rational behavior, they do not all mean the same thing. Some evaluate rationality in terms of a standard that they, as scientists, treat as independent of particular subjects but presumably applicable to all from circumstance to circumstance. For instance, they might suggest that to act rationally is to maximize one's gains and minimize one's losses, defining the substance of gains and losses either by fiat or by asking subjects about them. We, on the other hand, leave the definition of rationality to people's sense of it when, in the course of their action, it is an issue for them.

What is taken for granted to be reasonable (rational) by members of some situation has no existence separate from what is practiced there. In each situation, there are *background expectancies* or "life as usual" assumptions (Garfinkel, 1967) about what people do and say that make certain talk and deed reasonable to those who engage in them. What is glossed over depends on background expectancies, which vary from one occasion to another. What is taken to be rational is bound by circumstance. On some occasion, certain talk and gesture may be construed as irrational to members who as members of another occasion would assume them to be quite rational. Comparing what people treat as "perfectly reasonable" on one occasion with what they treat as equally "reasonable" on some other occasion suggests that what allows them to behave the way they do from place to place is their ability to gloss over the apparent inconsistency by naturally and tacitly attending to what are accepted as the realities at hand.

Take the practical rationality on each of the occasions in the following example. A new father is eager to see and hold his daughter in the nursery of an obstetrics ward of a hospital. As he enters the nursery, one of the nurses rushes toward him and cautions him first to don a hospital gown, mask, and cap. She provides him with the clothing, which he dutifully puts on, and proceeds into the nursery among the cribs toward his daughter. As this takes place, the nurse politely reminds him of the need for such precautions because "people can bring any kind of germ into the nursery."

The next day, we find the same father walking toward the nursery. As he approaches it, a man dressed in janitor's greens and carrying a screwdriver and pair of pliers precedes him into the nursery. The nurses look up, see who it is, and nonchalantly ask the janitor what he is going to fix. He answers as he pries open a window. The nurses perfunctorily return to their routines, glossing over the "fact" that the janitor is not wearing

sanitary clothing. One background expectancy of this occasion
is that janitors are not typified as belonging to the category of
people who may infect the nursery. Meanwhile, the father has
been handed his gown, cap, and mask. He enters the nursery
and proceeds toward his daughter's crib, which is near the janitor. Things seem as routine (rational, in practice) as usual.

Still later, as the nurses gather to chat on one of their
breaks, one of them recalls the "gall" of a father who "walked
right in there [the nursery] in street clothes and all" and how
"you have to watch those eager beavers or they'll contaminate
the whole place." At the moment, everyone gathered is attuned
to fathers who contaminate. The nurses' exasperation is "justi-
fiably" and "reasonably" aimed at such fathers. For all practical
purposes, theirs is "perfectly reasonable" talk. As members of
that circumstance, they take for granted the reasonableness of
their complaints and get on with their affairs. When one of the
nurses interrupts to remind the complainants of "what it *really*
means to watch for contamination," suggesting that the janitor
might also contaminate the nursery, her comments are glossed
over with teasing remarks about "what a know-it-all she has suddenly become!" One background assumption of the situation at
hand is that it is a place to complain about eager fathers. The
teasing remark is a reminder of this by one member to another.
It tacitly suggests that the nurse who interrupted should act reasonably, for all practical purposes. The rationality invoked is
bound to the working situation at hand.

The Reality of Life Change

We began this chapter by noting some assumptions about
life change that underlie our social phenomenological approach.
We delineated the meaning of select social phenomenological
concepts, particularly *negotiation, glossing, indexicality, member, accomplishing,* and *practical rationality.* Now that we have
introduced our point of view, what sense does it make of the
reality of life change?

Recall the reference earlier in this chapter to the possible
impact that living an upper-income as opposed to a lower-

income life might have on the likelihood of committing suicide. Just for the sake of argument, suppose we hypothesize that income is positively related to suicide; that is, the higher one's income, the more likely one's life terminates in suicide rather than some other form of death—other things being equal, of course. With due care taken for various kinds of bias in data, we proceed to use mortality statistics and occupational data to test our hypothesis. Depending on the data, we conclude that there probably is or is not a relationship between income-linked life experiences and demise. A style of life that differs from another in terms of income does or does not have some effect on the type of death that is likely to terminate it.

Social phenomenologists would have little or no argument with this as far as whether or not a relationship exists between the foregoing variables. It is not the relationship they would question. As a matter of fact, they are likely to wholeheartedly agree with whatever relationship is found (given that the research is technically sound). This is not where the radical difference between conventional sociology and social phenomenology emerges. The radical difference grows out of how each conceives of the *reality* of variables.

Returning to our hypothesis and data on income and demise, a social phenomenologist might conceive of them as referring to people's practical theory (the hypothesis) and the people-deduced products (mortality statistics) of such theory, respectively. Thus, any relationship found might be interpreted as something that people themselves believe about income-linked life experiences and demise. When a death occurs, it is by no means inherently self-evident what the nature of that death is (let alone the facticity of death as such). It must be defined as suicide, homicide, accident, or whatever. Someone does the defining. In the world of everyday life, people who do so (the police, coroners, and others at the scene of death, such as hotel clerks, janitors, nurses, doctors, and passers-by) hold and invoke any number of theories about such events in order to make sense of them.

Take an occasion when someone has plunged to his death from a fifteenth-story window of a building. After it has been decided that the man is dead, those at the scene deliberate about the cause of death. They try to make sense of it: Was it murder, accident, suicide, or what? Suppose that in the process of piecing together the so-called evidence—which includes information about the man's identity and background—talk among those at the scene indicates that *they* have a tacit theory about the likelihood of there being a relation between suicide and income. This may influence their evaluation of evidence in such a way that they conclude that the rich man who just plunged to his death "must have been a suicide," since "everyone knows" that the rich commit suicide. Those on the scene, with this theory, virtually talk (accomplish) the death into a factual suicide. The status of the death is a product of their practical deliberations in the situation at hand.

Lay theories of behavior may or may not be substantively the same as conventional scientific theories (in practice, they are identical). When they are substantively the same, conventional scientific arguments about life change are likely to be empirically supported. When they are not, such arguments are not likely to be supported. Since conventional scientific arguments about life change are often folk arguments, it is not surprising that many of them are in "fact" verified—and also considered "obvious" by laypersons.

The sense that a social phenomenological point of view makes of the reality of life change has two sides. The consideration of life change begins with a bracketing of belief in conventional realities, which is one side. This, of course, does *not* imply that we consider life change to be unreal for people. On the contrary, it is all too real to them—who may despair, argue, or conduct personal war over its reality. This is the other side. This two-sided conception of reality suggests the following. First, there is no such thing as life change separate from the public sense of it presented and negotiated by members of occasions when life change is being considered. Second, when members act as if change has or has not taken place, it is a product of the work they do in talk and gesture to make it seem so. Third, the reality of life change is located in the process of its accomplishment. And fourth, evidence of this can be found only in and over the process of accomplishment.

People's talk is central to social phenomenological investigation. The flowing reality of life change is located in it. Of course, gesture is also meaningful to people and is an integral part of the process by which they accomplish their worlds. The end products of people's talk and gesture—such as mortality statistics and income or occupation data—are empty of the practical phenomena of everyday life. Our most important involvement with the reality of data is *at the very point* of its generation, not before or after that.

In the next four chapters, we turn to people in concrete social situations who concern themselves with life change. Their talk and gesture are treated as working features of the situation at hand. Life change, in turn, emerges out of the social flow of talk and gesture.

Chapter Three

Being On
or Off Course

In considering events related to life change, people distinguish between those they believe normal and abnormal ones. More generally, they concern themselves with whether someone is on or off course. This chapter deals with the social phenomenology of such occasions. Our concern is with what people do and say, and how they do so, when behavior becomes a topic for conversation about a proper life course.

Typifying Events

Alfred Schutz (1964) presented an idea that is quite useful for our discussion of the propriety of life change. He conceived of the way that people treat events in their own and others' lives as part of a process of *typification*. In their day-to-day relations, people are confronted with any number of events or displays of behavior that they believe they must make sense of in order to get on with their business. How do they do this?

Schutz's answer is that people make sense of events by casting them as elements of one or another "ideal" category (type) of events that is part of their stock of knowledge at hand. Schutz's conception of types is more encompassing than Weber's. Weber distinguishes between concepts that are empirical generalizations such as genuses or species, on the one hand, and ideal types that are "tendential" concepts used for particular theoretical purposes, on the other. Schutz treats all concepts as types, relevant types being tacit emergents of the occasion at hand. As Schutz (1970a) states: "As Husserl . . . has convincingly shown, all forms of recognition and identification, even of real objects of the outer world, are based on a *generalized* knowledge of the *type* of these objects or of the *typical* style in which they manifest themselves. . . . Each of these types has its typical style of being experienced, and the knowledge of this typical style is itself an element of our stock of knowledge at hand. This same holds good for the relations in which the objects stand to one another, for events and occurrences and their mutual relations, and so on" (pp. 118-119).

Events are encountered by people who, either through deliberation or in a moment's duration, conclude that such-and-such occurrence is typically this-or-that. Events, in effect, make no sense to people until they have been standardized as "obviously" (at least for the moment) an instance of some known type of occurrence. To make sense of events is not just a matter of discovering the meaning of occurrences. It is more active and constructive than this. Events are judged and typified by people as an *intrinsic* feature of meaningfully responding to them. The reality or sense of events does not exist before the work that people do to understand them. It emerges out of the process of understanding. Needless to say, this places the study of life change in the midst of people's deliberative processes, what we have generally called "negotiation."

The way people make sense of the events of daily life has two sides. On the one hand, they perceive and ponder what occurs in front of them. Things felt to be "out there" puzzle them. On the other hand, answers to the ongoing riddles that they confront lie in their deliberations over them, deliberations that rely on knowledge (typifications) at hand.

People's work in dealing with events is not far removed from traditional notions of scientific work. Scientific work is said to be two-sided. It is empirical in that scientists focus their attention on some facet of a world tacitly accepted as real, considered to be separate from their own minds. Scientific work is analytic in that this real world is not simply perceived, but conceived, which means that thoughts about it are generated. These thoughts are assigned a variety of names such as hypotheses, theories, models, and the like.

Assuming that laypersons make sense of events in a manner analogous to the way scientific work is done, we shall treat both laypersons and human scientists as simply people. Thus, scientific theories, hypotheses, and analytic schemes may be thought of as typifications. They are the formal stock of knowledge that the scientist uses to make meaningful the events that he encounters in the world of interest to him. They constitute the set of ideal categories to which he, as a scientist, commits himself as being a way of looking at his subject matter, whatever it might substantively be.

Although we have drawn an analogy between the work of laypersons and that of scientists in the task of making the events of their respective worlds meaningful, it is important to keep some distinction between the two in mind. They differ from each other in at least two important respects that relate to their treatment of typification. First, scientists usually professionally commit themselves to the systematic elaboration of their typifications while laypeople do not. Second, conventional scientific etiquette urges scientists to make public their typifications.

Why should these distinctions be kept in mind? We shall only suggest a reason here since we will return to this later. Although both laypersons and scientists make sense of, and thereby construct events in, their respective worlds, they differ in their publicly expected and/or publicly professed commitment to the task. Scientists are constrained by others as well as they constrain themselves to use a rather specific vocabulary and to be more wide-awake to the task.[1] Such social and personal constraint—which, by the way, may serve as a behavioral definition of scientist—suggests that the scientist is likely to be more determined than the layperson in the invocation of acceptable typifications in making sense of events. When a scientist deals with human events and moral phenomena, there is a kind of professional determinism in his considerations. Laypersons, on the other hand, are more likely to entertain independent "moral pleas" from those people whose lives they judge.

All people distinguish between types of events in daily life,

---

[1]The visibility of scientific, life-constructing activities is the empirical ground for the social phenomenological criticism of conventional scientific approaches to life change. The conventional human scientist's concern with life change is the same as the layperson's except that the scientist is more consciously systematic and analytic about it. Thus, in order to see and understand the logic of people's talk and deeds about being on or off course, in all its nuances and implications, the most effective place to look is the conventional human scientist's or scientific practitioner's work in relation to the topic—for example, commitment and discharge proceedings on the so-called mentally ill.

There are, of course, degrees of scientific concern with scientific theories. This brings us back to Kuhn's (1962) argument about scientific revolutions discussed in Chapter One in relation to Piaget's conception of cognitive growth in children. If he were to use Cicourel's (1970a) terminology, Kuhn would argue that "basic" concern with scientific theories by scientists characterizes the revolutionary periods in scientific thinking and research in which paradigm assumptions are made visible as assumptions and opened to question. "Normative" concern with scientific theories characterizes what Kuhn calls normal science. Kuhn might say that normal science "glosses" over its basic (tacit) assumptions as such and must do so in order to carry on its business (research). Scientific research, therefore, could be said—like lay people's everyday lives—to necessarily rest on a kind of fundamental ignorance of itself. It cannot be continually, critically reflexive (compare Gouldner, 1970) and empirical simultaneously.

Kuhn's argument has its analogue in lay people's "theories" about life change. Like normal science, everyday living is a matter of lay people taking for granted (and thereby not being concerned with) their tacit "theories" of life change as theories. This is one way to define what Schutz calls the "natural attitude" (in science it might more appropriately be called the "empirical attitude"). Should lay people begin "basically" to be concerned with their "theories" of life change, it would be as revolutionary for them as it is in science. Durkheim may have had this in mind when he spoke of anomie. Anomie, like scientific revolution, is a state of existential despair at having seen through one's world and realized that all that was sacred (or unspoken) about it is of human design. Not speaking of it allowed one to go about its "real" affairs.

the typical order of such events, the typical circumstances in which order may be temporarily disrupted, and so on. Besides being or not being professional, people differ in how elaborate and technical their typifications are. Some hold simple, mutually exclusive, dichotomous typifications such as ideas of life as either good or bad or of its events as sacred or profane. Others bring an elaborate conceptual baggage with them in making sense of life. Indeed, part of their official work may be the task of constructing and elaborating developmental schemas with any number of components such as stages and/or critical periods. The more elaborate the typifications, the more variable and complex are life events; the more professionally conceived are the typifications, the more self-assured the acceptance of the meaning of events is likely to be.

Using Typifications. Typifications serve their users by providing frames through which events are made meaningful. For example, consider those who have typified people's acts as being either those of scoundrels or those of honorable men. A scoundrel may have typical characteristics such as hypocrisy, being prankish, and being untrustworthy. The appellation *scoundrel* suggests a category of acts that are logically and "obviously" related. Likewise, honorable men are defined as typically unhypocritical, not prankish, fair, and open-minded.

Now, consider those who carry this conception as they encounter behavior that they define as prankish. What do such pranks mean? At least for the moment, such behavior may be accepted as the acts of a scoundrel. The term *scoundrel* organizes a number of reasonable inferences. Pranks are distasteful because they are understood to be part and parcel of the behavior of a type of person who is obnoxious in that he is also implicitly untrustworthy and hypocritical. Of course, this may be only a momentary response to the prankster. With further evidence, pranks may become typical of something else. For example, they may suggest that the prankster merely has unsubtle humor. In the process, the prankster's acts take on different meanings for those observing and considering them; the acts become different "things" for them.

Depending on the occasion of their use, types differ in the

cognitive function they serve. All types serve to meaningfully assemble events. Sometimes, types are used simply as ordering devices. For example, to conclude that an event is trivial orders it in relation to more significant ones. At times, types serve to explain events. For instance, to suggest that an act is the normal, immature behavior of an adolescent boy explains the behavior as a manifestation of a normal, developmental process. At still other times, types serve highly rhetorical purposes, and so on. The particular emphasis that typification takes cannot be understood separately from its occasioned use in practice; the emphasis meaningfully constitutes the "content" of types. On one occasion, typifying an act as normal, immature behavior may serve to explain it, while on another occasion, this may serve as a means of dissuading others from chastizing the boy.

Typification has a number of practical features; let us consider four of them. First, as we have indicated, it is an important means by which people make sense of events, whether those events are finally conceived as comic pranks, politics, or symptoms. People not only see the world but organize it, which allows them to claim that what appears before them is thus-and-thus. When shared, such claims become social typifications or interaction devices (compare *institutionalization*). They serve as a means by which people together interact toward "things"—in a way reminiscent of Berger and Kellner's (1970) conceptualization of the emergent social reality of marriage.

Second, typification elaborates understanding. For example, if an event is defined as a typical instance of the normal, prankish acts of some type of individual, it can safely be concluded that—for all practical purposes, at the moment—the event is not "strange." If the behavior is not "strange," it is unreasonable to look for further events that might serve as symptoms of abnormality in the individual who displayed the original behavior. The conclusion might be reached that such an individual will "typically grow out of such things in time," and his behavior therefore dismissed. What has been encountered and defined as an act of prankishness by a single individual at a single point in time is elaborated as being an expected instance of some typical but more general and normal scheme of events.

This use of typification is not unlike the scientific function of theorizing (see Hewitt and Hall, 1973). Theories serve scientists in that they are the means of making sense of events in scientifically relevant worlds. Theories also elaborate understanding, independent of events. The internal logic of scientific theories implies any number of conclusions that stand on relatively small bits of empirical input. The same is true of laypersons' "theories." The logic of "theories" fills in gaps in the knowledge of things that have been only selectively experienced —often quite selectively. Both forms of theory are practical in that they are the working means by which people make sense of things.

Third, typifications serve as guides to action. By making events meaningful, typifications suggest behavioral programs to people. For example, should an event be defined as the typical, normal acts of someone at some stage of life, it follows that the acts should reasonably be dismissed as such. There is no point in making much fuss over them. After all, as might be concluded, "It's only natural, isn't it? What can you do but live with it?" The "same" event defined as a typical abnormal act suggests a rather different course of action. It would be reasonable to search for more evidence suggested by one's "theory" of madness or, at least, abnormality. Moreover, it would be reasonable to attend very carefully to the individual involved for clues that would lend further credence to his typical abnormality. Dismissing this type of behavior, under the circumstance, would be unreasonable. Lemert's (1962) description of the dynamics of interaction between people who have typified someone's acts as "suspiciously abnormal" shows how carefully attentive they are to other "clues" of abnormality. Their attention virtually becomes a part of the abnormality they seek out.

Besides guiding action, typifications serve as public rhetoric. This is a fourth use of typification. People actively use typifications to persuade and convince others of the proper meaning of their own and others' acts. For example, such use occurs when some untoward act has been or will be committed. A man may have been discovered by his wife to have spoken too frankly about his spouse among casual acquaintances. When she confronts him with this, she is, in effect, taking issue with the sense of order that she thought both tacitly agreed governed their lives, namely, an understanding that their intimate joys and trials were privy to no one but themselves. She is visibly disturbed by this breach of faith as she asks him, "How could you?" As her spouse explains that "something must have come over me" or that "I had to say those things in order to show my openness so as to find out something from them" he is constructing a definition of his alleged betrayal that typifies it as "obviously" reasonable and "in order," given the circumstance in his explanation.

This rhetoric of definition, centering on the meaning of making intimate information public, is, from our point of view, visible evidence of the negotiation of social order. Certainly, the order at stake is a small portion of what people feel is the total order in their lives. Nonetheless, on this particular occasion, it is *the* social order, for all practical purposes. The nature of that order eventually comes to rest on what typical event the alleged breach of intimacy is convincingly defined to be.

Mills (1940) and Scott and Lyman (1968) called this rhetorical use of typification "vocabularies" and "accounts," respectively. Not knowing what came over one and offering someone valued information in exchange for information of greater worth are vocabularies that serve as definitions for one's acts. They offer motives for what one has done.

The use of typifications as accounts is retrospective; that is, it serves to explain breaches in order that have already occurred and are considered to be in need of repair. Hewitt and Stokes (1975) have noted that people also attempt to typify impending awkward events in such ways that what they eventually do is defined as one thing rather than another. For example, rather than risking the definition of one's statements as being those of a racist, a person may preface them with "I'm not prejudiced—some of my best friends are Jews, but . . ." This suggests to members of his audience that, while what he will say would otherwise be construed as anti-Semitic, they should "really" typify his statements as those of an objective observer of the Jewish/Gentile scene who is simply commenting on what he has noticed, his statements being a way of interpreting his observations. Hewitt and Stokes call this prospective use of typification "disclaimers."

Typification Shifts. Typifying an event is like placing it within a theoretical frame. This may be quite fleeting. Consider people confronted with some simple occurrence that has no common meaning for them. Suppose that one of those confronted by the occurrence suggests that "that's just so-and-so doing such-and-such." Others may agree and nod in "obvious" certainty that such-and-such is "really" the case. For example, someone may glibly suggest, "that's probably true" because of what he saw yesterday. Another comments that "that's just Charlie," implying that Charlie *will* be Charlie, over the normal course of events. Perhaps finally someone concludes, "Well, you know him. That's just to be expected." This suggests that the event is to be treated as an inevitable part of the nature of things—in this case, Charlie's nature. These brief exchanges offer a history of the occurrence, a prognosis of things to come, and a philosophy by which to understand its logic.

The important thing to note here is not whether or not things happen in just this way. Rather, it is that out of and around an occurrence, in a flash, an entire world is made. Moreover, at the moment, it is within this world that people operate and lead their situated lives. Typifying the occurrence as such-and-such has, by the very logic of typifying (or theorizing), generated a whole conceptual edifice around the occurrence.

Now, suppose someone notes another event, relates it to the preceding one, and suggests that the original occurrence may be something other than it was presumed to be. It is suggested that "what happened, somehow, just doesn't jibe with how Charlie acted last fall at this same time." Others entertain the remark. It raises the possibility that, indeed, what has occurred may not be "just natural" and therefore, "just Charlie." This is an urgent issue because, first, thinking about Charlie, and second, knowing how to respond to him necessitate resolving it somehow—which way it is resolved not being as significant for us at this point as that the issue is resolved.

If the occurrence is defined as possibly unnatural, the search is on, as it were. Are there other events that support the "hypothesis" that the occurrence may be an expression (symptom?) of an unnatural (abnormal?) process? Given a "theory" of abnormality, what and where should we look for further evidence for or against the "theory"? The past? The future? Is the occurrence typical of normal or abnormal events given the circumstance and person being considered?

A world is being negotiated. It is being generated around the occurrence and is being elaborated. Its conceptual apparatus is being developed and its logical conclusions are being drawn. Contrary to the popular maxim against "jumping to conclusions," which suggests that such jumps may somehow be prevented so as to promote reason in daily living, "jumping to conclusions" is at the very heart of living a meaningful existence. People cannot help doing so in order to *get on* with the reasonable business of daily living.

Once an occurrence has been redefined as typically something other than previously believed, again, in a flash, another whole world is generated. Such qualitative shifts in the meaning and understanding of occurrences cannot be thought of as developmental. Rather, they are analogous to quantum leaps or gestalt shifts. Typification shifts abruptly alter the meaning of an event from one reasonable world to another. Such worlds are internally reasonable but not logically reducible to each other. In everyday life, people experience such shifts as natural and take them for granted. Should they experience them as definitional shifts as such, they would likely be shocked, to say the least. For us, as observers of daily life scenes, definitional shifts are amazing.

As far as conventional approaches to life change are concerned, the significance of typification shifts is that they *radically* challenge the analysis of life change as being a matter of development, growth, maturation, and the like. Rather than life being linear and continuous, in practice it leaps ahistorically and philosophically.

Typifying Life Change

We have spoken of typification in general as it related to how people deal with events in everyday life. We indicated uses

that people make of typifications. And we commented on the
shifting character of products of the typification process. In
light of this, what do we mean, concretely, when we say that
people typify life change as to its normality?

A Lay Example. Consider the following account of an
event reconstructed for one of the authors by a graduate student (who is the mother involved) after she recalled and "saw
through" an experience as a process of typification. Mother is
hurriedly preparing for an afternoon tea with the ladies of her
charity club. Her son, age thirteen, is in the midst of what she
considers to be a normal spell of the summer doldrums, putter-
ing around the house and complaining that there is nothing to
do. Mother halfheartedly listens to his complaints as he follows
her around the house. She begins to feel harried as time flies by.
He continues to complain, whining occasionally and fidgeting
with the decor his mother has fastidiously arranged for her
guests. It is hot. The two are gradually coming to conflict as the
mother presses on with her preparations and as her son annoys
her and undoes some of her presumably completed tasks while
he tries to pass the afternoon in some way.

Finally, she turns toward him and yells bitterly that he is
"such a child!" She caustically reminds him that kids like him
grow up to be pests, never knowing what to do with themselves,
and always hanging onto other people. He shouts back at her,
tersely mouthing some words about not being a child, and reminds her of how "grown up" she said he was yesterday. She
glosses over this and continues to elaborate her prediction about
what kids like her son (type) grow to be later in life. She calls
him a pantywaist and exasperatedly concludes that he will never
make it on his own.

The mother is now taken up with the way she has typified
her son's annoyance that afternoon. She hurries about the
house muttering to herself. On occasion she addresses her son in
curt phrases. He continues to hang about whichever room she
enters. She asks herself, in a tone loud enough for her son to
hear, what could possibly have made him into the kind of person he is showing himself to be. She half blames herself for
perhaps overprotecting him as a child. She then concludes,

while shouting at him, "Yes. That's why you're still such a child!" The doorbell rings. The episode is concluded, for the moment.

What are we witnessing here? We have described a few fleeting events involving a mother's preparations and a son's complaints. However, much more than this is understood to be meaningful by the mother and son as both continue to exchange comments and "jump to conclusions" about the reasons why the events at hand have come to be what they are as well as what "surely" is likely to follow. In typifying her son's behavior as overly dependent, the mother begins to construct an explanation. She is, in effect, constructing a theory of his behavior. An abnormal life course is invoked. Her son responds to her by talking about *the* course. He denies the stage at which his mother has located him. She glosses over this and elaborates her son's progress over the course, describing its typical history in terms of his behavior. The course she invokes is real at the moment.

The typical course the mother has invoked is a linear one. The mother turns from this implicit model to her son's childhood and "discovers" evidence for overprotection, evidence that, she suggests, reasonably explains her son's current behavior. She then elaborates the model. She informs her son of what he "obviously" will grow to be.

Let us return to our example. The doorbell has been answered. Mother and son politely greet the first ladies to arrive. The son bids them welcome and asks them to be seated in the living room. They begin chatting. Son interrupts his mother to inform her that he is going to see if he can "round up any of the guys to play ball." Mother urges him to do so and returns to her guests.

One of the ladies comments on what a nice young man the son is. She continues to say that he certainly knows how to be "*the* gentleman" and is certainly more mature for his age than many adolescents she has known. The other ladies concur. The mother does, too, and proceeds to provide her guests with examples of his resourcefulness. She even hints at what transpired immediately before her guests' arrival, saying that when he wants something, he's quite "hardheaded," glossing over her earlier interpretations of this. The mother then glibly suggests that such hardheadedness is a sure sign of independence. The guests agree and compliment their hostess on what a fine boy she is bringing up. She thanks them and concludes that, yes, indeed, he is a fine boy.

The conversation then turns to the more general topic of typical boys like her son. The talk of those gathered for afternoon tea elaborates the life course of such boys. One of the ladies asks the mother about the kind of "self-reliance training" she provided her children when they were growing up. Mother provides examples of what *she* did with *her* kids. One of the ladies, some time later, concludes: "Well, I guess that explains it, doesn't it?"

As the moments pass, the conversation about childhood development becomes quite serious. Some of the ladies, the hostess included, are visibly proud of their offspring and what their children are becoming. One or two of them are dismayed as they report on their own children's behavior and what prospects life holds for them.

Now what have we witnessed? The son has become typical of a different kind of person than what was "obvious" in the circumstance before arrival of guests. In a flash, his mother's description changes from his dependency to the fine young man that he is becoming. The son's life shifts from one course of development to another in a matter of moments. Life change is as fluid as conversation.

A Professional Example. The foregoing was an account of a short series of events so commonplace that, mostly, they pass for the trivial rather than the dramatic. They are largely unconscious[2] to those involved in them. However, in their construc-

---

[2] Consider Freud's contrasting vision of the unconscious. Freud considered the unconscious to be a source of "troubles" for everyday living, which, in being made conscious, allows a person to deal with "troubles." For us, however, the unconscious (seen but unnoticed) features of everyday life enable people to proceed with the business of living; being conscious of everyday life would seem absurd to people and, contrary to Freud, would make for "trouble."

tion and elaboration, from place to place, the very stuff of life change emerges.

Let us turn to another example, this time to professionals concerned with life change. One of the authors (see Gubrium, 1975) did extensive field work on the social organization of patient care in a nursing home. As in many patient care facilities, the professional administrative staff (top staff) of the home conducts weekly staffings, or more formally, patient care conferences (PCCs). Top staff includes administrator, medical director, director of nursing, assistant director of nursing, social worker, chaplain, occupational therapist, in-service director, activity director, and dietitian. On occasion, a member of the home's floor staff, such as a charge nurse or a nurse's aide, or an interested outsider, such as a patient's clergyman, is invited to attend.

Staffings serve as a means by which to discuss the medical and emotional status of specific patients and to develop and write individualized care plans for them. This presumably requires top staff to have information about patients. Although members of the top staff spend little time on patient floors, they do have access to four kinds of information that are accepted as data about patients: nurses' notes on patients' charts; "serious" interviews that some members of the top staff occasionally conduct with patients, typically lasting from five to ten minutes; anecdotes about "amazing" events in certain patients' nursing home lives that are part of the home's staff folklore; and the passing observations that some top staff members (especially, the administrative nurses) make when they briefly appear on patient floors, usually for purposes other than patient care.

Nurses' notes are written by nurse's aides close to or during shift change. Writing them is considered an annoyance at best. The standardization of entries is an efficient way to complete an undesirable but required task. The content of these entries is so uniform as to virtually homogenize variations in patients' daily lives. "Serious" interviews are usually chats about such subjects as the weather, how "good" the patient looks today, upcoming nursing home events, whether the patient plans to attend them, and the like. Patients define and treat these interviews as visits. Anecdotes focus on what staff considers to be the outstanding and/or rather humorous behavior of patients. For example, there are anecdotes about romances, boisterous quarrels, patients escaping from the home, and the distances that patients walked before they were found. Passing observation provides top staff with information about the physical decorum of a floor. In practice, top staff uses physical decorum as an indicator of the emotional status of patients.

Now, given the information that top staff has about patients, how does it conduct staffings so that the conferences are recognized as the planning aspect of patient care in the home? In staffing a patient, staff members must interpret the information to which they have access. Staff's interpretations involve typifying it. The meaning of the information arises out of the schemes and "theories" used by staff to order it. For example, recollected anecdotes may suggest that someone is "obviously" this or that type of person. Or the results of a serious interview might imply that this or that "theory" of behavior is "certainly" applicable in the case at hand.

The practical relationship between the information top staff has and its members' typifications of patients is two-sided. Garfinkel (1967) calls the practice a "documentary method of interpretation." On the one hand, certain bits of information about patients are treated by top staff as documents of a wider scheme of things, such as a personality type or a disease syndrome. On the other hand, once these types, syndromes, "theories," or schemes are discerned, they, in turn, are used to decipher other information that is available or speculated about.

Top staff typifies patients in various ways. For example, information on a patient's behavior may typify him as "really sick, you know what I mean," or as "a real leader." Such typifications meaningfully frame a patient's behavior and prompt those who use them to look for or recollect other evidence about the patient who is "really sick" or the one who is "a real leader." Typifications may be ensconced in rather technical language. For example, a patient's behavior may be defined as an example of "typical regression" or he may be seen as a "typical introvert."

Once patients are typified in some way, in a flash, a whole world of meaning emerges. Suddenly, the information is sensible in terms of a "theory" of the events being considered. The "theory" not only *makes* the information meaningful, but elaborates its meaning and guides further consideration of the patient. Typifications become tacit programs for how to talk and proceed in the coming course of interaction.

Once typified, events take on an increasingly rational character. A staffer who suggests that a bit of information shows that someone is a "typical leader" virtually implores others who accept the suggestion to search for and/or recollect select clues about his leadership qualities. A staffer who suggests that someone is "really" mentally ill in one way or another is tacitly suggesting to others present that they elaborate this "theory" of mental illness. It is taken for granted to be the job of reasonable persons to reach (jump to) "logical" conclusions. The purifying feature of typification leads people to "rationalize" events. This means that untypical information tends to be glossed over as more "obvious" information is gathered and integrated into a gradually emerging portrait of "perfect leadership," "perfect insanity," and so on.

Once begun, the purification process gains momentum until some other typification is proffered. The process tends to reach closure by its *own* momentum—that is, by the logical actions of rational men and women who reason together. Thus, to some extent, people's deliberations about the meaning of events are independent of the empirical content of those events. Deliberation, in effect, rushes on to its reasonable conclusion. A professional staff that claims to be in the business of caring for the physically and emotionally sick tacitly is enticed to "find" (make) illness, on which it subsequently uses its expertise in rehabilitation.

The following are excerpts from two patient staffings. Much of what we have delineated in the preceding paragraphs about the nature and process of typification occurs very quickly. Regular staffing participants are (all pseudonyms):

Mr. Filstead	Administrator
Dr. Cosgrove	Medical Director
Miss Timmons	Director of Nursing
Mrs. Singer	Assistant Director of Nursing
Mrs. Boucher	In-service Director
Mrs. Smith	Activity Director
Miss Erickson	Social Worker
Reverend Edwards	Chaplain
Mrs. Walsh	Occupational Therapist
Mrs. Hoffman	Dietitian

The first excerpt is from Joan Borden's staffing. Note the shifts in how staff typifies her: from being independent to being mentally deteriorated, agitated, self-sufficient and a leader, and finally to being subject to "spells." Each typification is briefly elaborated in staff members' deliberations. Varied bits of anecdotal, casual, and formally recorded information are recounted as "documentary" evidence of who Borden "really" is. The reality of Borden's life and changes in it lies not so much in objective fact as in the tacit theories that staffers invoke to organize what they accept as fact. The negotiation of Borden's life ends, for all practical purposes, as time runs out. Staff considers its business closed when a goal has been agreed upon.

JOAN BORDEN, 72 YEARS OLD

Singer: Joan's a very independent lady. She's quite active and participates in all the sing-alongs. The reason we decided to discuss Mrs. Borden is that she's recently had two strokes. She was watched closely. Dr. Savoy [*Borden's personal physician; not present*] feels comfortable at this point that she remain on the first floor. [*The first floor of the home is for "residents" who are considered in need only of personal care while the other floors are for "patients" who are considered in need of various levels of skilled nursing care.*]

[*Singer then reviews Borden's medical history, frequently glancing at Dr. Cosgrove. Then, Father O'Brien speaks.*]

Father O'Brien [*Borden's priest*]: She's been very active at St. Barbara's. I saw her in bed here and then I saw her later when she was up and around.

Timmons: Mentally, also, she has deteriorated. [*Note typification shift.*] She doesn't continue with her personal care. She has trouble with putting her clothes on.

[Several participants nod in agreement as Timmons' characterization is elaborated by others.]

Smith: She has trouble with crafts. She can't see the calendar right. She seems confused.

[A number of side conversations take place noting Borden's physical symptoms as evidence of her "mental deterioration," whereupon Dr. Cosgrove offers a suggestion.]

Cosgrove: We should try to limit the demands on her. We should try to lighten an already taxed mind. This is not a time for new things for her.

Singer: I'm worried about her activities outside the building. *[Borden has planted and cares for a flower bed next to the building, among other things.]*

Cosgrove: We should limit her outside activities. But, I don't want you to take this as final. This recommendation is only for discussion.

Smith: I find her considerably agitated. You know Joan.

Timmons: Her hearing must be getting worse. She picks up certain things and interprets them wrong and then spreads them. You remember . . . like she spread the rumor that someone had died and spread that. *[Alleged death was reported incorrectly to the home's receptionist. Borden overheard correctly.]*

[Chuckles. Many asides which recount various aspects of the rumor. Erickson continues.]

Erickson: You're not thinking of moving her to the third floor, are you?

Cosgrove: I think that that would be too sudden.

Reverend Edwards: Well, I saw her helping someone in the parking lot.

Cosgrove: Well, this indicates that she thinks of herself as a leader. *[Note alternate typification invoked.]*

[Staffers begin to elaborate alternate typification.]

Erickson: That's why we better be careful about moving her, because we'd threaten her and she'd flip out.

Father O'Brien: Joan, to my knowledge, has been very alert.

Cosgrove: I think if we should look at this over a period of time . . . maybe we should lighten the burden.

Erickson: The family has noticed these trends also. She's also a leader. When I first came here, Joan gave me my first sock in the stomach. *[Several staffers ask for details.]* She said that nursing homes are not for her. *[Other participants are reminded of similar comments they have heard from Borden and recount them for the staffing.]* Now, she's a real promoter of Murray Manor *[the nursing home]*.

*[More reminding and recounting of events that typify Joan as
a leader and alert. Then Timmons suggests another characterization.]*

Timmons: Miles *[Borden's roommate]* says that her personal hygiene
has gotten worse.

Smith: I think she knows that she can't do the things she used to do.
She's had a few seizures . . .

Cosgrove: By the way, we should get out of the habit of calling these
things "seizures." Maybe "spells." That's bad, too. Let's call them "thing."
Someone is having their thing.

Filstead: Father O'Brien, do you think these things *[PCCs]* are helpful
to you?

Father O'Brien: Yes. I think that this is very helpful. We have a real practical problem in any church. When they go into a nursing home, we lose
contact with our older members. So, when a funeral comes up, because of
change in personnel in the parish, we don't know who this member of the
parish was who was here ten years ago.

Filstead: We do want you to be here at the meetings. You may agree or
disagree with us, but at least you know what we're doing. You can get an
insight into what we're trying to do here. We are trying to do what we
profess to do when I first talked to you.

*[Considerable public relations talk. Borden's care plan is lost
in it. Finally, the social worker interjects.]*

Erickson *[rushed]*:   Then, the goal for Borden is to curb burdensome activities and encourage realistic independence. Right?

*[Everyone nods in the midst of side conversations about other
affairs. Time is running out. The next case is introduced.]*

The second excerpt is taken from Eileen Radke's staffing.
Here again, note typification shifts and the practical reasoning
and acceptable "facts" that elaborate each characterization of
Radke invoked. In a matter of minutes, Radke's life shifts from
being aimless and morbid, to being withdrawn, and finally to
being religious and "philosophical" as well as concerned for
others' needs. As with the Borden staffing, Radke's staffing
ends with someone's concluding statement of a care goal.

EILEEN RADKE, 86 YEARS OLD

Erickson: First patient to consider is Eileen Radke. Dr. Resnik *[Radke's
personal physician]* can't make it.

Jane Schuman [*floor nurse*] : Trying to find things out from her is like pulling teeth. If she can develop a need to report symptoms to us, then we've something accomplished. She speaks of dying. She doesn't have a goal.

> [*A competing "theory" of the "real" Radke is invoked by Singer.*]

Singer: I disagree with that. She has a very definite interest in maintaining herself at her present level. Jane, why don't you go on and give a patient profile.

> [*Schuman continues briefly, whereupon Erickson introduces yet another characterization of Radke.*]

Erickson: She's an introvert. She's very family-oriented and withdrawn. I don't want to put a psychological emphasis on it.

Walsh: She really wants to stay by herself. I think we really have to draw her out.

> [*Other participants submit personal anecdotes about Radke that "confirm" her alleged introversion. Then, Smith invokes still another typification.*]

Smith: She doesn't really feel depressed about being alone. It's a problem for us, but may not be a problem for her.

Erickson: That's right.

Reverend Edwards: When I interviewed her this morning, I found no depression. She was really being very philosophical about her life.

> [*This elaborates the character being constructed. Staffers now recount evidence for Radke's "philosophical" character.*]

Timmons: I see her as a very religious person. She takes a very existential role about "you die to live."

Hoffman: I've interacted with her at lunch. She's very concerned with the other patients' needs . . . whether they get their trays or not and so on.

Erickson: I don't think we should try to force our life style upon her.

Walsh: Yes. I feel that if she wants to be alone, then that's her choice and we should respect it. Don't you?

Cosgrove: She may not think in terms of her body. The other possibility is that she understands very well what you're trying to do and is simply not clinically oriented.

Erickson: We have to think of her generation as different than ours. Her generation never learned to relax. Her life is empty because she has no work to fill it.

Cosgrove: Let's just treat her like she wants to be. That'll be our care goal.

Filstead: What's the meaning of "treating like she wants to be"?
[All staffers sigh and exasperatedly assure him that he knows very well what that means, glossing over his question.]
Cosgrove: I think that these conferences are good. They enable us to get away from our bird's-eye view of things. [*Note the positivistic or "natural" attitude implied.*]

The Range of Normality

People vary in what they consider to be normal events of life. On occasion, their view is very narrow. In Chapter One, for example, we saw fairly distinct differences in the narrowness of definitions of normal human development among conventional approaches to life change. On other occasions, people assume the range of normal living to be quite wide. Any number of events might typify people as being on some normal course of life.

Whether an event is typified as normal or abnormal, the fact that it is typified at all instantaneously opens up a panorama of meaning that "obviously" follows from the typification at hand. For example, a man whose behavior of late has been considered rather "strange" but who is still typified as normal, is conceived as idiosyncratic, moody, under pressure, or the like as part of the meaningful integration of his actions into the type of person he is taken for granted to be. However, the instant that he becomes, through definition, a type of abnormal person, all his erstwhile "strange" actions are now symptoms of his madness, sickness, pathology, or whatever. His personal history and future qualitatively leap from one type of life course to another—in this case, from a normal course to an abnormal one.

Dealing with "Strange" Actions. How do laypersons deal with the actions of others that they feel are rather unseemly, given past actions? Consider the following. Yarrow and her associates (1955), in evaluating the meaning of mental illness for family members, analyzed the typifying processes of wives who encounter unusual behavior in their husbands. She cites the case of a husband, Robert F., a thirty-five-year-old cab driver, who was admitted to a mental hospital with a diagnosis of schizophrenia. Yarrow's question is: How did Robert F. get to the hospital?

Robert's wife, Mrs. F., recounted how she responded to her husband's intermittent unusual behavior. Among the things she noted as not typical of him were: his complaint of the TV set being "after him"; talk about his grandfather's mustache and a worm growing out of it; his statement that his genitals had been blown up and that little seeds covered him; and reporting that he had killed his grandfather, asking his wife to forgive him, and then wondering if his wife were his mother or God.

Her husband's talk and actions, of course, did not immediately lead her to conclude that his behavior was "strange." The occasions on which these events occurred were interspersed with times when Mr. F. was believed well and working, when Mrs. F. "never stopped to think about it," namely, his unusual behavior. When unseemly events occurred, however, his wife was surprised at them, and was always somewhat puzzled at why her husband should say such things. In trying to make sense of his behavior, she persisted for some time in attempts to integrate it into what she knew and felt would be typical of a person with his typical background and character, as she had come to define them. Thus, after some thought, she dismissed his reference to the worm growing out of his grandfather's mustache as just the normal kind of mix-up that he "must" have had after watching little worms in the fishbowl in their home. She normalized his shaken cries about having killed his grandfather as "probably due" to the fact that such wartime experiences as her husband had had would, understandably (typically), lead most people to talk like her husband did. For a few years, her husband's intermittent unexpected behavior and talk were considered to be just the kinds of things that any *normal* person would "really" do under the circumstances and not "really" that strange at all.

On each of the foregoing as well as other occasions, Mrs. F. continued to use the notion of normal to typify her husband. Her long-term knowledge of his actions, some of which she considered not unlike, or at least understandable antecedents of, the present ones, sustained her commitment to his normalcy.

Moreover, her "knowledge" of what (typical) people like her husband must go through because of their typical experiences (for example, typical soldiers) served to further corroborate his normalcy. What Mrs. F. "knew" about her typical husband as well as what she "knew" about typical people like her husband "obviously" meant her husband was really normal but had occasional "troubles."

Finally, a few days before Robert F. was admitted to the hospital, and after a number of episodes of unseemly behavior, the following was reported:

> Three days before admission, Mr. F. stopped taking baths and changing clothes. Two nights before admission, he awakened his wife to tell her he had just figured out that the book he was writing had nothing to do with science or the world, only with himself. "He said he had been worrying about things for ten years and that writing a book solved what had been worrying him for ten years." Mrs. F. told him to burn his writings if they had nothing to do with science. It was the following morning that Mrs. F. first noticed her husband's behavior as "rather strange" [Yarrow, 1955, p. 15].

With the definition of her husband's behavior as "rather strange," a whole new "theory" emerged for making sense of her husband—a "theory" that typified him as abnormal.

The process of typifying normality or abnormality and the use of typification to deal with "strange" actions, of course, does not necessarily occur in the particular sequence in which Mr. and Mrs. F.'s did. There is no particular patterning to the negotiation of normality, although the product of negotiation may be highly patterned. In the case of the F. family, in a matter of moments, an entire life history changed from having had a normal course to one that had been abnormal "all along." It is not unreasonable to conclude that the reverse also occurs.

Dealing with "Sick" People. Elsewhere in this chapter, we stated that typification is practiced by all people, lay and professional. Psychiatric, psychological, sociological, and other scientific theories and their applied counterparts may be considered typifications. For professionals, as for people in general, the meaning of the behavior of persons whom they claim to be in the business of evaluating or rehabilitating is not obvious (although they may claim that it is). In practice, its meaning is generated by defining it as an instance of one typical form or another. However, compare the range of events considered normal in the following staffings with the range in the preceding example.

Consider two transcriptions of patient staffings in a mental hospital which Perrucci (1974)[3] studied in a year of fieldwork. As he describes his work: "Its central purpose is to examine the way in which becoming mentally ill, being mentally ill, and becoming normal again are related to communal definitions and relationships" (p. xiii). The following transcriptions provide data about the "becoming normal" phase of this work.

When a patient, his family, or his physician desires that the patient be discharged or obtain a leave of absence (L.A.) from the hospital, the patient appears before the hospital disposition staff, which is composed of all physicians having responsibilities for a particular treatment service. This is called "going to staff." On occasion, the group may include other professionals (for example, social worker, minister, or nurse) who may have a special interest in a case. The disposition staff decides whether or not the patient being staffed is well enough to be discharged or to go on leave.

What is evident in the following transcriptions is how significant the matter of "structuring" is (as Perrucci calls it) in obtaining a discharge or L.A. *Structuring* refers to the way patients present themselves to the staff as far as their illness is concerned. In order to talk of and evaluate the patient, staff needs evidence, in talk and gesture, from the patient that he is "indeed" a patient and was "indeed" ill so that the staff, in turn, can do its business of processing the patient being staffed as dischargeable or ready for a leave. Staff typifies all those who come to staff as having been abnormal and now possibly ready for release. The typical patient is believed to have a life course

---

[3]The transcriptions on the following pages are reprinted from Robert Perrucci, *Circle of Madness: On Being Insane and Institutionalized in America*, © 1974, pp. 140-142, 155-158. Reprinted by permission of Prentice-Hall, Inc., Englewood Cliffs, New Jersey.

that runs from developing illness through institutionalization and rehabilitation to potential release. Staff is ready to talk the language of this course of life in terms of abnormality/normality at staffings. Its discharge or leave considerations and deliberations are framed in that language only. When a patient "structures" his behavior and talk in a language other (for example, a political one) than what staff is prepared to talk (namely, abnormality/normality), the business of discharge or granting a leave is not likely to be considered an appropriate request. When patients structure their talk and gesture in other than "normalizing" terms, it is considered irrational or sick. Such patients, thereby, are not believed properly releasable.

Perrucci argues that in staffings in which a patient does not structure his behavior so as to give clues to his "unwell" status, he is less likely to be discharged or granted leave than in those in which patients provide such clues. His argument is one about people's (in this case, patients' and professionals') "reasoned" use of typification.

The first transcription, Case 511, ends with the patient being granted a leave of absence.

Dr. Hand: The next one is ——————— .

Dr. Stone: Oh, she'll be here. She's a live one, "hellzapoppin" with her.

[Dr. Hand reads briefly from patient's folder, indicating age, sex, race, date of admission, diagnosis, previous hospitalizations, previous leaves, current treatment program. The progress note written by the ward attendant especially for staff is read also. This note usually indicates patient's relationships with others in the ward, and her general cooperativeness or non-cooperativeness with ward staff. Dr. Stone recommends a leave of absence.]

Dr. Hand: Will you call her in, Dr. Craig, and question her? I have to step out for a minute.

[Patient enters and sits down.]

Dr. Craig:

Q.   How long have you been here?

A.   About two years.

Q.   Have you got a family?

A. No.

Q. You sure you won't have any kids now if you leave?

A. No, I had one of those operations.

Q. Are you going to be an out-patient here?

A. I don't know.

[Dr. Hand returns at this point, and Dr. Craig turns patient over to him.]

Dr. Hand:

Q. Have you ever been on an open ward?

A. No.

Q. You taking any medicine now?

A. Yes.

Q. What are your official plans?

A. I want to go home to my husband.

Q. Are you anxious to go home?

A. Yes.

Q. Does anything bother you?

A. No.

Q. Do you think you need to be here?

A. That's for the doctors to decide.

Q. What happens when you have your nervous breakdowns?

A. I just get all upset, and sometimes I hear voices.

Q. How's the world treating you?

A. O.K.

Dr. Hand: Do you want to ask questions, Dr. Miller?

Dr. Miller:

Q. Is your husband working?

A. No, he gets social security checks.

Q. How much does he get?

A. I don't know.

[Dr. Miller indicates he is done.]

Dr. Kirk [*staff psychologist*] :

Q. You say you heard voices—tell us about them.

A. Oh, most of the time they're not too clear.

Dr. Hand: When did you hear them last?

Patient: Couple of months ago.

Dr. Kirk:

    Q.   Do the voices make you angry?

    A.   No.

    Q.   Are there any other signs of mental illness that you have?

    A.   Sometimes I think my periods may be some of it. I bleed an awful lot, and just feel terrible that time.

    Q.   Do people talk about you?

    A.   No.

Dr. Hand: Dr. Stone, you want to ask anything?

Dr. Stone: No, that's all right.

Dr. Hand: O.K., you can leave now, Mrs. _____. Thank you for coming. [*Patient leaves.*]

Dr. Hand: She takes Thorazine now, 150.

Dr. Stone: She just cooled down. She was high as a kite before.

Dr. Kirk: Do you think there's anything significant about her comments on menstrual flow and her illness? Freud said something about it . . .

Dr. Stone [*cutting off Dr. Kirk*]:   Sure he did. I'll give you a lecture on Freud; he was as crazy as a bedbug.

Dr. Hand: What shall we do?

Dr. Stone: Can't we get Social Service to check on the home before giving her an L.A.? They want her, but I didn't think the home situation was so good.

Dr. Craig: Let her go home before she gets sicker. She's all right now.

Dr. Hand: Let's put her on three months' L.A. instead of six months. That all right with everyone?

    [Everyone gives general support to the director's suggestion (Perrucci, 1974, pp. 140-142).]

Now, note the difference in structuring in the second transcription, Case 63, in which no release is granted. The patient frames her plea in political terms, an approach that, to staff, is not characteristic of someone who is releasable. Rather, it is "obviously" typical of a "really" sick individual.

Dr. Hand: The next one is _____, a discharge request. She says she can get a lab job in Benton Hospital. Would you tell us something about her, Mrs. Rand [*the patient's ward nurse*]?

Mrs. Hand: Well, _____ has been after a discharge for a while now. I asked Dr. Powell if we shouldn't try, and he said maybe we should. I think it's a shame to keep her here. She's a very bright girl, and she's really learned her lab work. Lately, she has refused to take her medicine. She says it doesn't help her; and besides, she says she doesn't need us to take her medicine.

Dr. Hand: I have a note here from her work supervisor indicating that she works well in the lab and has picked up a great deal.

Dr. Miller: Shouldn't we wait for Dr. Powell before we handle her case?

Dr. Hand: No, he won't be able to make it today, so we'll have to go on without him. Will you show her in, Dr. Craig?

[Patient enters.]

Dr. Hand:

- Q.   I see where you want to get a job at Benton Hospital.
- A.   Yes, I talked with their lab director last time I was in Benton and he was interested.
- Q.   Do you think you would like lab work as a permanent job?
- A.   Oh, yes, I enjoy my work here very much.
- Q.   It's really not easy work running all those tests. Are you bothered by the blood tests?
- A.   No, I don't mind them.
- Q.   Do you know who the governor of _____ is?
- A.   *[Appropriately answered.]*
- Q.   Do you remember when you first came to Riverview?
- A.   *[Appropriately answered.]*

Dr. Craig:

- Q.   How do you know you'll get a job at Benton if you're discharged?
- A.   I told you I talked to the lab director, and he was interested.
- Q.   Suppose he's not as interested as he appeared to you? Where will you work if you can't get in at Benton Hospital?
- A.   I think I know my lab work well enough to get a lab technician job somewhere.
- Q.   Well, let's see how much lab work you really know.

[Dr. Craig asks the patient more questions pertaining to various procedures and lab tests. After the last response, Dr. Craig indicates that the patient does know her lab work.]

Dr. Hand:

- Q.   How do you get along with the other patients?

A. Not very well. I have a few close friends, but I don't socialize with the other patients.

Q. What bothers you about the other patients?

A. Oh, I don't know. I just don't like living in the hospital.

Q. Do you think we've helped you while you've been here?

A. No, I don't.

Q. What kind of treatment have you had here?

A. Lobotomy and shock.

Q. Do you think it's helped you or tortured you?

A. I think it's tortured me.

[This response brings a stir from others present at staff.]

Q. You mean that we did these things just to torture you?

A. Oh, no, I'm sure that when they give shock they mean to help. I don't think they have.

Dr. Stone:

Q. Besides not liking it here, why do you want to go to work?

A. For one thing, I want to start earning my own money, and making my own way.

Q. If you want to make money, we can probably find plenty of opportunities for you to make money right here.

A. You mean like washing cars. I'm already doing that.

Q. *[In an annoyed tone]*: No, I don't mean washing cars. You could probably work full-time in the lab right here on a work placement.

A. I already asked Dr. Galt about an opening in histology, and he said there wasn't any. Anyway, I'd do much better if the hospital would free me.

Dr. Hand:

Q. What do you mean, "free you"?

A. Well, it would be just like the other work placements I've had. You're never really free.

[It was at this point in the staffing session that the observer noted the beginnings of the change in staff behavior. The patient's response about "never really being free" was followed by the exchange of glances among the physicians. These glances indicated that they had, so to speak, "picked up the scent." Staff participation at this point no longer followed the orderly procedure of the staff director asking individual members if they had any questions. The physicians spoke whenever

*they wished, sometimes cutting in on each other, and some-
times several speaking at the same time. The normal speaking
tone vanished as pronouncements and accusations were directed at the patient.]*

Q. But if you stayed here on a work placement you'd be free to
come and go on your own time. It would be just like a job.

A. No. You would still be controlling me if I stayed here.

Dr. Craig [*cutting in*] :

Q. Do you mean we control your mind here?

A. You may not control my mind, but I really don't have a mind
of my own.

Q. How about if we gave you a work placement in _____ ;
would you be free then? That's far away from here.

A. Any place I went it would be the same set-up as it is here.
You're never really free; you're still a patient, and everyone you
work with knows it. It's tough to get away from the hospital's
control.

Dr. Stone [*cutting in*] :   That's the most paranoid statement I ever heard.

Mrs. Rand: How can you say that, [*patient's first name*]? That doesn't
make any sense. [*Nurse is standing at this point.*] It's just plain crazy to
say we can control your mind.

[Nurse Rand turns to Dr. Stone, who is looking at her.]

Mrs. Rand [*still standing*] :   I had no idea she was that sick. She sure had
me fooled. [*Turning to patient again.*] You're just not well enough for a
discharge, [*first name*], and you had better realize that.

Dr. Stone: She's obviously paranoid.

*[Immediately following Dr. Stone's remark, Dr. Craig stood
up, followed by social worker Holmes. Dr. Stone himself then
stood up to join the others, including Nurse Rand, who had
been standing for some time. It should be noted that this took
place without any indication from Dr. Hand, the staff director,
that the interview was completed. He then turned to the patient and dismissed her. After the patient left, the standing
staff members engaged themselves in highly animated discussion. Nurse Rand was involved in making general apologies for
having indicated support of the patient's discharge request at
the beginning of the staff meeting. Drs. Stone and Craig were
engaged in monologues interpreting and reinterpreting the patient's statements. Amid the confusion, Dr. Hand managed to
comment, "I guess there's no need to vote on her; it's quite
clear" (Perrucci, 1974, pp. 155-158).]*

The outcomes of the foregoing staffings significantly "influenced" the life courses of the patients involved. Members of the staff deliberated over each case as if to judge whether a stage in some well-known course of abnormal or normal living had been reached, thus indicating that the person involved "obviously" was still too sick or was now "obviously" well enough for release. Depending on such deliberation (negotiation), in a matter of moments, life is on or off course.

Chapter Four

Predicting Growth

Interaction has a prospective as well as a retrospective dimension. People may consider a past that is different from the present and a future in which the present will be altered. Such considerations condition the present. Immediate events are seen in light of what has transpired and what will likely develop. For people, interaction is not wholly constrained or determined by present circumstances since the interpretation of "what is going on" is affected by beliefs about "what has already gone on" and "what will go on." For example, a husband's approach to what he believes to be the unfaithfulness of his wife will depend on his beliefs about her past indiscretions and future behavior as well as on her present revelations of sorrow, guilt, and promises of change. A father's interpretation of his son who flunked out of college will include the consideration of his past academic record and his future chances as well as the current definition of the problem and its solution offered by the son and others.

People provide direction to their own and others' lives

87

through practical theories that they have about living. All theories (both those of laypersons and those of scientists) are practical in the sense that they are used to conveniently summarize, categorize, and interpret a vast and otherwise unmanageable array of impressions and observations, to identify cause-and-effect relationships, and to predict new relationships or unexplored areas in which old relationships can be discovered. The practical theories of laypersons enable them to make sense of what has happened in their personal worlds and the worlds of others, to discover continuities or discontinuities between past and present, and to predict how past and present will develop into a future. These theories then allow them to discover and interpret change. In an important sense, change is created by them as they filter life experiences through the categories that their practical theories identify as useful. In the same way, formal scientific theories tell the researcher what variables are important, how they are related, and what to predict. In both situations, life is interpreted, in fact invented (Cicourel, 1970a; Garfinkel, 1967).

The *use* that people. make of theories of life change requires them to constantly articulate interpretations of the past with interpretations of the present and the future. The meaning of present happenings is not self-evident. Their meaning is contingent on the *interpretation* made of events in the past as well as expectations of events in the future. Likewise, events in the past are reinterpreted on the basis of present happenings, and future events will be seen as developments from past and currently present events. The point is that theories of life are not simply conveniently packaged reflections of the "past," "present," and "future" events of people's lives. Rather, people engage in extensive practical work to make them seem so and to claim them as such. Although in their actions, people take into consideration their sense of the past and their assessment of things to come, they do this as a practical feature of the present (see G. H. Mead, 1932). In this chapter, we focus on some practical features of theorizing about individual futures. How do people accomplish the prediction of future happenings and how do interpretations of the future affect the present?

The Future as Work

Human behavior is vastly more subtle and active than conventional theories would warrant. Certainly, in some sense we are rational beings, weighing alternative routes to desired ends and making reasonable choices from possible means. In the sense that people complain of being (as they claim) determined or controlled, they might be said to be products of such things as their personal histories, class backgrounds, and religious and educational experiences. What the more abstract, conventional depictions of human behavior miss, however, is that people are also beings who are continually in the process of negotiating their existence, of interpreting their past, defining their present, and predicting their future. Individuals are active in this process but they are not alone. Others join them, and they join others, in constructing theories of the past, present, and future. They all create their worlds together; the process of having been, being, and becoming is a social undertaking.

People have theories of life change that include notions about what kinds of persons are likely to change in what ways, what steps can be taken to manage change, what past and present behavior can tell us about change, and so on. Prediction is a continuous job, a process that is ongoing. Judgments are rarely final. They are tacitly conditional decisions, made on the basis of occasioned and "reasonable" estimates of future alternatives that are seen as more or less probable. Predictions generally contain an implicit "if" clause. That is, guesses are contingent on things staying the same but can be altered on the basis of new circumstance.

The business of prediction involves a great deal of work. For example, the prisoner tacitly negotiates the interpretation that guards make of his behavior. His behavior may lead the custodial staff to believe that he is trustworthy, harmless, a good prospect for reform. However, the prisoner also negotiates his image, or what he typically is, with other inmates (compare Hewitt and Stokes, 1975). The cues he uses to convince the guards that he is a good fellow may lead to a negative interpretation by other prisoners. Likewise, the guards may desire to

portray a lenient, humanitarian image to the prisoners in order
to make everyday life with them more bearable and less dan-
gerous. Yet, they balance this with their attempt to negotiate a
favorable image of their work with the captain or warden, who
may be primarily concerned with security. Thus, the reasonable
future that is "predicted" by inmates, guards, and others, is a
matter of considerable negotiation and tacit circumstantial competence.

Settings for Directing Growth

There are social settings in which the future officially receives special attention, in which some participants claim to
have a formal responsibility for directing the future lives of
others who are in their charge. Many of these settings are places
where the work that sociologists generally describe as "socialization" goes on. These are places in which the normative order of
a society is presumably passed on from one generation or group
to another. Families, schools, and certain types of youth organizations are claimed to provide such settings for children and
adolescents. The armed services, colleges and universities, personnel and training divisions of business organizations, and
rehabilitation prisons are said to provide them for young adults
and older persons.

The future is more than a set of possibilities to consider or
manipulate in calculating one's own best interest now or later.
Although personal interests are certainly important, as we shall
see, there is also the official claim of performing specialized
work for "society." Schools are officially organized and li-
censed, for example, to teach skills, attitudes, and habits that
are thought to be important for adult members of a society.
The armed services claim that they are training men for future
citizenship as well as for possible combat roles. In these future-
oriented settings, present behavior assumes special meaning in
terms of what it is thought to indicate about behavior to come.

Models of Schools as People-Making Organizations. In this
chapter we will focus on schools. As formal organizations,
schools are said to show the essential elements of the legal-

rational bureaucratic model presented by Weber (1958). Abstract rules are established to govern and guide actors' behavior in the coordinated pursuit of rational ends. Rules of behavior as well as goals are presumed to be clear and unambiguous. Duties and authority are located in a set of hierarchically arranged offices or positions sanctioned by a set of administrative rules. Regulated procedures are available for filling official positions. Policy decisions, administrative acts, and routine business are recorded in writing and maintained in a filing system.

This portrayal of organizational rationality misses much of the dynamic internal life that exists in complex organizations, such as schools, according to Gouldner (1959a). Complex organizations can also be viewed from what Gouldner calls the "natural system" model. This view stresses the importance of spontaneous, unplanned activity within the formal structure of the organization. The words *spontaneous* and *unplanned* refer to the many actions that cannot be understood from the perspective of a rational-legal model alone. People have "latent social identities" that are not rationalized in the official demands of the organization. They have very personal problems, concerns, and ambitions that are not treated in the ideal model. For example, people must deal with jealousies, career anxieties, sexual desires, headaches, and angry feelings as well as with formal goals. People also are faced with "situational problems" that are not easily articulated with the formally stated means and goals of the organization. Events are not so standardized as to exclude personal interpretation based on biography, the occasion, and previous events of similar kind. Rules and expectations are ambiguous and leave room for spontaneity and official nonrational behavior.

The two models, then, present rather different "images of man" in complex organizations. One depicts rational persons who know the ends to be achieved and the acceptable means for achieving them. They are able to identify alternative courses of action and to estimate probable desirable and undesirable consequences in terms of well-defined organizational objectives. The second model stresses the limits of completely rational behavior where goals may be unclear in specific circumstances. In addition, situations may present opportunities for conflicting goals, the range of viable alternatives may not be known, and the probable consequences of alternative means may be difficult or impossible to estimate. This model stresses the more informal aspects of organization behavior as opposed to the more calculated, mathematical image of the ideal-rational model.

Following Gouldner, both models would be needed to explain the complexities of life in schools. On some occasions, behavior appears to be unplanned and spontaneous, not formally articulated with educational goals. At other times, official calculation and consideration of alternative actions appear to dominate. Yet, neither model provides us with a perspective by which to fully understand the practice of schooling, that is, how members of school settings generate predictions of educability and meaningfully accomplish their official tasks. Behavior that appears to be spontaneous may in fact be thoughtfully constructed and responsive to past interaction and future expectations. Behavior that appears rational may not originally have been oriented to official methods or goals, but, on a later occasion, it may have been interpreted to fit legitimate categories of organizational rationality.

Life in the School

Let us consider two views of organizational life as they specifically relate to school life. One set of views, which we label conventional and which includes both models delineated by Gouldner, sees the school as an entity that in some way affects the behavior of its members. The other view, a social phenomenological one, sees school behavior as a practical product of the work done by those who conduct schooling.

Some Conventional Views of School Life. Many commentators on classroom life are looking for ways to improve its rational organization following what Gouldner calls the legal-rational model of organization. Behaviorists study the stimuli and reinforcers provided by the teacher and curriculum materials and the responses of students. Their goal is to understand the learning process and to make it more efficient in the service of school objectives. Educational technologists have a similar objective although they may not adhere to the behaviorist perspective. Educational psychologists develop tests, study teacher and student characteristics, and conduct research in the areas of learning and motivation, again with the aim of improving the learning process.

Proponents of open classrooms, free schools, and alternative learning programs have been more concerned with improving the life of the child. The immediate goals of organization take a back seat to mental health and happiness. It is generally assumed, however, that organizational goals will be fostered when the child is free of the constraints and pressures generated in the classroom.

In this search for a more rational or humane school, the day-to-day routine problems of "doing" classroom life have been largely ignored. Missing is a serious look at how teachers and students practically organize their daily lives, the routine problems they speak of, and how they routinely convince themselves and others of their solution. So much serious and earnest attention has been given over to theorizing about how "real" problems can be solved (that is, make schools more efficient and productive) or how to make school life more satisfying for the child that the question of how life is actually accomplished in schools has been neglected.

A few observers have given us a more intimate look at day-to-day life in classrooms (Jackson, 1968; Smith and Geoffrey, 1968). Their descriptions reveal a host of social processes that have been barely touched in educational theory or research. Jackson (1968) describes the world of a teacher and twenty-five to thirty students as a world constrained by the significance of the trivial. Life goes on day after day in a standardized environment marked by repetition, redundancy, and ritual. The children are the same, as are the curriculum, the class periods, and the organizational rules and procedures. It is a crowded environment that requires management of supplies, time, space, attention, and distractions. Evaluations are constantly being made of children based on test scores, daily performances, judgments of motivations, and character traits. These judgments are difficult

to make since performance may be different in several contexts
and children may be feigning interest and motivation. The immediacy of classroom events constantly intrudes on the best-
conceived plans. Moment-to-moment events cannot be anticipated; teachers do not know what weight to attach to
alternative actions or even what the range of possible alternatives is. Yet they manage to use fleeting behavioral cues to interpret and manage the immediacy of classroom events. In practice, they come to know "what's happening" because they have
observed similar behavior before and they extend the various
alternative possibilities into the future. However, their solutions
are never permanent; they are open to new interpretations as
things develop.

Smith and Geoffrey (1968) also see classroom life as an
ever-changing reality. They describe the teacher as subjectively
rational, as orienting means to desirable ends in a situation in
which decision making is constantly adjusting to changing
assignments, situational perspectives, and multiple and often
conflicting goals. The job of teaching involves much more than
the processing of rewards and punishments for desired ends.
Events from the past are interpreted in light of current behaviors, predictions are, made about future behavior, and preparations are made for alternate future contingencies. The teacher
may invoke "continuity" from the past into the present and
estimate the course and meaning of present events into the future. Awareness is constantly demanded if the teacher is to stay
on top of the multiple and simultaneous events in the classroom. The shaping of future events and a smooth transition
from the present into the future depend upon accurate information about a number of realities in the present. The teacher sizes
up the situation from moment to moment, projects current
behavior into the future, and makes tentative decisions on how
to maintain current development and how to institute changes.

The writings of a few people like Smith and Geoffrey and
Jackson provide us with much-needed intimate detail about life in
schools. Analysis has risen above pure advocacy or efficiency to
focus on the critical problems of how teachers see the complexity of their jobs and how they manage day-to-day problems

in the classroom. Yet, while they have broadened our perspective, the practice of school life remains to be documented.

Conventional sociologists have largely ignored the daily life and routine of schools in order to look at the end products. Schools are seen as places *for* socialization, *for* preparing students for later life. Students arrive at school with widely varying backgrounds and potentials. The school personnel then, relying on a blend of technology and art, attempt to convey certain positive cognitive skills, "real" motivational characteristics, and normative preferences. Schools are shown to more or less succeed with pupils depending on the children's background and intelligence and the technology or instructional resources available to the school. If the children are from poor backgrounds, the school is not likely to have as much success with them as with children from middle-class families. Likewise, if the child's intelligence or motivation is lacking, performance in school will suffer. The school is then said to be constrained by the type of student it serves (Coleman, 1966; Jencks, 1972; Boocock, 1972; Averch, 1974). Presumably if a lower-class school suddenly received a deluge of middle-class or upper-middle-class children, its services would be used much more effectively.

Of course, the career of a student is not tied just to background or ability characteristics. Decisions about placement and progress are made throughout the period a child spends in school, and these decisions affect the future options available to the child in the school as well as the occupational world. The daily experiences of school personnel with the child provide additional information, which is used to evaluate and place students. For example, some children are said to be "underachievers"; their performance does not match their capacity. Others are "overachievers"; they do much better than test results indicate that they should. This sort of information contributes to the more or less rational process of deciding what is both best and possible for a particular child.

In this view, students are said to possess characteristics that can be developed in the school to varying degrees, given the current state of instructional technology. Unfortunately, this technology is not considered powerful enough to make up for social, cultural, and personal disadvantages of background, race, and intelligence. Thus, the more advantaged have the resources to make more of their time in school and subsequently reap the rewards of a better education in the occupational and professional world. It is claimed that public education could provide a powerful force for more equality of opportunity if only students had more equal resources with which to take advantage of the opportunity.

The Social Phenomenology of School Life. In recent years, the sociology of education in Britain, much more so than in the United States, has been influenced by a social phenomenological perspective (Young, 1971; Esland, 1972; Dale, 1972; Hargreaves, 1972; Flude and Ahier, 1974). This "new" educational sociology rejects the conventional market model in which schools link the supply of talent to the demand of the market and thus focuses sociological interest on the barriers and obstacles to equal educational opportunity. Conventional variables, such as intelligence, race, class, and organization, are retained for analysis but their significance is quite different. Rather than treating these variables as external or constraining, in the new sociology, these variables become the elements of commonsense typifications that school personnel consider and use to make sense of and to justify their activity. Sociological work then focuses on the documentation of the processes whereby actors generate and maintain their view of the social world (Hurn, 1976).

The future status of children may be seen as a process of continuing interaction and negotiation between and/or among them and school personnel. Background characteristics, test scores, and personal encounters are not simply neutral or self-evident facts; they are subject to definition, judgment and interpretation. Judgments or interpretations stem from typifications and practical theories about people and what can be expected from them. From this perspective, the critical problem is to understand how classroom reality is constructed in the school. Students do not present problems or opportunities that are independent of the meaning and evaluation assigned to them by personnel in the social organization of the school. We need to know how events and behavior displays are given meaning and shared among school personnel, how they come to be seen as important, and how various criteria are negotiated and used for making judgments about children and their qualities.

Depending on whether personal or cultural characteristics are emphasized, theories about educational problems lead to propositions about deficient intelligence or disadvantaged environments. Both sorts of theories are glosses. That is, they unwittingly fail to make explicit the connections between personal or cultural characteristics and events in schools. Observers of the day-to-day intimate life that occurs in every school have clearly told us that schools process and differentiate students (Holt, 1964; Kozol, 1967; Kohl, 1968). They do not simply present opportunity. Teachers, administrators, and other school personnel judge, evaluate, and reward and punish. They make decisions about which group a child should belong to, how much attention he should receive, what instructional materials he should have, how fast or slowly he can work, and so on. Decisions are made against a complex and fluid background of personal beliefs, test results, daily behavior, and organizational expectations and constraints. These decisions are seen as "routine" jobs in the line of teaching and administering, decisions that are based on the strengths, weaknesses, or problems presented by a child or a group of children. They are "routine" or "mundane" because they are hardly thought about or reflected on by those who make them. The decisions are hardly routine or mundane in their consequences, however, for they are the very stuff of children's futures.

Predicting Growth on the First Days

Several years ago, one of the authors (Buckholdt) did intensive observation of a first grade class in an inner-city school of a major Midwestern city (Hamblin, Buckholdt, Ferritor, and Kozloff, 1971).[1] All of the children and the teacher were black.

[1] The work reported in the Hamblin book is primarily experimental and based on a social learning paradigm, rather than a social phenomenological orientation. The conversational data reported here were collected for, but not presented in, that work. The definition of data and the interpretation of events are quite different in the present context.

Within ten days after the beginning of school, the teacher had arranged the children into three "ability" groups. When asked about her reasons for assigning children to one group or another, the teacher explained that she used several criteria. The kindergarten teachers had passed on reports on reading readiness, ability to listen and work on assignments, behavior problems, and attendance. A group intelligence test had also been administered near the end of the kindergarten year and the results were given to the first-grade teacher. The teacher claimed that she had used this information from kindergarten as well as her own observations and evaluations during the first two weeks.

Accounting for Terry. The observer then asked the teacher about particular children. The following dialogue was recorded:

Interviewer: OK, I'd like to find out about some particular children. Why did you put Terry in the lowest group for example?

Teacher: Ha! That's an easy one. Look at what Jones [*kindergarten teacher*] said about him. He should have stayed in kindergarten if there weren't so many new kids this year. And his IQ, 57. He probably won't be with us long.

Interviewer: What do you mean?

Teacher: I know his parents, both winos and poor. His brother was here two years ago but we had to send him to "special." Terry's a sure candidate, too.

Interviewer: Were there any other reasons why you put him in the bottom group?

Teacher: Well, you've seen how he acts. He just sits there and stares into space. At least he doesn't bother anybody. You know, I haven't heard him say one intelligible word since school started.

The teacher claims to have used several indicators for the decision that Terry should be in the lowest group. His parents were alcoholic and poor. The home environment was bad, causing problems for both Terry and his brother. Terry had not acquired the necessary readiness skills in kindergarten and his IQ was extremely low. Also, she claimed, she could see from his behavior in first grade how unprepared and/or incapable he was.

Terry remained "sullen" and "unresponsive," according to

the teacher, for the first six months of first grade. He rarely answered questions from the teacher or completed more than a small fraction of his work. Interaction with other children was rare and, when it did occur, was generally marked by physical and/or verbal fighting. By February, the teacher was planning to have Terry placed in a "special" class for the following year. She invited the principal and several other teachers into her class to observe him and to confirm her judgment as well as to advise her about the best placement for Terry.

At the end of February, however, a series of events caused the teacher to briefly reconsider her evaluation of Terry. All of the children in the low group had made little progress in the first grade. They did not appear to recognize the letters of the alphabet, or, more importantly, the phonetic associations for the letters. At that time, Buckholdt was interested in finding out if young children could teach one another. He asked the teacher to allow him to pair children from the "advanced" group with the "slow" children for about twenty minutes each day. The more able children were to teach letter names and their associated sounds to the other children. The pairs of children were taken from the room and allowed to work together in the privacy of a small office. The observer either remained in the office with the children or listened to their conversation from outside the room. After twenty minutes of work, the observer tested the children to see how many new letters and sounds they had learned.

One day shortly after this experiment had begun, the observer, who was listening outside of the room, could not recognize the voice of the child who was serving as instructor. When he entered the room, he found Terry helping the supposedly more advanced child with letter recognition. Terry continued to switch between the tutor and tutee role with his partner for several days, until they both knew all of the letter names and sounds. At first, the teacher did not believe the reports about Terry. Finally, she came to see for herself and found that it was true. She asked Terry and his partner to give a demonstration to the other children in the class and invited the principal and several other teachers to observe his performance.

Terry made many other unexpected advances during the remainder of the semester. He became a leader in spelling, reading, and arithmetic. He was tested again at the end of the year and received a score of 131 on a group-administered intelligence test. Yet, ironically, the teacher kept him in the slow group. When she was asked why she had not allowed him to move to another group, she responded, "It takes more than a couple of weeks of work to get out of that group."

The observer followed this same group of children into the second grade. Unfortunately, Terry had moved from the area and was no longer enrolled in this school. Several teachers reported that his aunt had taken him to live with her after his parents had beaten him; others claimed that his parents had been evicted from their home and had moved from the neighborhood. Near the end of the school year, however, Terry returned to the school and entered the second grade with his old friends. Once again, he appeared sullen and unresponsive to the teacher. He did not read nor would he identify letter names or sounds. His official record now showed that his intelligence was "untestable"; it was too low to assign a score from the norming chart. He was assigned to a "special" class for learning and emotional problems for the following year.

The second-grade teacher was aware of Terry's progress during the last part of his first-grade year. Yet she dismissed this as unimportant since, as she claimed, he had received so much personal attention. "He won't make it in the regular classroom," she asserted. "We can't give special attention with so many kids. With his home and IQ, he won't cut it." So a boy who for a few weeks had risen to the top of his class was now assigned to a special terminal-track class for children who school personnel judge do not have the background or talent to succeed in the regular classroom.

Terry's case is interesting for several reasons. First, it shows the practical work of teachers in locating and understanding the "problems" of children. One could construct innumerable explanations for Terry's behavior, but the teacher's tacit model led her to discover the source of his difficulty in the family situation. Problems in the home accounted for his low

IQ and inadequate cognitive and interaction skills. The teacher's typification of Terry as a classic deprived child allowed her to interpret the meaning and source of his behavior. The theory of the teacher thus mirrored the more professional theories that explain many educational problems in terms of cultural disadvantage.

Second, Terry's case illustrates the reality-sustaining logic of the typification process. While both the first- and second-grade teachers admitted that Terry had shown remarkable improvement during the latter part of first grade, they dismissed this evidence as irrelevant to his standing. Using an argument similar to one that we will encounter again later when we discuss the work of probation officers in estimating the dependability or trustworthiness of delinquents, the first-grade teacher argued that a few weeks of outstanding performance provided insufficient evidence for removing Terry from the group of children that she saw as essentially uneducable. The second-grade teacher similarly dismissed any attempt to retypify Terry by attributing his apparent gains to the individual attention he received, attention that could not be provided in her classroom. Terry's tested IQ of 131 was not his "real" IQ. Her theory of intelligence apparently demanded that IQ be evident in large, noisy classrooms where children receive little individual instruction from the teacher. Intelligence, as measured by a test, had little relevance for her unless it could "really" operate in the context of the classroom as structured.

Finally, the typification of Terry reveals the predictive dimension that we have discussed previously. The teachers were able not only to locate the sources of his problem and to understand their meaning as evidenced in his behavior but they were also able to envision his future school career. The first-grade teacher saw his assignment to a special track as inevitable. The second-grade teacher made a similar prediction of Terry's future: "With his home and IQ, he won't cut it."

Terry's case, of course, is unusual in that few teachers are confronted with information that is apparently so discrepant with a public typification. The problem for the teachers could have been especially severe in that the information arose from officially recognized sources, intelligence and performance tests, not simply from parents' and students' pleas that one is more able than he appears. The unusualness of this case, however, serves to highlight the reality-making and reality-sustaining work of teachers. Moreover, we cannot answer who the "real" Terry is except that his intelligence is realized through the ongoing work that people do to make sense of it. Our purpose is to argue that the teachers handled this problem matter-of-factly. Their typification of Terry allowed them to casually dismiss apparently contradictory information about him and to continue with the business at hand without any extended disruption of schedule or instructional program.

Practical Reasons for Tracking. Rist (1973) has reported similar processes of student differentiation and tracking in the kindergarten of an all-black urban elementary school. The teacher possessed four pieces of information about each child as he or she entered school for the first time: a form showing preschool experience and medical history; a questionnaire in which parents reported on behaviors of their children, such as bedwetting, lying, and disobedience; a list of children from families who were receiving public funds; and gossip and reports from other teachers about the parents and older siblings of the kindergarten children. The teachers had no information about language skills, intelligence, or special talents or problems. Yet, by the eighth day of school the teacher was able to assign each child to one of three ability groups. Rist observes that the three groups could be distinguished on criteria of clothing and other aspects of physical appearance, body odor, interactional behavior among themselves and with the teacher, and the use of standard American English. The teacher had begun to evaluate student behavior and appearance from the very first day. When this information was combined with what she already knew about family and social-class background, she was able to typify and group children into supposedly homogeneous ability tracks. Certain criteria were used as indicative of future success and others as indicative of failure, and these judgments were leveled after only a few days in school.

Tracking or assignment to ability groups is a common practice in many schools. While student differentiation is justified as a rational process by school personnel, formal rules of assignment are inevitably too vague to accomplish this task. Teachers must rely on practical theories in order to identify signs of competence, motivation, and the like to make assignments in particular cases. In this instance, physical appearance, body odor, and the use of standard English apparently "told" the teacher something about the academic potential of children.

These early judgments had serious consequences for the quality and amount of instruction and attention that the three groups received for the remainder of the year. Rist reports that the leading group received two to three times as much of the teacher's time as the members of the other two groups. Members of the first group were more likely to be assigned positions of responsibility and authority in the classroom, to sit closer to the teacher during large group instruction, and to receive praise from the teacher. Members of the other two groups were much more likely to be the targets of control statements, threats, and ridicule. They also more often did "busy work" while the teacher presented new concepts or instructional material to the first group.

Once the groups were formed, there was no movement across castelike lines. Further evaluation apparently convinced the teacher that her initial judgments were correct. "Facts" she had tacitly accomplished out of practical reasoning were corroborated in the same ground—like an unwitting conspiracy, as P. L. Berger (1963) might put it. Near the end of the year when Rist (1973) asked the teacher about the performance of the children in the various groups, she replied as follows:

> Those children at table one gave consistently the most responses throughout the year and seemed most interested in what was going on in the classroom. The children at table two and most all of them at table three, at times, seemed to have no idea of what was going on in the class and were in another world often by themselves. It just appears that some can do it and some cannot. I don't think it is the teaching that affects those who cannot do it, but some are just basically—I hate to say it—low achievers [p. 176].

> I guess it is that parents do not pay any attention to the children and take no pride in the work that the children bring home from school. The children just do not get encouraged. Did you notice at the play yesterday how so many of the children came so nicely dressed and clean and their hair was combed? And did you see how Lilly came? She was dressed in a dirty dress, dirty socks, and her hair wasn't even combed. It must be that some parents just have a different set of values. The child can be no better than his association with his parents. Maybe some of the children will change when they get older, but most of them will be in a rut for their whole life [p. 177].

Rist followed these children into the first grade. The group assignments were almost identical to those first made in kindergarten. Now, however, the differentiation was made on more "objective" grounds. In addition to observed behavioral and attitudinal characteristics and records of progress in kindergarten, scores on intelligence tests and reports from the kindergarten teacher were available for the evaluation of each student.

The separate groups continued into the second grade. Now the groups even had names to designate their status: the Tigers (presumably referring to the Detroit Tigers who had recently won the World Series), the Cardinals (the team that finished second), and the Clowns. When Rist asked the second grade teacher about the children in the three groups, the teacher responded with the following kinds of descriptions/explanations.

In response to a question of whether the term "cultural deprivation" applies to her second grade children:

> Yes, definitely.... I think most of these children get their cultural experiences through school. They really wouldn't have any cultural education if it was not for the school because most of these children are in families that don't have the time, money, or interest in their children [p. 216].

> They come to school and they are absolutely filthy. I can never remember so many ragged kids as now. Some of these kids even come to school without underwear [p. 216].

In response to a question about the futures of children in
the three groups:

> [Tigers] . . . Well, they are my fastest group. They are
> very smart. . . . They all feel an education is important and
> most of them have goals in life as to what they want to be.
> They mostly want to go to college [p. 217].
> [Cardinals] . . . They are slow to finish their work . . .
> but they do get finished. You know, a lot of them though,
> don't care to come to school too much. . . . But I guess most
> of the Cardinals want to go on and finish and go to college. A
> lot of them have ambitions when they grow up. It's mostly the
> parents' fault they are not at school more often [pp. 217-
> 218].
> [Clowns] . . . Well, they are really slow. You know,
> most of them are still doing first grade work. . . . They are
> playful. They like to talk a lot. They are not very neat. . . .
> They are always so restless. . . . I don't think education means
> much to them at this stage. . . . For example, take Nick. He is
> not going to do anything. . . . Curt won't amount to very
> much and neither will Orlando. Amy tries, but she hasn't got
> it. Lilly is the type that will drop out and go to work [pp.
> 218-219].

The preceding accounts have come from urban schools
which serve poor, mostly black, families and children. The social differentiation processes that begin from the very first days
of school, however, occur in all schools. As Jackson (1968) has
noted, there are few social contexts in which behavior is subject
to such continuous and multidimensional evaluation. Students
are continually being tested, sorted, and classified. The result is
a stratification of students within schools, a within-school variation, which is larger than variation between schools (Smith,
1972; Jencks, 1972). Thus, schools may create differences between students on the various dimensions that they choose to
measure. The differences between the top and bottom students
in both rich and poor schools are large, larger than the average
overall differences between rich and poor schools. Conventional
approaches generally locate the source of between- and within-
school variations in the child's intelligence or his family or other

background characteristics. The child is viewed as the important unit of analysis, since it is his characteristics that determine his life course in the school. These approaches gloss the practical differentiating or sorting processes that allocate children to relative positions of superiority or inferiority. Characteristics of children are not self-revealing in behavior, performance, or scores on tests. Rather, teachers and other school personnel interpret behavior based on theories about what sort of child this is and what can be expected from him. Practical theories of competence filter the variety of information that could be available for each child and select for use only a fraction as relevant for present purposes, that is, school purposes. Thus, dirty hair, tattered clothes, family on welfare, and poor language skills are viewed as relevant predictors for children who are seen as having these characteristics. They indicate what "type" of child this is as well as enable teachers to "reasonably" predict what he will become. The fact that children may appear as highly verbal in other contexts or may display what could be interpreted as imagination and curiosity on occasions outside the classroom is tacitly ignored, or at least not looked for, since, obviously, "that's different." The teachers' theories thus not only identify important characteristics for predicting growth, but also tacitly specify the "obvious" contexts in which they can be "discovered."

From the very first days, then, children are subject to evaluation, classification, and typification in schools. Background characteristics and personal qualities may indeed provide powerful predictive information for measures of outcomes of schooling but these relationships can only be understood in light of the processing that takes place there. Students do not simply take more or less advantage of school. Rather, their future in the organization is a negotiated placement based on interpretations that people charged with the task of predicting growth make of their characteristics defined as relevant to the task.[2]

[2]We are aware of the debate on the effects of tracking students. The current resolution appears to be that tracking has little influence on learning outcomes (Goldberg and others, 1966; Boocock, 1972). Our argument, however, addresses a fundamentally different question. We are asking how

"Measuring" Growth Potential

When children first arrive at school, school personnel have little information about them except what they know about background characteristics. As time passes, however, teachers come to "know" more about individual children, their strengths and weaknesses. This information, however, is not easily articulated with theories of child development, language acquisition, or instructional technology. Daily events are too complex and occasioned to interpret or evaluate simply in terms of competencies or deficiencies. The children's behavior appears to change from day to day. It is not readily apparent where they have been or where they are going.

An organization that claims to teach and change lives by means of a rational process of instruction, however, cannot afford to justify its behavior or plan its activities on fleeting impressions or vague evaluations. Parents and other community members want to know more than "Johnny is doing poorly in math" or "Jane doesn't seem to be motivated." The significant audiences of the school as well as its own internal planning and evaluation functionaries demand more precise, informative, and "objective" reports on what is going on. Schools provide this information in a variety of ways, standardized tests being among the most prominent and important.

Standardized tests yield a single total score or a set of subscores, which provide an evaluation of a child in relation to other children (the children on whom the test was standardized) either on the dimension of general intelligence or on several dimensions of learning. Test scores are generally considered to provide a clear and accurate interpretation of a child's capacity or intellectual progress. They are seen as more reliable and valid than the nonuniform, subjective evaluations made by teachers.

Several tacit assumptions are made when school personnel

---

student differentiation or tracking is accomplished as a practical activity of classroom operation. Exclusive attention on outcomes glosses the typification processes and interpretive work of teachers that constitute the practical reality of student differentiation.

interpret test results (Mehan, 1973). First, test questions are assumed to be unambiguous stimuli that elicit responses that are indicative of the respondent's knowledge. The meaning of the stimulus-response event is shared by the person who constructed the test, the person giving the test, and the person taking the test. Given this presumed standardization of meaning, there can be only one correct answer to a question. Correct answers result from adequate knowledge and search procedures while incorrect answers can be traced to faulty reasoning and/or insufficient knowledge, ability, or understanding. Second, the relationship between the stimulus and response is assumed to be context-free. That is, factors such as frequent interruptions, time of day, experience with this kind of test, are ideally not relevant to the final score. Factors other than underlying abilities and acquired information and skills are extraneous. In other words, one testing situation is, in principle, the same as another. Third, the tester is assumed to passively and objectively record each response from the child and assign it the status of a correct or incorrect answer.

These assumptions, and thus the notion that tests directly measure some real, positive, underlying ability or skill, have been questioned on several grounds. The motivational conditions surrounding the test, including the reasons given for taking a test and the incentives or reinforcement offered, can influence scores (Zigler, 1970; Ayllon and Kelly, 1972). The race and sex of the teacher-tester may affect expectations and performance of students (Entwisle and Webster, 1974). Also the language of the teacher-tester and the linguistic structure of instruction and testing may artificially limit student performance, particularly if the student normally uses nonstandard English or is bilingual (Baratz and Baratz, 1970; Cazden, 1970; Labov, 1970).

Objections to the adequacy of test scores as indicators of cognitive processes, learning potential, or acquired skills generally stress problems of motivation, cultural bias, and setting. The assumption is that test scores will be more valid and reliable if tests are administered by the right people, in appropriate contexts, and in relevant cultural settings. While these objections are probably valid, they do not address the heart of the problem. Meaning is never an inherent property of a test item.

Meaning and Measurement. When we speak of "meaning," we are referring to an ongoing, emergent process. The meaning assigned to a social act is located in the occasioned, negotiated interpretations of actors. The production of "meaningfulness" in social behavior is worked out by partners in interaction as they signal, through talk and gesture, what they are intending or how they are "defining the situation" at some time, in some place. Of course, persons who engage one another regularly or who share the same culture develop role expectancies that guide and articulate their interaction. Yet these normative rules are never adequate for "getting through" any specific interaction or event.

What someone is doing or asking is not self-evident, since occasions twist and alter meaning. People must interpret behavior displays, assign some sense or meaning to them. In short, they must typify them. Often, further information is needed before meaning gains some practical, momentary stability. Likewise, what an appropriate or acceptable reciprocal behavior is, is not self-evident. An individual considers alternative behaviors in light of what he thinks is being communicated and what he estimates the probable response will be to alternative actions. The selected response is received by a person and evaluated in light of what he was "really" asking and how he expected the other to respond. He may accept the behavior as responsive to his initiating behavior, as evidence of misunderstanding, as unresponsive but leading to a more intriguing line of interaction, and so on. The other receives verbal and gestural forms of feedback, assigns meaning to them, and continues the exchange of behavior and negotiation of meaning.

The above statement is a highly general and oversimplified description of human interaction. The intent is not so much to show the complexity and subtlety of human interaction but to point out the inadequacy of the stimulus-response model that dominates much of our current thinking about human behavior in schools, particularly concerning testing events.

The Emergence of Appropriate Answers. During the routine of the classroom, teachers often present children with problems or questions that are similar in form and content to items found on a standardized test. The teacher asks what appears to be an obvious question that should elicit a "correct" answer from children who understand the concept or have learned the skill. The behavior of the child should provide a clear indication of understanding; that is, the answer will provide a correct or incorrect response to the question or direction. The child's evaluative process, however, which appears on the surface to be so straightforward and objective, is actually a practical affair involving considerable interpretive work. The question must be viewed in a context of constantly changing features that cannot be entirely anticipated. The way the question is asked, the behavior of other children, previous lessons, gestures and facial expressions of the teacher, and other highly variable conditions can affect the meaning engendered by the child. Also, the questions do not provide a child with a description of the work or behavior that will be judged to be following the rules. Thus, a child must select from alternative ways that are available to answer almost any question.

The child's response will often indicate that the initial question was incomplete or that unstated assumptions need to be made explicit. So, additional information or feedback is provided and children are asked for further answers. Once again, children interpret the request in light of previous experiences, present contexts, and anticipated events. Their response is interpreted in turn by the teacher as an indication of the need for more information, additional examples, correct answers, and so on. The point is that the children and the teacher continually engage one another in ongoing negotiation in which the "meaning" of questions and answers is determined as the lesson unfolds, in terms of what seems practically reasonable.

Consider the following lesson segment that was observed by one of the authors (Buckholdt). A teacher and eight first-grade children are sitting in a circle. The teacher is holding a box that contains plastic forms of various sizes, shapes, and colors. In previous lessons the children have learned to identify several characteristics of the forms. The teacher begins the lesson:

Teacher: Today we will select shapes that have several things alike. Watch me now. I have the small blue triangles [*Holds up the objects for the children to see*]. Now I have big red squares. Now I have small green rectangles. Now you try it. Johnny, can you come over here and select the small green squares?

> *[Johnny approaches the teacher and points to some objects in the box.]*

Teacher: Good, Johnny, those are small green squares. Show them to the children.

> *[Johnny picks up two small green squares and holds them in his hand.]*

Teacher: Are there any more in the box? I want you to find all of them.

> *[Johnny looks in the box and points to several objects.]*

Teacher: Are those small green squares?

Johnny: Yes.

Teacher: Will you show them to the children?

> *[Johnny has put down the other two objects. He now picks out three small green squares from the box and holds them in the air.]*

Teacher: I want you to show all of the green squares. What happened to the other two?

> *[Johnny now picks up the other two and holds all five of them.]*

Teacher: Good, now tell us what you have.

Johnny: Green squares.

Teacher: Are they small or big?

Johnny: Small.

Teacher: How many do you have?

Johnny: Five.

Teacher: So tell us, "I have five small green squares."

Johnny: I have five small green squares.

Teacher: Good.

The teacher's evaluative criteria for this lesson became evident only as the interaction with Johnny proceeded. She wanted the children to select all of the items of a particular shape, color, and size, hold them in the air for the other children to see, and finally construct a complete sentence of a particular form describing what they were holding. These several criteria were not clear in the initial instructions.

The lesson continues:

Teacher: Rose, will you find the big red triangles.

[Rose comes over to the box and points to several objects in the box.]

Teacher: Children, when I say "find" some objects, I want you to pick them up and show them to us. Now Rose, find the big red triangle.

[Rose selects and shows four big red triangles and one small one.]

Teacher: Is that a big red triangle? [*Teacher points to the small one.*]

Rose: No.

Teacher: Well, see if you can find another big red triangle.

[Rose searches for and finds another big red triangle and continues to hold the four other big triangles as well as the small one.]

Teacher: Rose, put the small triangle back in the box.

[Rose complies.]

Teacher: Now, tell us what you have.

Rose: Big red triangles.

Teacher: Say "I have five big red triangles."

Rose: I have five big red triangles.

Teacher: Fred, find the big yellow circles.

[Fred gets up from his chair but instead of approaching the teacher, he heads toward the back of the room.]

Teacher: Fred, where are you going?

Fred: To get the big yellow circles.

[There are several cardboard circles on the desk at the back of the room that are much larger than the plastic circles in the teacher's box.]

Teacher: Come back here, Fred. We are only interested in the shapes in this box. Now show us the five big yellow circles. [*Note that the teacher now says, "show us" and tells Fred how many to show. Fred picks up and shows five big yellow circles.*]

Teacher: Now tell us what you have.

Fred: Five yellow circles.

Teacher: Say, "I have five big yellow circles."

Fred: I have five big yellow circles.

Teacher: Fred has five big yellow circles. You say it, David.
David: Fred has five big yellow circles.

When she began the lesson, the teacher assumed that she had a definite plan for what the children should do and how they should demonstrate their knowledge of size, shape, and color. She felt that her initial explanation was clear. As the lesson unfolds, however, it is clear that some elaboration is needed, that what she might have initially described as her plan is not adequate to the task, in practice. The children are not only to select the appropriate shapes following her directions but also to show them to the other children. The showing is to be accompanied by a complete sentence using the pronoun "I" plus numerical, size, color, and shape descriptions. The shapes selected are to be taken only from the box that the teacher holds. The appropriate form of the correct responses and the criteria for judging the responses thus emerged as the lesson proceeded.

The material presented above shows how unstated expectations gradually become clear as children respond to questions posed by the teacher and as the teacher redefines and adjusts her expectations and criteria. The directions given by the teacher do not provide the children with sufficient guidelines to show what the teacher desires. The needed information emerges only during the interplay between the teacher and the children. The children tacitly inform the teacher how to teach as they interact with her. They are as much a part of the instruction as is the teacher.

"Practically" Adequate Solutions. Mehan (1974) and Cicourel (1974) argue that most questions or directions presented by a teacher can be interpreted in a variety of ways. For example, the question, "Where is the triangle, Joey?" could be answered with any of the following responses: "On the paper," "in the room," "right here," "right above the square," and so on. The question presents the child with more than the problem of simply providing "a" correct response. He must find the one answer among several alternatives that matches the teacher's

unstated assumptions concerning what the right answer is and how to determine its correctness. Mehan (1974) summarizes the problem of emergent reality in the following way: "Because the teacher's instructions are indexical expressions, their meaning changes for the child as the lesson unfolds. This emergent sense of meaning defies a static description which presumes that the meaning of instructions is clear at the outset of an exchange and remains constant throughout; it requires a description which openly includes retrospective and prospective assignment, indefiniteness and indeterminacy as features of meaning" (p. 126).

Standardized tests are allegedly free of ambiguity. They should not require the child to interpret what is being asked or to search for meaning. It is assumed that a stimulus in the form of a picture or a set of directions should lead the child to the one correct answer, if he has developed the skills to perform the task. If he selects or constructs the correct answer, it is assumed that he possesses the skill. Likewise, if his answer is incorrect, the child supposedly does not have the required skill. He is not asked why he selected a particular "wrong" response or rejected the "correct" answer.

The simple model depicting right answers flowing from proficient skill and wrong answers from deficient skill is problematic for the child. The author of the test had a specific rationale for the connection between stimulus and correct response but his reasoning is not open to discovery or negotiation by the child. So, the child must interpret meaning, based on his experience and background.

Mehan (1973) asked children why they had selected particular items on a basic language and concepts test. The answers revealed considerable linguistic and interpretive ability that was hidden by the test score as an indicator of ability. For example, one test item showed children with heads obscured. The task was to choose the tallest child. The "correct" response was to not make a selection since relative heights could not be determined. Numerous children, however, selected one of the pictures. They justified their decision on the perceived fact that "his feet are bigger." The children thus understood the thrust of the question, to discriminate and compare, but they were not using the same criterion of correctness as the test developer. Although their answer was marked wrong, their response was an indication of a different scheme of interpretation rather than a lack of skill. In another item, children are asked to mark the "animal that can fly." The picture shows a bird, an elephant, and a dog. Many first-grade children selected the elephant. When later asked about their selection, they reported that the elephant was Dumbo, the flying elephant from Walt Disney stories. Again, although these children were "wrong," they used logical and interpretive skills in arriving at an answer that, given the meaning they provided, was reasonable. After all, they were not told that the worlds of fantasy and cartoons were to be excluded from the testing situation. In still another item, the test presents a picture of a medieval fortress, with moat, drawbridge, and parapets. The child is to select the initial consonant in the word which describes the picture. The alternatives are *D, C,* and *G.* Many children chose *D* (rather than *C* for *castle*) because the picture was *Disneyland.*

MacKay (1973) reports a similar analysis of the inherent ambiguity in test items and the practical ability of children to "fill in" meaning. In a test designed to measure reading ability (by marking the picture that illustrates the situation described in a preceding phrase, sentence, or paragraph), one item shows a boy apparently swimming, a boy presumably walking, and a car. The stimulus phrase reads, "I went for a ride." The car is to be marked, supposedly because it "obviously" provides the best illustration of the phrase. However, this one correct association is not so obvious if a child recognizes the past tense of the phrase and the current action shown in the picture. Certainly the interpretation "I went for a ride but now I am walking" might lead a child to select the second picture. Reading would be accurate and considerable interpretive skill would be used, but the response would be arbitrarily marked as incorrect. A second example taken from MacKay demonstrates how a correct answer can result from an interpretive process that is creative but considerably different from what the test developer intended. The stimulus phrase reads, "The bird built his own house." The phrase is followed by three pictures that presumably show tree branches, a man-made bird house with a small entrance, and a nest containing several eggs. The child selected the third picture, the correct alternative. When an interviewer asked the child to reread the stimulus phrase and explain his reasons for choosing the third picture, the child read *owl* rather than *own*. He then explained that the hole in the second picture was too small for an owl so he picked the picture of the nest. This was an imaginative and reasonable answer for the child, one that he constructed in response to his interpretation of the question. The child displays inferential abilities in arriving at his answer. Yet the "correctness" of the answer was not obtained by means of the reading and inferential process "intended" by the test developer.

Glossing over Alternate Realities. We could provide numerous additional examples but the argument now, we hope, is clear. Meaning is an emergent, negotiated property of everyday life, including life in the classroom. Meaning is occasioned. Through talk, gesture, and other symbolic activity, persons signal what is intended, relevant, and expected in a particular context. While general, presumably context-free rules (normative rules) may orient persons to patterns of interaction, these rules are never sufficient guides for behavior. Persons must interpret symbolic messages as they arrive at definitions of the situations in which they are members. The job of interpretation requires considerable cognitive and interaction skill from participants.

Teachers see instruction, in principle, as explicitly unambiguous. Children gradually acquire knowledge as they listen to instructions and practice skills. Yet, in their interaction with children, teachers deal with the ambiguity of rules, instructions, and assignments. Teachers and students continually engage one another through questions, requests for further information, and requests for feedback and evaluative comments in search of additional information. Teachers and students are continually orienting and reorienting themselves to one another based on past experience, the interpreted meaning of the present context, and anticipated future events.

This process of the emergence and negotiation of meaning

is glossed over in the construction and interpretation of achievement and intelligence tests. The test developers construct items that are presumably clear to them and that are thought to tap underlying language, cognitive, and other skills. Correct answers indicate the presence of these skills while incorrect answers indicate deficiencies. The number of correct items is tabulated and used as an index of development and learning. Reliance on a test score, as an indicator of ability, obscures the social practices through which the score was created.

Testing is a social occasion, an occasion with emergent properties that are created and managed by participants. Testers provide a rationale for the occasion and a more or less controlled set of stimuli or directions. Yet, these "standard" conditions are often altered by teachers-testers (Mehan, 1973; Friedman, 1968). Teachers provide their own versions of the standard directions, allow more or less time than the directions allow, and provide subtle clues to the children on some items. They may also allow children to practice with similar tests and provide "rules of thumb" for guessing, reading directions, and figuring out what the test developer intends for them to do. In other words, teachers tacitly know of the difficulties children have in searching for meaning in test situations where interaction and negotiation are restricted. They try to provide more clarity, but testing occasions and test items nevertheless remain highly ambiguous and subject to a wide variety of individual interpretations.

Test scores are taken as valid indicators of ability and skill development, thereby being useful in "predicting" intellectual growth. The fact that a child may have utilized rather complex conceptual and analytic skills to arrive at a reasonable but "wrong" answer, given his interpretation of the item, is glossed over. Likewise, the possibility that a child may have arrived at a "correct" answer by way of an unanticipated reasoning process is not considered. The score provides an image of the child based on the model used to construct and administer the test. The model glosses the situational and contextual intricacies of testing events as social occasions and forces a standard interpretation of results. That is, responses to test items supposedly allow a clear inference to underlying traits. Describing a child's ability from his test score is like judging an iceberg by its tip (Jennings and Jennings, 1974).

Negotiating Placements

One of the authors (Buckholdt) attended a series of conferences between a principal, several teachers, and a social worker. The participants were deciding which eighth-grade students were to advance to an academic high school and which to a terminal program. The discussion revolved around students who, the participants believed, could possibly be assigned to the terminal track. The principal had asked the teachers and the social worker to submit a list of names of students who should be considered. The records on these students were available for the meeting. They included academic history, scores on intelligence and achievement tests, family information, and reports from teachers and other professional school personnel.

The principal asked the group to first select the children about whom there was "no doubt." One teacher suggested that the principal should provide them with the criteria they should use, so they would not be making judgments on different grounds. The principal replied: "Two things are important. If the IQ isn't 80 or above they have to go to terminal. And if their achievement scores are bad, they should be in terminal." The teachers decided to organize their job by first separating all the children with IQ scores of 80 or lower. They then began inspecting the records of the children with "acceptable" intelligence quotients. "How bad do they have to be?" one teacher asked. "Well, that depends," the principal replied. "Generally, if they're below fifth-grade level they won't make it. But you know these kids, you tell me." So the teachers began making decisions. Usually the teacher who presently had a child in her class made the decision. The others generally concurred, but occasionally there was debate:

Teacher 3:   Michael Phillips, he can do it if he'll come to school. Let's send him on.

Principal: He wants out. He told me he wants a full-time job.

Teacher 3:   I know, but he's a bright kid. He just doesn't apply himself. Give him the chance anyway.

Principal: OK.

Teacher 1:   Lonnie Briggs is a tough one. His scores are low but he's had problems. Those boys he runs with—well, if only he had other friends. I think he can do the work.

Teacher 2:   I don't. I had him last year. He's hopeless. We've had the same smart-ass behavior from him for four years now.

Principal: Yeah, he won't change. We can't just pass our problems on.

Teacher 1:   OK. You're right.

The meeting continued until a decision had been made about each of the children. Before concluding the meeting, however, the principal reopened the cases of two children who were originally placed in the terminal category because of low intelligence scores:

Principal: Let's look at Earl James and Brenda Washington again. They're in the low IQ pile. I don't think their tests were any good. They both do fairly well in school and I know their families. They have big hopes for the kids. I want them tested again and I will give them some extra help.

Teacher 3:   OK with me. Why not test Morris Wright again, too?

Teacher 2:   Yeah, and Sylvia, too.

Principal: OK, the tester from the board will be around in three weeks. Get your kids ready.

Seven children were retested and six of the seven scored above 80 on the second trial.

Leiter (1974) reports occasions on which implicit typifications are shared and used as the basis for promotional decisions. On one occasion, two kindergarten teachers and their principal met to decide how to distribute the kindergarten children across three first-grade sections for the following year. The principal had a picture of each child from each of the two kindergarten classes. The teachers were to write two or three descriptors of each child on the back of the picture and then place the child's picture under the name of the first-grade teacher who was most "appropriate" for the particular child. The conversation proceeded as follows:

Principal: Now what I want you to do is take each one of these and on the back with a felt pen or something write two or three descriptors. [*Picks up a picture.*] What's outstanding about this child, Pa (_____): sunny, cheerful, aggressive, retiring?

Teacher 2: Would you please write a long list that we could choose from, those are great [*laughs*].

Teacher 1: Now, she's outgoing, an' strong academically strong.

Principal: Okay then that goes on the back here. Now recognizing that . . . [First-Grade Teacher A] is a different kind of person, what would be good for this child? Now does this child need somebody strongly oriented academically? Does she need that kind of strong hand? Here's a warm mother [*tapping First-Grade Teacher B's card*]. . . . Now we're going to have some kids in here who are going to need a Momma-type. All right, here's your Momma. . . . Here's a gal we want to protect [*pointing to First-Grade Teacher C's card which is actually going to be the new teacher's class*]. We don't want to give her really tough ones. I will not have her picking up all the kids that are difficult [Leiter, 1974, pp. 34-36].

The teachers then proceeded to divide the children into three groups, the strong, the average, and the weak. The strong students were given to the teacher who was typified as "strongly oriented academically," while the average went to the new teacher and the weak to the "warm mother."

For our purposes, it is useful to view characteristics of children, as judged by school personnel, as situationally bound products of the practical theories and procedures used by these personnel to gather information about their students. This notion differs from the traditional view that children either possess or do not possess abilities or traits, or possess them to varying degrees, and that school personnel simply observe, measure, and record them. Children do not just present themselves for judgment and evaluation. They participate in social occasions in which there are rather general expectations and guidelines for behavior. They work on lessons, answer questions, listen to the teacher, play, take tests, line up for recess, and so on. These activities constitute the routine activities of life in schools. Teachers and other school personnel structure these occasions, supervise their emergence, and monitor the transitions from one occasion to another. They also use the behavior of children during these occasions to evaluate their intellectual growth and potential and to identify them according to common-sense typifications.

The teacher is involved both in making things happen and in deciding or interpreting what is happening. He or she is, in practice, part of the child's intelligence and conduct. Appropriate or acceptable behaviors are generally determined by school policy, lesson plans, curriculum guides, shared understandings, and the like. Interpretation of what is happening is based on common-sense, practical theories about how various types of children behave on routine school occasions. These theories are constructed around the everyday, practical circumstances of life in the classroom. They tend to focus on the behaviors of children that make life easier or more difficult for the teacher. Evaluative typifications, then, are embedded in the trivial, yet essential, work of organizing school routine. The typifications used by the teacher are grounded in the work needed to accomplish everyday life in schools.

Common-sense typifications include categories such as "lazy," "immature," "bright child," "slow learner," and "troublemaker." The use of such typifications depends largely on the demands that children make on the resources of the teacher and other school personnel. The "slow learner," for example, requires more instruction, repetition, and review than do other children. "Immature" children are those who do not display the behavior that the teacher's tacit developmental model predicts should be evident at a particular chronological age; extra resources are required to keep them involved and prevent them from disturbing other children. The "bright child" demands a minimum of time and effort from the teacher; he learns new concepts quickly and requires little repetition or review.

We have argued that schools do not simply provide opportunity for or respond to supposedly objective characteristics of children. School personnel are active in the process of "discovering" what these relevant characteristics are and in processing children based on the meaning they attribute to the abilities and traits they discover. Within the classroom, the teacher typifies children in the process of managing daily tasks of instruction. The typifications describe the ease or difficulty that teachers have with particular children in working through daily routine. They also influence the behavior and feelings of the teacher toward children of a particular type. Typifications transcend particular classrooms and also other occasions when decisions, such as placements and promotions, are made. Criteria relevant to the decisions are interpreted and negotiated. Teacher reports, test scores, information on family life and peer-group affiliation, and other "data" about the child that school personnel see as relevant "in this case" may be used. The dynamics of this processing, however, are not available in official records, which report only the outcome of practical decisions. The records may show varying stages of development and the decisions that were presumably based on measures of development. The interpretive processes that school personnel have used to generate meaning from events and the use of information relevant to decisions are not revealed in official documents or official accounts of what has happened.

The Predictive Work of Experts

Although selection and differentiation occur at varied levels in educational settings, the outcome of these social processes is narrower and more definitive when managed by "experts" than by laypersons. More than a decade ago Cicourel and Kitsuse (1963) described how the professionalization of the counseling function brought more students with presumably more serious problems to the attention of the school. Previously, teachers had treated most problems as the "normal" ones of living and growing up. Professional counselors, however, viewed the same behaviors as surface manifestations of deep-seated inner conflicts that required expert diagnosis and treatment. The problems were viewed as serious enough that counselors could no longer depend on students with problems to seek help. Counselors began to actively search for the problems that they had been trained to service. Other "experts" also have gotten into the business. Psychologists, social workers, physicians, psychiatrists, and special school personnel have become involved in the testing and diagnosis of children and in the design and maintenance of special programs to meet student "needs."

While all people typify in order to make sense of and manage their lives, certain persons or those in particular positions apply definitions of behavior that are taken by others as more definitive or authoritative because of accepted claims to their expertise. Professional agents of social control, for example, can define young people as delinquent and this definition will have more force than if the same or a similar term is applied by the man who lives next door. In schools, these "serious" and professional labels are managed by "experts" such as the school psychologist, social worker, or psychiatrist. Their conclusions are given special status because of their training, scientific apparatus, and supposedly "objective" procedures of identification and classification. They are given credit for being able to "spot" problems that others may not see, name them with authority, and provide remedial alternatives that are relevant to individual problems of particular kinds.

To date there has been little research on how this "expert" function of processing and differentiating children in schools is accomplished. There is some evidence, for example, that many "deviant" categories, such as behavioral disorders, learning disability, and educable mentally retarded are not descriptive of the general abilities or behaviors of children but are categories that are invoked and negotiated as teachers and other school personnel gradually "discover" that some children do not fit easily into the routine of the classroom (Goldstein and others, 1975). Children may be indistinguishable from friends and playmates except for a few differences in the classroom, as perceived by teachers and other experts; but these few differences are enough to result in a deviant label or typification[3] and

---

[3]The difference between a labeling perspective and a phenomenological one is apparent in the notion "delabeling" (see Trice and Roman,

assignment to special programs if they are available (President's
Committee on Mental Retardation, 1970). If the same characteristics that are used to identify mentally retarded children in
school were used on an adult population, many adults who are
functioning quite adequately would be classified as deficient
(Mercer, 1974). Once children are placed in special classes, the
likelihood of returning to regular settings is slight. Gallagher
(1972) estimates, for example, that in large city school systems,
special track traffic goes in one direction, and less than 10 per-
cent of the children placed in special education classes are ever
returned to regular education.

One of the authors (Gubrium, 1975) has reported elsewhere how aides in a nursing home control the diagnosis of
problems and prescription of medication for elderly patients in
what allegedly is a professional function. When a patient becomes a "nuisance" for the aide, it is not uncommon for the
aide to "persuade" a nurse to contact a physician and request
medication for the patient's "disorientation." The aide provides
the label as well as whatever supportive evidence is needed to
convince the doctor that there is a problem and that something
should be done. The doctor often prescribes medication without ever seeing the patient. His immediate intervention is indirectly a product of the request of the aide who wants to solve
a practical problem. Later accounts of the intervention, however, inevitably stress the relevance of the medication for the
resident's, not the aide's, "problem." We suspect that the
process of labeling and classification by "experts" in schools
occurs in much the same way in many instances. Teachers "dis-

1970). Delabeling suggests that something can and should be done about
the assumed "injustice" of the labeling process so as to avoid the use of
labels in what presumably could be a more rational social processing of
persons. From a phenomenological perspective, on the contrary, labeling
and delabeling (as typifications) are necessary features of everyday living.
They make meaningful the events of everyday life and provide "recipes"
for people's activity in it. Because labeling is an essential feature of everyday life, we suggest that the terms *labeling*, *delabeling*, and the like are
misleading. The term *typification* is more appropriate to describing the
organization of meaning in daily life, and the conception *typifying
processes* is more conducive to organizing its general exploration.

cover" problems as children interfere with what teachers desire to be an orderly and efficient daily routine. They report their problems with particular children to school psychologists, counselors, or social workers and define these nuisances as indicative of some "problem" (Goldstein and others, 1975). One of these experts may test the child, review his past academic performance, and briefly observe his behavior in the classroom before classifying the child. Special services or classes may then be "made available to the child." Later accounts emphasize the problems of the child and the services that are being offered, but they gloss over both the teacher's routine problems and the social process through which the problem was created and invoked. The label becomes a practical explanation of the source of the problem as well as a justification for the "treatment" that is being offered.

We are not suggesting that ordinary people such as parents or coaches have less "influence" on the developing skills and attitudes of children than experts do. However, typifications (which may be reinforced, for example, by parental or teacher desires) made by certain school personnel are accepted as more "authentic" since they are constructed by "experts." Moreover, these "scientific" typifications are *used* to manage and justify processes of student differentiation, including promotion, retention, and special placement. In turn, differentiation is used by people in determining the future opportunities made available to children both within and outside of the school.

The "meaning" of student behavior and the course of student intellectual growth emerges in interaction as teachers, experts, and others interpret behavior, using a variety of theories of what children of a particular age, background, ability level, and so on should be able to do. Past behaviors are reevaluated and reinterpreted as the present emerges and present images guide expectations and actions into the future, all done around the practical needs of getting on with evaluative and predictive business, in schools and other settings.

Chapter Five

Negotiating Competence

Maturity is a term widely used for describing a standard of human growth and development. For the philosophers of human development, from Aristotle through John Amos Comenius and Jean Jacques Rousseau to the developmental psychologists, like G. Stanley Hall, Sigmund Freud, Erik Erikson, Jean Piaget, and Lawrence Kohlberg, movement from one stage of life to the next is described, either by the theorists themselves or by their interpreters, as increasing maturity. Physical growth provides a model for the development of psychosexual, cognitive, affective, and moral aspects of the person: from relative simplicity to greater complexity of structure and differentiation of function. Human growth may be stimulated or retarded by the physical and social environment but the sequence and hierarchy of stages are determined by the biogenetic characteristics of mankind.

126

Maturity, then, is the gradual unfolding or emergence of a "gift" of the species.

Other psychologists, while not denying the developmental determinism of human growth, have been more interested in variation in human behavior. Some individuals apparently "mature" more quickly or make more developmental progress than others. This interest in individual differences has led to a number of studies both on the personality characteristics of the mature person and on the environmental conditions that stimulate human growth. Personality correlates of maturity include such characteristics as allocentrism (orientation to others) (Heath, 1965); taking others into consideration (Elkind, 1967); personal integration and openness to new experience (Rogers, 1964); stability of self-image, values, interests, and interpersonal relationships (Carlson, 1965; McKinney, 1968); and a plethora of other traits (see Symonds, 1961; Cox, 1970). Those who have stressed the importance of environmental influence on human growth have emphasized such ideas as the "teachable moment" (Havighurst, 1951) and "critical periods" (Hunt, 1961) to argue that human development is not an inevitable unfolding of biological potency but a process that depends on the proper mix of human potential and environmental stimulation.

Sociologists have generally worked with the concept of socialization, rather than human development. In general, this concept has included both the content of what is to be learned and the procedures for changing people. The content includes a wide variety of norms, values, skills, and expectations that are required for both the social integration of the person and the stability of society. Socialization is considered to be functional for both the person and his social order if it provides for individual integration into a particular social world and mutual integration of persons in a society. Infants are incomplete, irrational, incompetent, and asocial. They are not yet human since they have not yet been socialized. They cannot yet participate in the integrative work of society, that is, its network of interdependent roles and positions. Through experience gained within a variety of formal and informal settings and institutions, they gradually acquire the cultural baggage and social under-

standing by which they both recognize themselves and are recognized by others as competent members of some social order
(Clausen, 1967; Elkin, 1960; Inkeles, 1966; Parsons and Bales,
1955; Brim and Wheeler, 1966).

The writings of sociologists and social historians have
pointed out great variations in age classifications across time
and across societies. Ariès (1962) has argued, for example, that
the notion of a period of childhood did not emerge in Western
society until after the sixteenth century. Before then, young
persons were abruptly moved into the adult world after a brief
period of physical dependence on the mother or nurse. For
Eisenstadt (1956), cultural definitions of age and age differences are affected by the social division of labor in a society and
the relationship between the family and economic order.
"Youth" as a transition stage has tended to develop in societies
where kinship provides neither the major criterion for assigning
adult status nor the rationale for organizing major social institutions. Coleman (1974), Keniston (1968), and Havighurst and
Dreyer (1975) have written about the origin and problems of
the youth in modern America where they are shut off from useful social roles and isolated in special institutions (schools)
created for them but run by adults. Numerous others have also
treated the cultural and social aspects of age or age-group status
in society (Davis, 1940; Friedenberg, 1962; Roszak, 1969; M. B.
Berger, 1963; Parsons, 1942; Moller, 1968; Lofland, 1968;
Flacks, 1970; for example). While these writings are diverse in
content, method, and argument, an underlying theme is clear:
the gradual unfolding of human biological development or
maturation is interpreted in a cultural context.

Conventional Maturity

Despite their many differences, psychological notions of
human development and sociological ideas about socialization
share a strikingly similar view of the child and the adult, of the
immature and the mature. The fully socialized or developed
adult provides the touchstone from which to judge competence.
Change is "developing" or "socializing" if it appears to be in the

direction of greater maturity, rationality, and responsibility. Lack of change or movement off course is seen as faulty socialization, inadequate development, personality defect, immaturity, and the like. The child is deficient vis-à-vis the adult. Although the child may have his own set of interpretive skills or culture, they are valuable only if they contribute to further development. If there is perceived continuity between the current behaviors and skills of the child and desirable future states, growth is evident. Perceived discontinuity between the present and the desired future signals problems for the person as well as for his social order. The warning is indexed with the labels *immature, irrational, incompetent,* and *unenculturated,* depending on whether the interpreter is an ordinary citizen, teacher, psychologist, sociologist, or anthropologist (MacKay, 1973).

There is a political undertone to such concepts as *mature, socialized,* and *rational*—they are all quite conservative. Human scientists who organize their theories around such concepts, judging people by their implicit standards, are fundamentally partisan and not as objective as they often methodologically claim. They are partisan in that all behaviors of people that do not adjust to "acceptable" standards of conduct are treated as somehow abnormal. This lumps together people's mistakes, passions, and radical sense of justice. Like many people, human scientists who accept the conventional realities of these concepts, in effect, act as apologists for the status quo—in their specific case, as expert apologists.

Human scientists, in their studies of child development and socialization, take for granted what "everyone already knows." That is, there is change in human behavior and change can be differentially evaluated, depending on whether it appears to be moving in the proper direction, toward greater maturity, personal and social integration, and cognitive differentiation and elaboration. The topic of human growth and development is taken over by the scientist as something real and factual, an objective thing that can be studied with scientific precision to reveal process and effect. The contrasting terms *adult/child, mature/immature, competent/incompetent, development/retardation,* and others, are taken from the common-sense world and elevated to the status of scientific concepts by the human scientist. The fact of either biogenetic or culturally defined stages is taken for granted, along with the assumption of fundamentally different orders or stages in the cycle of life. The result is a rigid and common-sense view of human growth and change. The acceptance by human scientists and laypersons of important "topics" such as life change has resulted in a glossing of the dynamic social processes by which change or lack of change is defined, evaluated, and shared by people.

The Acquisition and Recognition of Competence

Developmental psychologists traditionally focus their attention on the particular skills, general abilities, and personality characteristics that children acquire at sequential stages of life, while sociologists usually center interest on the structures and processes by which children learn to internalize the norms, values, and attitudes of their society. Both approaches miss the active elements of the emergence of a child into what is claimed to be a full or mature member of society. First, they neglect to study the acquisition and use of interactional competencies by children in concrete situations (Speier, 1970). Second, they fail to articulate competencies with their recognition in situated activities. That is, there has been little attempt to investigate the "developmental theories" of, and their uses by, practicing societal members, which allow them to recognize behavioral displays as indices of adequate development, maturity, competence, and so on (Cicourel, 1972).

We are not dismissing the importance of biogenetically determined potentialities. Developmental theories alone, however, are not sufficient for our understanding of how social structure is made and maintained in the daily interaction of people. Developing biogenetic competencies have no inherent or self-evident meaning. They are interpreted and given meaning by those who witness behavior and interpret it in specific contexts based on tacit and shared expectancies or understandings of human growth and development.

The notion of socialization as the "acquisition of interactional competencies" (Speier, 1970) implies that children gradually acquire a sense of social structure. That is, they develop the interpretive ability and behavior repertoire to continually negotiate their social worlds in a more or less successful way. A sense of social structure apparently requires the simultaneous development of two parallel competencies (Cicourel, 1970b). First, surface or normative rules specify general policies that apply to a wide variety of contexts and situations. These are assumed to be well-known and agreed-upon rules in particular groups or subcultures. They are what sociologists and anthropologists generally refer to as "norms," "values," "roles," and so on. Second, and fundamental to normative rules, basic or interpretive rules provide a means for negotiating interaction around norms, values, roles, and such on particular occasions. Normative rules are never sufficient for guiding ongoing interaction. The articulation of surface rules within particular situations is open-ended and problematic, depending on the meaning assigned and reassigned to motives, objects, ideas, and so forth. While normative rules may be invoked after the fact to account for behavior in particular situations, they are never sufficient for the negotiation and management of ongoing behavior. Cicourel (1972) has summarized some essential elements of basic rules which we have adapted as follows:

1. *The Reciprocity of Perspectives.* The child learns to interpret the "surface rules" of others and thus to reconstruct their intentions and to assume that others are similarly interpreting his intentions. Actors assume that others would have the same experiences of the immediate scene if they were to change places.

2. *Immediate and Retrospective-Prospective Uses of the Et Cetera Assumption.* The speaker-hearer learns to tentatively assign meaning to immediate scenes, based on the assumption of common understandings of a normative order which may be ambiguous in particular situations. There is a willingness to suspend any final judgment or decision until later events unfold or to decide on an interpretation in retrospect. Interaction does not break down simply because the meaning of an immediate encounter is unclear. Interactants take for granted that unclear things (et cetera) will become clear as interaction unfolds.

3. *Normal Forms.* We have previously discussed the idea
of typification. The notion of normal forms is similar. Certain
"normal forms" of talk, objects, and events are relied upon to
link moment-to-moment scenes with the more general, taken-
for-granted or presumed network of normative meaning. The
actor can retrospectively categorize specific events as instances
of more general normative rules and assume that others are
assigning meaning or typifying events in similar ways. The
more general rules allow interaction to continue without continual pauses for the negotiation or arbitration of terms or
meaning [pp. 150-155].[1]

What man has lost genetically in instinctual responses has
been amply compensated for in his symbolic or linguistic capacity (compare Berger and Luckmann, 1966; Berger and Kellner,
1965). This capacity presumably has a psychobiological basis
and emerges in each life in a more or less patterned way. This
developing capacity, however, is shaped and interpreted in diverse ways from culture to culture. While we all develop the
ability to participate in social organization due to our capacity
to learn to use normative and interpretive rules, we differ
widely as groups of people in the structure and form of the
rules we employ to create a substantive sense of social order.

We have briefly mentioned two models of development
and socialization. The first model, the conventional one, focuses
on the structure and properties of symbolic skills that presumably develop from a biogenetic base but that take form and substance in particular and diverse social orders. The child takes the
opportunity to practice and develop abilities on social occasions
marked by increasing complexity, opportunity, and expecta-

[1]Taylor and others (1973, pp. 204-205) note that while normative
or surface rules are rather easy to identify, basic rules are especially problematic and vague in the writings of Cicourel and Garfinkel. In fact,
Cicourel merely provides the reader with a reiteration of Alfred Schutz's
inventory of rules presumed necessary for ongoing social interaction. While
normative "rules" are more rulelike in the sense of providing preexisting
interpretive schemata for guiding and making sense of experience, basic or
interpretive "rules" are less programmatic, less directive in their use by actors. Since these rules are not essentially of the same sort, we would prefer
the use of a term like *interpretive skills*, or *procedures* (see Mehan and
Wood, 1975, p. 101).

tion. The child thus gradually develops a more adultlike sense of social order, feels himself to be a part of organized society, and is recognized by others as an increasingly competent societal member. The second model turns our attention to the procedures that adult or nonadult members use to judge relative competence or incompetence, and the occasions on which particular judgments are made. We will take the perspective of the second model and discuss how competence, maturity, rationality, responsibility, and so on are recognized and dealt with in the ongoing work of members who assign significance to growth.

The Situated Negotiation of Competence

From here on we will use the term *competence* to refer to a collection of similar terms such as *maturity, wisdom, ability, realism,* and the like. Of course, these terms have a variety of different technical meanings in the professional literature on socialization and human development.

Leiter (1974) describes the typifications used by several teachers for characterizing their students and for justifying placement in ability tracks or promotion to different kinds of classrooms or a classroom with particular student "characteristics." Leiter summarizes the social types as follows: (1) *Immature child*—he is easily distracted, cannot sit still during a lesson, and has a short attention span. Boys are more likely to be immature, as are children who are physically smaller than other children their own age. (2) *Bright child*—he learns quickly and without demanding much time or effort from the teacher. His social behavior may be poor but if he learns quickly and his verbal skills are good, he is considered to be bright. (3) *Behavior problem*—he is usually a large boy who fights with other children for "no reason at all." (4) *Independent worker*—he can work with little supervision and finishes tasks before beginning other tasks.

As we have argued previously, it is important to note that typifications developed and used by teachers (such as those described by Leiter) deal with their practical problems with children. In other environments, these same children may be typified somewhat differently, as "basically a good boy" at home or as "irreverent" at church, for example, again depending on the practical problems of the context. Our treatment of competence and similar notions refers to the social processes through which they are recognized and negotiated in multiple settings and not to a more or less stable set of personal characteristics that inevitably "rise to the surface."

The teachers described by Leiter were able to assign children to a "mature" and an "immature" class in one case and into personality or academic types (mama types, strongly academically oriented, and weak academically) in another. Further, teachers were able to accomplish this classification without apparent embarrassment about or wide-awake sensitivity to the ad hoc, situated nature of its production. This was "serious" business for them, a sort of professional diagnosis that was carried out with precision. They did not question one another's diagnoses, in principle, nor did they argue about the appropriateness of categories. Leiter did not study the process whereby these typical categories are constructed and shared in teacher talk. Yet the apparent ease with which teachers used them makes it clear that a system of surface or normative rules was referenced, allowing teachers to sense they were "talking the same language" and pursuing the same business in an orderly and rational way.

It is apparent that the teachers possessed the interpretive skills to "see" behavioral displays as particular examples of general types of children as well as the accounting skills to explain their competency classifications to the interviewer. Consider the following dialogue between a teacher and an interviewer (Leiter, 1974):

Teacher: Now this is Pa, . . . a very interesting child because he's one of the ones who's extremely bright but he is a behavior problem in school. And umm one of the reasons he's a behavior problem is because he—well, I guess I really shouldn't say he's a behavior problem but he's immature. Because he's young and we probably expect too much of him. He's an October birthday which would make him one of the youngest in the class . . . .

Interviewer: What are some of the things that give you the impression that he was bright?

Teacher: Oh, he has a fantastic memory. In the group I can read a story and he can be looking out the window or talking to his neighbor and I can ask him the question and he knows the answer like that, you know. At first I would, he would be talking so after I read something or if we'd been discussing something I would say "Pa, what have we been talking about?" And I was doing it because I figured he wouldn't know—and he did.

Interviewer: Um humm.

Teacher: And so it was in the total group that he's catching a lot of what they're hearing and if he's a child who can talk to his neighbor and still know the answer you know you've got a bright child on your hands . . . .

And again:

Teacher: Well I guess I really shouldn't say he's a behavior problem but he is immature because he's young and we probably expect too much of him. He's an October birthday which would make him one of the youngest in the class . . . [pp. 44-45].

Other teachers were able to talk about the same child or similar types of children and to provide convincing (to them) accounts of how they interpreted the behavior of particular children to indicate placement in one class or another.

In discussing the problems college students have in determining how to study for each of their several instructors, Becker, Geer, and Hughes (1968) have described a similar process of negotiation. Students come to understand that each professor has a somewhat different, yet implicit, scheme for assigning importance to aspects of the course (lectures, text, outside reading, and so forth). The students work to break the code or read the intent of each professor in order to know how to competently prepare for tests. This interpretive work is apparently needed because, given the multiple demands of several courses, students feel that they cannot prepare for all possible test questions and testing formats in all subjects. Thus, they strive to typify each professor, to predict what he is likely to emphasize and what form questions will take. The following conversation between two students reveals student problems and strategy:

Anne said, "And then the assignments they give can confuse me. I mean, I don't know what I have to learn here. They

say, 'Read Chapter One.' All right, Chapter One is 20 pages
long. How do I know what I'm supposed to remember with all
that stuff. I don't know what kind of questions they're going
to ask about it. I can't tell what to study."

Kathryn said, "I don't think that's so hard. I mean, it
might be until the first quiz, but after that you can tell what
kind of questions the professor is going to ask, and then you
know what to study. You can usually tell pretty soon, I think"
[Becker, Geer, and Hughes, 1968, pp. 84-85].

Students, either individually or jointly, develop a hypothetical, but tacit, model of how the professor constructs exam-
inations, what he thinks is important, and what sorts of answers
please him. Professors likewise typify students. They come to
see particular students and even entire classes as "lazy,"
"bright," motivated," or whatever, as evidenced by their performance on tests, behavior in class, and other "indicators."
Tacit models of student "types" allow professors to find evidence for one sort of student or another in their behavioral displays. It is interesting, however, that the student's skill in
typifying his professor is not recognized by the professor as a
legitimate or important element in his typifications of students.
Student ability and motivation are what count. The implicit
process of bargaining or negotiation goes unrecognized.

We have sketched some basic notions of our social phenomenological view of competence. Rather than attempting to
locate or measure competence in objective traits or characteristics of individuals, we have instead stressed the importance of
looking at how people tacitly negotiate typifications of one
another in practical situations. Let us examine several specific
aspects of the common-sense reasoning process used by people
to locate or identify competency, maturity, or rationality in the
behavioral or linguistic displays of others.

Imputing Readiness

For developmental psychologists, the notion of readiness
refers to the necessity of mastering the skills or dilemmas of one
stage before one can successfully move on to the next. In

Piaget's theory, for example, the child cannot begin to perform concrete operations (stage 3) until he is able to extract concepts from experience and make intuitive use of them, the developmental tasks of stage 2. Although stages are not strictly defined by age, they are thought to conform generally to age periods. For example, stage 2 in Piaget's theory continues from age two through age seven. Notions of developmental readiness are not the exclusive property of human scientists, however. They are given serious attention and used by lay people in the management of their everyday affairs.

Age and Size as Criteria of Readiness. Assumptions about relationships among age, training, experience, background, and other biographical characterizations and competence to perform adequately in a variety of settings guide much of our practical thinking about everyday affairs. Many teachers, for example, believe that children are not "ready to read" until they are six and a half years old (see Hamblin, Buckholdt, and others, 1971). The rationale for this belief is located, by teachers, in the developmental readiness of children and not in the historical development or organizational structure of the public school. Another example is the "theory" of a relationship between age and the ability to be an "informed" voter. Until recently, a person had to be twenty-one to vote. Now, apparently because our younger citizens are developing more quickly, have more education, and the like, we as a society have decided that 18-year-olds have the capacity to participate rationally in the democratic process. Or, as still another example, a friend of the authors was recently in the running for the chairmanship of the sociology department in a major state university. His teaching and publication record were apparently good enough to allow him to be among the final few contestants. When he visited the campus, however, department members commented on how "young" he was (thirty-one) and on how young he looked. Presumably a desirable chairman is more mature or at least "looks" more mature. This person did not get the job. We are not suggesting that the applicant's age and appearance were the only or "real" reasons for rejection. However, the practical reasoning of the department members, linking "age" with competence to be a chairman, was used to recruit a desirable chairman.

Implicit notions about the relevance of individual characteristics such as physical size and chronological age are used for
imputing readiness in schools in much the same way as educational credentials are used in employment decisions. Consider
the following rationales of teachers both for placement decisions and for explaining behavior (Leiter, 1974) [emphasis
added] :

> Then we have had one other *little* boy who is very, very
> immature and he was a *November birthday*. Just a little, little
> boy [p. 43].
> Maybe I ought to put her five plus because she does have
> a *May birthday* [p. 33].
> Because he's *young* and we probably expect too much of
> him. He's an *October birthday* which would make him one of
> the *youngest* in the class [p. 44].
> She's a *large* child. Now, here's a case where even though
> she would not be ready for first grade—she's ready for a low
> first grade—but even if she were not ready in other ways, I still
> would pass her on to a first grade because that girl . . . another
> year in kindergarten? Look how *big* she'd be before she went
> into the first grade [p. 63].

In Leiter's examples, intuitive theories that link age and
size to behavior allow teachers to "make sense" of readiness
decisions in practical situations. In this instance, the decision
was who would go on to first grade and to what "type" of first
grade particular children would be assigned. Age and size criteria were invoked both to make the decision and to justify and
explain it.

Training as a Criterion of Readiness.   Age, of course, is not
the only means used to make decisions about readiness. Training or, more importantly, the certification of training is also
considered relevant. Persons are not presumed to be ready or
qualified for most important work unless they have the proper
credentials such as a college or graduate degree, professional
license, or certificate of apprenticeship, for example. Common-
sense reasoning tells us that education has a strong positive (and
desirable) relationship with both personal well-being and economic productivity. This notion is supported by the so-called

"human capital" economists who inform us that improvements in the quality of human resources are one of the major sources of economic growth (Schultz, 1962).

In a very important but largely neglected (in sociology) book, Ivar Berg (1971) questions the validity of both the scientific theories and common-sense reasoning that imply a simple, direct relationship between education and performance in jobs. In interviews with personnel directors, managers, and foremen, Berg discovered a strong intuitive feeling that better educated workers were better employees. They are presumably more "promotable" and possess more "stick-to-it-iveness." The actual content of their training was not as important as the fact that they had "completed" a program and thus supposedly demonstrated desirable personal qualities. Only a small fraction of the firms studied by Berg had ever tested their tacit assumptions by examining personnel records to document the presumed relationship between education and job performance. Berg proceeded to study this relationship and concluded that there was little if any evidence for the hypothesis. In fact, on several measures such as absenteeism, turnover, and job satisfaction, less educated personnel had a better record (from the point of view of the company). Berg further shows that job criteria shift over the course of the year and appear to be geared to semester endings and commencement exercises. The proportion of jobs requiring at least twelve years of education increased sharply in February and May and declined substantially in April and August. Berg concluded from this, and a substantial amount of additional research, that educational requirements for jobs have increased dramatically as much due to the increasing availability of better educated people as to the increasing complexity of jobs (compare Collins, 1971).

One additional point from Berg (1971) is worth mentioning. In discussing educational credentials from a managerial perspective, he reports: "Interviews with highly placed executives responsible for personnel policies revealed the same bewildering behavior concerning educational credentials that has been endlessly recounted by social scientists who have patrolled the shops and offices of business and government ever since the

days of the classic experiments at the Hawthorne works of the
Western Electric Corporation. These discussions with managers
evoked the same question-begging responses that were obtained in investigations of business decision making, including
pricing decisions and decisions to subcontract" (p. 72). Berg
then goes on to illustrate his point by quoting a section of a
report produced by three Brookings Institution economists in
which they describe pricing decisions in "a representative sample of large enterprises," decisions that officially require a good
deal of training and technical skill. Berg notes (p. 73) that decisions were indeed made but they were of the "it seemed like a
good idea" variety rather than decisions based on the application of general rules or formulas acquired from educational
training.

Our interest in Berg is not to join in the debate about the
relevance of educational credentials or to argue with the
"human capital" economists but rather to show how educational criteria are used to typify persons as one sort or another.
In Berg's study, managers and personnel directors recognized
that important skills are learned on the job. Educational attainment is used more to decide about a person's "readiness" to be
a mature, trustworthy employee. Better educated persons are
presumably better gambles for the company. The fact that
nearly half of the college recruits left the companies within the
first five years did not lead to a reassessment of the typification
process; rather, companies merely recruited twice as many college graduates as they thought they needed. The ones who left
were said to "think they are better than they are," or to be
"kids who want too much," or "who haven't yet learned the
facts of life, that you have to bide your time." In other words,
despite their education they "really" are not yet mature.

Using "Theories" of Incompetence

Much of the work of modern sociology involves the highly
technical investigation of the processes by which background
variables such as social class, race, intelligence, and family situation influence both individual and group life and the inde-

pendent and interactive contribution each makes to the fate of individuals and the structure of society. In contrast to this, let us consider the practical procedures used by people in particular contexts where they take these background factors into account, using them to "make sense of" behavioral displays or to "explain" behavior. In this perspective, background factors influence people through the significance that others "find" in them rather than in any deterministic fashion.

Negotiating Delinquency. Juvenile delinquents are believed to be a group of persons incompetent in terms of various personal and social criteria. Psychologists generally "locate" their problems in emotional conflicts of one sort or another, while sociologists investigate factors such as the family, adult community, and peer influences and/or the structural inconsistencies that have led them to delinquency. The "fact" that delinquency exists—as indicated by police, court, school, and other records—is more or less taken for granted. Yet, the social process of "recognizing" delinquents and reaching some decision about their official classification is by no means a straightforward application of legal statutes to behavioral displays.

Piliavin and Briar (1964) report, for example, that police exercise considerable discretion in encounters with juveniles. Five alternative dispositions are available: outright release, release and submission of an interrogation report, official reprimand and release to parent, citation to juvenile court, and arrest and confinement. Police discretion is supported by an unofficial belief among policemen that correctional or rehabilitation alternatives would not help most young people as well as by the official training manual, which states that "age, attitude, and prior criminal record" should be considered in all but the most serious offenses. The "character" of the juvenile, in most cases, rather than the specific offense, is officially used to determine disposition. Piliavin and Briar note, however, that in the field, officers have little or no information on the past offenses, school performance, personal adjustment, or family situation of particular juveniles. Decisions are based on "cues" that emerge from the immediate encounter and that are used to assess "character." These cues include age, race, grooming, dress, and particularly demeanor. Juveniles who are contrite, show fear of sanctions, and are respectful are judged to be "salvageable" and are released with only a reprimand. Those who display nonchalance, rebelliousness, or impenitence are seen as "would-be tough guys" or "punks." Black males are judged to be particularly problematic and are most likely to be stopped and interrogated, and to receive more serious dispositions. Even in cases judged to be serious, police exercise considerable discretion in the disposition of them. Consider the following two situations involving alleged sex offenses observed and recorded by Piliavin and Briar (1974):[2]

> 1. The interrogation of "A" (an 18-year-old upper-lower-class white male accused of statutory rape) was assigned to a police sergeant with long experience on the force. As I sat in his office while we waited for the youth to arrive for questioning, the sergeant expressed his uncertainty as to what he should do with this young man. On the one hand, he could not ignore the fact that an offense had been committed; he had been informed, in fact, that the youth was prepared to confess to the offense. Nor could he overlook the continued pressure from the girl's father (an important political figure) for the police to take severe action against the youth. On the other hand, the sergeant had formed a low opinion of the girl's moral character, and he considered it unfair to charge "A" with statutory rape when the girl was a willing partner to the offense and might even have been the instigator of it. However, his sense of injustice concerning "A" was tempered by his image of the youth as a "punk," based, he explained, on information he had received that the youth belonged to a certain gang, the members of which were well known to, and disliked by, the police. Nevertheless, as we prepared to leave his office to interview "A," the sergeant was still in doubt as to what he should do with him.
>   As we walked down the corridor to the interrogation room, the sergeant was stopped by a reporter from the local newspaper. In an excited tone of voice, the reporter explained that his editor was pressing him to get further information about this case. The newspaper had printed some of the facts about the girl's disappearance, and as a consequence the girl's

[2]The following excerpt is reprinted by permission of the University of Chicago Press. © 1964 by the University of Chicago.

father was threatening suit against the paper for defamation of
the girl's character. It would strengthen the newspaper's position, the reporter explained, if the police had information indicating that the girl's associates, particularly the youth the sergeant was about to interrogate, were persons of disreputable
character. This stimulus seemed to resolve the sergeant's uncer-
tainty. He told the reporter, "unofficially," that the youth was
known to be an undesirable person, citing as evidence his membership in the delinquent gang. Furthermore, the sergeant added
that he had evidence that this youth had been intimate with the
girl over a period of many months. When the reporter asked if
the police were planning to do anything to the youth, the sergeant answered that he intended to charge the youth with statutory rape.

In the interrogation, however, three points quickly
emerged which profoundly affected the sergeant's judgment of
the youth. First, the youth was polite and cooperative; he con-
sistently addressed the officer as "sir," answered all questions
quietly, and signed a statement implicating himself in numerous
counts of statutory rape. Second, the youth's intentions toward
the girl appeared to have been honorable; for example, he said
that he wanted to marry her eventually. Third, the youth was
not in fact a member of the gang in question. The sergeant's
attitude became increasingly sympathetic, and after we left the
interrogation room he announced his intention to "get 'A' off
the hook," meaning that he wanted to have the charges against
"A" reduced or, if possible, dropped.

2. Officers "X" and "Y" brought into the police station a
seventeen-year-old white boy who, along with two older com-
panions, had been found in a home having sex relations with a
fifteen-year-old girl. The boy responded to police officers'
queries slowly and with obvious disregard. It was apparent that
his lack of deference toward the officers and his failure to evidence concern about his situation were irritating his questioners.
Finally, one of the officers turned to me and, obviously angry,
commented that in his view the boy was simply a "stud" interested only in sex, eating, and sleeping. The policemen conjec-
tured that the boy "probably already had knocked up half a
dozen girls." The boy ignored these remarks, except for an occasional stare at the patrolmen. Turning to the boy, the officer
remarked, "What the hell am I going to do with you?" And again
the boy simply returned the officer's gaze. The latter then said,
"Well, I guess we'll just have to put you away for a while." An
arrest report was then made out and the boy was taken to Juvenile Hall [p. 211].

The presumed "character" of the person is not the only consideration that influences police discretion in particular cases. Investigators have reported, for example, that other situational factors, such as the presence of an audience or a complaining witness, or a satisfactory place, other than jail, to deposit the person may influence the decision to arrest or release (Sudnow, 1965; Bittner, 1967a, 1967b). For our purposes, however, the important consideration is that "practical theories of criminology" are used to interpret the meaning of the penal code in particular situations. One cannot predict the disposition of cases merely from a knowledge of the law. Practical theories about types of people, including hypotheses about "why" kinds of people behave as they do and what they can be trusted to do in the future, articulate behavioral displays with the penal code. In an important sense, the law is used to justify whatever practical decisions or character imputations criminal justice personnel have made. If the person is judged to be a "good risk," a way can be found to avoid formal booking and detention. Likewise, the law can be used to legitimate more punitive treatment for "bad risk" cases. The work of law enforcement personnel in interpreting the "meaning" of behavioral displays and in articulating behavior with legal rules is an important example of the more general negotiation process through which persons are judged to be incompetent, immature, and such, activities in which circumstantial demands are considered.

Another excellent example of this negotiation process is described in Cicourel's *The Social Organization of Juvenile Justice* (1968). Cicourel has studied the decision-making process and strategy of probation officers who must decide the "meaning" of the particular actions of a young person on probation. Cicourel argues that the probation officer and youthful offender implicitly negotiate between them a certain sense of "trust" that includes expressed feelings of regret about previous behavior, admission that it was wrong, and promises to try to do better. Future behavior is interpreted in light of this implicit trust. The probation officer, for example, may "reread" past behavior and conclude that there was actually no basis for the trust or that the present incident really does not require any basic reinterpretation of the trusting relationship but only a reminder of its existence (see Chapter Six, "Reconstructing Biography").

Consider the following dialogue, recorded by Cicourel (1968), between a female probation officer and Audrey, a fifteen-year-old female juvenile who had been reported by school officials for fighting. This part of the conversation comes after the girl has admitted that it is wrong to fight and has promised that in the future she will simply "walk away" from situations where a fight may be brewing.

Probation Officer: Well, Audrey, you've overcome a lot of your problems, you really have. But now that we see maybe another problem is going to start getting you in trouble, this is the time to start handling that problem [*pause*]. Right? Not wait until it becomes so serious that it is difficult to tell other people that you're going to stop doing it. Now they'll still believe you like Mr. James. If you're not going to fight any more or not get mixed up in this stuff any more, he'll believe you. But if you went on doing it for a couple of months, you know, he'll find it difficult to believe you, wouldn't he?

Juvenile: Yes.

Probation Officer: So you stick by what you've told him [*pause*], that you're not going to get in any more trouble, all right? [*Cut off as "all right" uttered.*]

Juvenile: You know, I could have went to juvie again, but Mr. James say uh [*cut off by Probation Officer*].

Probation Officer: I know it. He helped you.

Juvenile: I know, 'cause he said I hadn't been in no trouble since I had been in.

Probation Officer: See [*pause*], so that good time helped you. If you had gotten in trouble right away he wouldn't have known if you could behave yourself. And he probably would have, you know, let you go to Juvenile Hall, but since you had all this—how many months?—six or seven months?

Juvenile: I figured eleven months.

Probation Officer: Eleven months.

Juvenile: At the home.

Probation Officer: Eleven months with no real difficulties either at home or at school, right?

Juvenile: Yeah.

Probation Officer: So that's why he knew if you said you won't get in more trouble he knows you can if you stick by that.

Juvenile: You see I gotta [*cut off by Probation Officer*].

Probation Officer: He trusts you, Audrey, so it is up to you to keep his trust.

We now pick up the conversation again.

Probation Officer: I, I would have to figure out what would be best for you, Audrey. I don't know what would be best, but if you don't stop having these problems that you just started having, I'd have to think up something.

Juvenile: Oh, I can stop having problems.

Probation Officer: Well, then you'd better. You show me that you can and then I won't have to make any decisions. Right? I'm coming out here today mainly just to warn you about what can happen if you do any more of this. Do you understand that?

Juvenile: Uh, hmm.

Probation Officer: You have anything you want to talk about? If you want to stay there, well, this is fine with me. I go along with that. I think it's a real good idea. I'm not saying forever. I can't promise you forever either. Right?

Juvenile: Yeah.

[Cicourel, 1968, pp. 153-157.]

Cicourel notes that the probation officer has not chosen to see this incident as a violation of probation. Yet the officer makes it clear that further troubles may force her to a different conclusion. The juvenile apparently displayed a "cooperative" or "right" attitude on this occasion but there is a warning that future problems may cause the officer to reevaluate her interpretation of "what is best" for the juvenile.

The probation officer must now articulate her interpretation about the meaning of Audrey's recent behavior and her decision about what should be done about it with general policies or rules of the criminal justice system. The articulation is accomplished through the production of a report, a portion of which is presented below, which manages the impression or interpretation that the probation officer wishes to give

(Cicourel, 1968): "A couple of minor incidents since—yesterday she and some other girls jumped on a laundry truck at school and Audrey didn't obey bus driver on bus. However, Mr. J. reports that Audrey's attitude was good—admitted everything and promised she wouldn't any more" (p. 163).

The description of the situation as "minor" and of Audrey's attitude as "good—admitted everything and promised she wouldn't any more" justified the decision to treat this incident as insignificant and not to reevaluate the current disposition. Audrey had earlier been placed in a foster home after she had been accused of several thefts. The probation officer discovered "a lack of adult and parental supervision and control. Both parents are employed and either unable or uninterested in having Audrey properly supervised." To the probation officer it was "obvious that Audrey has quite a problem with thievery and should have some type of professional help." Hospital authorities agreed: "She has an . . . extremely low self-esteem which she compensates by stealing" (p. 131). Audrey was thus typified as a clinical type, a girl with "deep underlying problems" that cause her to break the law. Her current behavior is seen as one more unfortunate example of her difficult, but potentially victorious, battle with emotional problems, rather than an additional transgression in the developing career of a hopelessly "criminal" type.

The production of a delinquent career is not the sole responsibility of the juvenile. Probation officers, police, school authorities, and parents participate in the work of deciding what has "really" happened and what the behavior means in terms of the "kind" of person this is and what can be expected from him in the future. The young person behaves in ways that are judged to show good character, cooperation, rebelliousness, defiance, and similar typifications. The talk of the parents, their personal appearance and the appearance of their home, and their expressed concern or lack of concern for their child is interpreted by police and probation officers to "reveal" positive resources for change or continuing contributions to delinquency. The police, using their practical theories of criminology, view some juveniles as "kids with normal problems" and others as "future criminals" who need to be dealt with now. The probation officers, armed with "practical theories about juvenile problems and rehabilitation," see deep, emotional problems rooted primarily in the family and cultural environment and secondarily in schools and peer relationships. The legal future of the child depends on the negotiation and resolution of meaning among these contending parties.

Cicourel (1968) has described the production of delinquent careers in several detailed case studies. In the following pages we will describe the practical theories about one boy as they are revealed in written reports, collated or produced by the police and probation officer. The boy is named Smithfield. He is a black male who has been accused of burglary, petty theft, and defiance of school authority on at least eight occasions over a period of three years.

From the school:

> Smithfield is mentally retarded, or at least appears that way. He would profit from placement in a special class. Smithfield responds well to praise and recognition, and these methods should probably be used in teaching self-control and acceptable social behavior [*sixth grade*] [Cicourel, 1968, p. 204].
>
> During the time that Smithfield has been in the room his adjustment has been very ineffective. His social values seem to be functioning at a different level than the rest of the class. He appears to have no personal goals and does not appear to recognize significant problems which face him. The antagonistic attitude with which he meets both students and teachers aggravates all of his social situations [*seventh grade*] [p. 207].
>
> Would rather tell a lie than tell the truth. A typical sentence: "I didn't do it. Besides you did not catch me." Has a hard time keeping his hands off other people's property. I have changed his seat in class several times, hoping he would improve, to no avail. . . . What suggestions can one make for a boy who is dishonest, a chronic liar, a very poor student and a constant trouble maker [*eighth grade*] [p. 217].

The several accounts provided by the school give a rather clear picture of Smithfield. His academic progress is poor and he is considered disruptive, a chronic troublemaker, and a liar.

From juvenile authorities:

> Smithfield appears to be an emotionally disturbed boy
> who has considerable difficulty relating to peers. He is loud
> and aggressive, and has a tendency to pick fights with the
> smaller and less physically adept group members. He refuses to
> accept authority of any nature. When counselled, concerning
> his negative conduct and attitude, he becomes emotionally up-
> set using crying tactics as a means of getting sympathy instead
> of admonishment [pp. 218-219].

From the reports above and many similar "descriptions"
provided by Cicourel, it is apparent that the police and school
officials agree that something is wrong with Smithfield. He is
described as a poor student, mentally retarded, emotionally disturbed, aggressive, and disrespectful of authority. The "underlying problems," however, are not revealed. They are left to the
diagnostic skill or interpretive ability of the probation officer
who determines not only "what is wrong" but "what should be
done."

From the probation officer:

> Mrs. Elston [*Smithfield's mother*] is handicapped in
> coping with her son's problems, primarily because of her in-
> ability to be firm. She does not realize, after firm counselling,
> that it is her responsibility as a parent to work with agencies
> that are attempting to assist her. It is encouraging to note the
> mother figure has taken a firmer attitude in the matter of her
> delinquent son and will attempt to be more realistic in the fu-
> ture [p. 211].
>
> There is little the Probation Officer can add to the above
> remarks and at this point, it would appear a change of environ-
> ment as well as schools, possibly will assist those concerned in
> rehabilitating this child [p. 211].
>
> It appeared to this writer that Mrs. Elston was able to
> control Smithfield's activities and companions for a long
> period of time but that during the current year Smithfield ac-
> quired undesirable companions without the knowledge of his
> mother. Consequently, his general attitude regressed. The
> School personnel have acknowledged that they are willing to
> continue working with Smithfield and the minor's mother has
> acknowledged a desire to continue working with him and fur-

ther acknowledges that she will contact the Probation Officer
if the minor does not conform, therefore, the Probation Officer is recommending that Smithfield be continued on probation and allowed to remain in the custody of his mother, but it
is further recommended that the Court instruct the minor and
his mother regarding their responsibilities and inform them
that if they are not able to meet them the Court will find it
necessary to remove the minor from his home and place him
elsewhere [p. 221].

The official reports do not reveal the complete range of
practical information used by police, school officials, and probation officers to interpret Smithfield's behavior as exemplary
of a "type" of person. For example (although not indicated in
the foregoing excerpts), Smithfield's racial and social-class characteristics were used by the police to account for their claim
that he would be a source of trouble and a likely suspect whenever there is a crime. They assumed that he would lie about his
involvement and would attempt to conceal evidence. An un-
happy marriage that ended in separation and the supervision of
"trouble-prone" children by an overburdened mother is useful
information for the probation officer. Such knowledge apparently allows one both to "understand" how such behavior and
attitudes could develop and to suggest remedial intervention.

We have not been concerned here with the "facts" of
Smithfield's case. The behavioral bases of the accusations of stealing and lying and the diagnoses of mental retardation and emotional insecurity have not been examined to determine their
accuracy or validity. The reports do not provide sufficient detail
to allow us to know what Smithfield actually did or said on particular occasions. Even if the reports had provided more descriptive material on Smithfield's "actual" behavior, however, our
interest would still have been on the interpretation of the behavior made by police, probation, and school personnel. This
approach is in keeping with the theme of our argument that
individuals do not simply possess immature, incompetent, delinquent, or similar characteristics that are self-evident in their
behavior, although they may be reported by people as self-
evident. Rather, characteristics are attributed to persons by

others who observe them directly or who have access to reports about their behavior. Practical theories about development, deviance, abnormality, and the like, allow others to meaningfully "recognize" personal characteristics and to produce convincing rationales (to themselves and for others) for their judgments and remedial intervention. Smithfield's case was made "understandable" through the application of common-sense theories about "boys like Smithfield." Race, family problems, cultural deprivation, bad peer influences, and other undesirable influences are believed evident or easily "read" from his behavior. Police, school, and probation personnel basically agree on this interpretation. There may be some disagreement about what should be done with Smithfield, however. The police believe that probation officers are too "soft" on delinquents, that punishment is called for in more cases. The probation officer is reluctant to recommend punishment because he has identified the "reasons" for the problems and he feels sure that some remedial action can be helpful. In official reports to the court, he downplays the significance of the delinquent activity as such and argues for a clinical interpretation of "deep problems," which may be corrected with appropriate treatment. For the practical purposes of the probation office, Smithfield is "salvageable," while for the police he is on the course of an inevitable "delinquent career." Our purpose is not to show who has made the "correct" diagnosis of Smithfield but to demonstrate how his past, present, and future have been negotiated by those who interpreted his behavior.

Typification not only provides classification schemes for locating types of people but also generates motivational explanations ("theories") of behavior and rationales for seeing behavior as exemplary of one type of person or another. As we have emphasized several times before, typifications are situated constructions that persons develop and use to work through the affairs of their everyday, practical lives. The job of the probation officer, for example, is presumably to salvage young people who get into trouble with the law. In order for a person to be salvageable, the origin of his problem must be found in some set of conditions that are correctable. Home, school, or peer group becomes a target of the therapeutic process. The typification of a juvenile as an "emotional problem" provides the probation officer with a ready-made explanation for a variety of problematic behaviors as well as a general strategy for intervention.

The juvenile, and possibly his family, may concur with the probation officer's diagnosis. Agreement is communicated in several ways. First, the juvenile does not challenge the probation officer's interpretation of why things have happened as they did. He may debate the "facts" of a particular case but the "underlying causes" are not challenged. Second, there must be some recognizable sign of willingness or intent to change. Third, there should be some basis for the probation officer to "see" progress over time. The trust relationship is always a tentative one, a relationship that is continually reinforced or renegotiated as new situations emerge. If the probation officer and juvenile cooperate to generate an image of the juvenile as a person who deserves therapeutic help and who is making progress, the young person probably escapes the more punitive consequences of the legal system. If the probation officer or others "recognize" that the cooperation effort has failed, however, there are persons (with their own practical problems) waiting in the wings to argue for different interpretations of the kind of individual this is, what motivates him, and what should be done with him.

The Denial of Rationality

The dictionary tells us that *rationality* is the ability to reason logically, as by drawing conclusions from inferences, and the term often implies the absence of emotionalism. Some synonyms for *rational* are *reasonable, sensible, sane,* and *well-advised.* Lay, as well as conventional social science, notions of rationality are similar to the dictionary usage. While certain extreme conditions are believed to stimulate unreasonable or irrational behavior (mob violence, for example), most persons are generally thought to be able to behave in a sensible way and maintain control of themselves.

Common-sense notions of rationality, however, fail to specify the social processes through which rational behavior is identified as such. "Rational" behavior, as a feature of competence and maturity, is a construction of people's interpretations. Rationality is identified in the everyday, occasioned activities of people who "know" generally how one should behave in this or that situation. Of course, allowances are made for variation in behavior in most situations and explained by notions such as experience, immaturity, fatigue, physical illness, or personal idiosyncrasies. Such "explanations" for behavioral variation are provided in common-sense typifications that allow people to interpret the meaning of behavior in particular contexts and to share or negotiate meaning as they comment on or talk about behavior together.

In this final section of the chapter we will deal with one interesting aspect of the social construction or identification of a person as irrational or out of control. Specifically, we will look at the interpretation made by professional counselors or therapists of the verbal disclaimers of persons who have been classified as mentally or emotionally ill.

Suchar (1975) offers a sample of talk among a professional child therapist and staff members in training during a session in which the latter are being taught how to make "correct" interpretations of, and provide therapy for, children in a state mental health clinic for emotionally disturbed children. At one point in a training seminar, a therapist in training offered the following description and account of one child whom she had been treating.

"What's happening with you?" And he [*the child*] said that two of the counselors had told him that he didn't belong here and I said, "What does that mean to you?" and I said, "Do you think you belong here?" and he said, "No." He said, "I've solved all my problems." And I said, "How'd you do that?" [*laughing*] and he said, "Well, the first problem we had was with school (and he's a very bright boy and he knows that) and I was flunking out of school and I was just goofing off." He said, "Now I'm doing really well in school. The other problem I have" (he only has two) [*laughing*] was that he didn't get along with people and he said, ". . . right now I'm spending more time around people and that's solving the problem." I said, "How's that work?" [*laugh*] He said, "Well, I

spend more time around people, I feel more comfortable, I
don't feel as uncomfortable or something like that." He said,
"Like you, I feel a lot more comfortable with you, but it took
me a long time, you see. I had to spend some time with you
and get to know who you were and what you were like." And
he said ". . . so I think that I've really solved all my problems
and dealt with it and I want to know when I'm going to get to
go home." I said, "Well, that's wonderful." [*laughing*] I said,
"Well, I couldn't tell you when you're going to go home. He
said, ". . . that's what you're here for; you go back to those
meetings that you have . . ." and he got into a whole long
thing about how I make the decisions whether he's to leave or
not and this is not at all true and I said, "That's not the way it
works, John, I do not make the decisions on whether you
leave or not," and he said, "Well, who does?" And I said, "It's
the entire staff." And he said, "I told my mother" (he had just
had a visit) that he wanted to go home and that he had solved
all his problems and his mother had told him that he hadn't
solved all his problems and he said, "I want to know what
she's talking about, she knows about some problems I have
that I don't know about." And I said, "How could she do
that?" And he said, "Well, she told me I had some that I
hadn't solved yet and I want to know what they are cause
maybe that's how I can get out of here . . ." *Well, he was just
being too logical,* I just couldn't take it here . . . He said that
he didn't know how he could solve any of his problems in the
situation that we were in, that just coming and talking to me
was not going to do him any good [*that is, get him out of the
institution*] [Suchar, 1975, p. 16].

In another context, this conversation may have been interpreted as the talk of a rational, mature young person. Such an
attribution of competence was apparently not possible here
given the "obvious seriousness" of the boy's emotional problems. The therapist held on to a diagnostic typification of the
boy's "actual" disturbed behavior, one that emphasized the
need to look behind overt behavior to discover "why" the disturbed child "needed" to say what he did. Behavior that might
appear to be rational in other settings is here judged to be
"symptomatic" of real but hidden problems. Nothing the boy
could say would make him "rational."

A second example of the denial of rationality comes from

Haydon's (1974) study of self-definition in an alcoholic rehabilitation center. Patients are referred to the center by employers, family, police, and others for stays of up to thirty days.
In addition to abstinence, the program requires patients to participate in a series of therapy sessions. Therapy is conducted by
counselors who structure their activities around a twelve-step
treatment program as developed by Alcoholics Anonymous.
Any patient is presumed to have an underlying, emotional problem that has led to his or her addiction. Because this problem is
often hidden to all but the trained counselor and other such
professionals, the patient is expected to deny the problem's
existence. In fact, "denial" is interpreted as a confirmation of
the problem. Progress begins when the patient admits to the
official interpretation of a problem and surrenders to it. Consider the following dialogue:

Patient: I'm setting up tests for myself.

Counselor: What do you expect to gain if you win?

Patient: Control over my drinking—sobriety.

Counselor: Control is not the same thing as winning, you're not serious
enough, you haven't accepted step one—you haven't surrendered.

Patient: Surrender to what?

Counselor: Surrender at the gut level that you're no longer able to control your compulsion to drink. Once you've quit fighting step one, surrendered, and really do take it in yourself—well, you could be swimming in
it and you wouldn't drink it. You lose if you try to control. You win when
you surrender.

The term *surrender* apparently means both admitting to
the overwhelming and personally unmanageable nature of the
problem of alcoholism as well as accepting the therapist's definition of the problem and the correct solution. Other patients
may even support the "official" explanation of the therapist
when a patient persists in denying that he is an alcoholic.

Patient 1:   I'm convinced I'm not an alcoholic. I'm not addicted to
booze.

Counselor: That's a lot of bullshit. You should talk to your wife.

Patient 1:   I only drink under mental anxiety or stress.

Counselor: What's that?

Patient 1: If I'm an alcoholic, I'm only one to a certain extent. I'm not upset all the time. [*Patient chuckles.*]

Counselor: What the hell you smiling for? Is this all funny to you? You've been smiling since you came into this group.

Patient 1: You'd smile, too, if your facial nerves had been cut like mine. [*Patient points to scars on his face.*] Knife fight. Believe me brother, right now I'm not smilin'.

Counselor: It seems like you know all about yourself. You seem to be saying, "People are confusing me." But that's not it. You know? You know right where you are. You're an alcoholic. [*The counselor pauses, then extends his arm, finger pointed, and sweeps it around at the other patients.*] Take someone else right now and compare yourself to him.

Patient 1: Maybe they won't like it.

Counselor: I don't care. I told you to do it.

Patient 1: Man. The thing that separates me from them is that they can't pass up a drink. They're addicted.

Patient 2: How the hell can you say that! [*Begins screaming.*] You beat your wife every time you got drunk, and you were drunk most of the time. You . . .

Counselor: Well, he only drinks when he's under mental stress, you know.

Patient 3: You must be under mental stress a lot.

Counselor: There are no degrees of alcoholism. You're either an alcoholic or not. There are different phases, but let's get that straight right now. You're either an alcoholic or not.

Patient 1: I know you think I'm denying.

Counselor: I see you with the big smile and you're having a good time. Let's get you to reality. Jesus Christ! Quit playing games. Why the hell do you stay here?

Patient 1: Maybe I'd like to find out something about myself.

Counselor: Hell! We can send you to a psychiatrist for that. You drink every day. Most of the time you get shit-faced plastered. You spend your money on booze. You beat your wife when you're drunk. Damn it! You're an alcoholic.

Patient 4: I think if you can't smother them in your brilliance you give them bullshit. You're looking for someone to blame. Anyone but yourself. . . .

Counselor: The way you're goin', you'll be ready for help around 1980. Tell us something about yourself.

Patient 1:   I'm determined. When I start something I'm determined to finish.

Counselor: I call it denial [Haydon, 1974, pp. 37-38].

We have not discussed the question of how disturbed children or alcoholics are identified as such in the first place or how they came to be in a therapeutic program. These are extremely important research questions but in the preceding circumstances, they do not appear to be problematic for the counselors. For them, one background assumption is that a person in a program is proof enough of the existence of a problem. Their logic appears to be something to the effect: "If he is in here something must be wrong with him." Again, no amount of rational "evidence" alters the denial of rationality embodied in diagnostic typifications.

Chapter Six

Reconstructing Biography

We began our considerations of life change by distinguishing conventional approaches from our social phenomenological viewpoint. We then turned to the meaning of *normal* and *abnormal* from the latter point of view. In Chapters Four and Five, we explored a number of issues of two time-orientations that people assume in talking of life change: the future and the present. Let us now turn to people's sense of the past. What sorts of accounts do they construct as intelligible portrayals of that which took place in what seems to have passed, and how is this done?

The Conventional Past

People refer to past lives in many ways, among them: one's past, a life history, a life course, a personal history, childhood, adolescence, middle age, old age, and one's life story. These terms suggest that the past is a series of completed events in a person's life; most do not imply that the past—whether in personal reminiscence, collective ruminations, or professional reconstruction—is an essential part of the present. The past to most people is regarded as *what has happened* to an individual up to some current point in time.

For the most part, to discover one's past, childhood, life history, or the like is to search for what "really" happened over, or in some portion of, the lifetime of an individual. It is taken for granted that certain events have occurred in someone's past, that these may be discovered, and that to do so is a matter of locating and reporting them. Conventionally, the crucial task in knowing a past life is to dis-cover it.

There are, of course, two elements in the matter of knowing someone's past: the past itself and the knower. Conventionally, emphasis is placed on "the past itself." The knower is considered, at best, a passive net that gathers the real facts of an individual's past. At worst, the knower interferes with, misinterprets, or unwittingly distorts what has "certainly, really" gone by in someone's life. To know one's past, personal history, life story, or whatever is a technical affair once it is taken for granted that an individual has a real past that has gone by and that is knowable.

What is the outcome of failure to consider the knower beyond possible inaccuracies of his representations of a past? Such failure involves systematically ignoring the tacit reality work of the knower in representing someone's past life, what we referred to earlier as his "practical procedures." For example, we ignore what he glosses over in gathering conventionally relevant data, what seems so obvious to him that it is seen but not noticed by him.

We began this section with a list of conventional names for past life or portions of it. None explicitly suggested that those who attempt to know someone's past contribute to its realization as part of the process. In exploring the social phenomenology of past life, we shall use the term *biography* to mean not a published book written about a more or less significant person, but, rather, a description or account of events in someone's past.

Biography

It is important to distinguish between two important senses of *biography*, one more conventional than the other. On the one hand, *biography* is used by both laypersons and human scientists to refer to the depiction of *a* life history, that is, *a* biography. While this usage acknowledges the fact that people write or describe life histories, emphasis is placed on what is written or described, not the process of writing and describing. We shall, on the other hand, consider biography to be an activity of biographers. For us, what is real about people's biographies is the work done (that is, practical procedures) to generate them, which emphasizes the *graphic* part of the term.

As Goffman (1963) suggests, people assume that each individual has a single biography: "Anything and everything an individual has done and can actually do is understood to be containable within his biography, as the Jekyll-Hyde theme illustrates, even if we have to hire a biography specialist, a private detective, to fill in the missing facts and connect the discovered ones for us. No matter how big a scoundrel a man is, no matter how false, secretive, or disjointed his existence, or how governed by fits, starts, and reversals, the true facts of his activity cannot be contradictory or unconnected with each other" (pp. 62-63). How is it possible, though, for people to accept the "obviousness" of single, individual biographies, on the one hand, while occasionally encountering the seeming multiplicity of individual lives, on the other? For example, what sense does a young woman make of her boyfriend, whose devotion is obvious to her and whom she describes as "a real man," when she learns of his long history of homosexual encounters?

People work to make their knowledge of others consistent with their assumption about the singleness of biography. They refer to and account for apparent inconsistencies in biographies with such terms and explanations as *passing, covering, going incognito,* and the like. Thus, for our young woman, the heterosexual devotion of her boyfriend is now seen as "really" his way of "passing as a real man." She reconstructs her entire biography of her erstwhile boyfriend to be consistent with his homosexuality. For example, she sees his athletic successes as "really" a way to cover up what she claims should have been obvious all along. What may appear biographically contradictory is, on the contrary, taken to be quite consistent and continuous when seen in the light of a person's ability (often said to be subtle) to manage to separate what is "certainly" a single lifeline.

Biographical work is a search for integrating accounts that lead to overall intelligibility. This process of integration requires a good deal of glossing, because the biography being considered is always the biography at hand. In some place, at some time, an individual's past is being considered. This limitation in space and time is meaningful to biographers in that the tacit background of specific situations defines "relevant" biography. For example, in situations in which grammar school teachers are to assign themselves to a number of students, the pasts of individual students are relevant to teachers in that students' "biographies" should make it obvious who should be assigned to whom. For all practical purposes, to the teachers concerned, the "complete" biography of each individual student is a school-centered one, which, by the way, to teachers may substantively encompass much of the student's formally nonschool life. Or, for example, as Kai Erikson (1962) implies about biographical glossing practices in the social construction of deviance: "When a community acts to control the behavior of one of its members, it is engaged in a very intricate process of selection. Even a determined miscreant conforms in most of his daily behavior—using the correct spoon at mealtime, taking good care of his mother, or otherwise observing the mores of his society—and if the community elects to bring sanctions against him for the occasions when he does act offensively, it is responding to a few deviant details set within a vast context of proper conduct. Thus a person may be jailed or hospitalized for a few scattered moments of misbehavior, defined as a full-time deviant despite the fact that he had supplied the community with countless other indications that he was a decent, moral citizen" (p. 308). Erikson couches his description in the language of social control, which is a conventional language. His description, however, may be read as a portrayal of the "reasoned" use of biography by people trying to make sense of someone's "strange" behavior. In this case, the biography being suggested is a deviant one. In this or any other case, it still would be a biography, casual or formal, with all its practical undertones.

Like Erikson, Ichheiser (1970) speaks of what he calls "misinterpretations of personality," citing the following example of the reasoned integration of certain facts of a man's life into a single biography of "perfect" criminality: "A man is under suspicion of murder. During the investigation certain definite abnormalities of his sexual behavior come to light, even though there is no evidence that they are related in any way to the committed murder. Again, the frequent reactions in many people, if verbalized, would read something like this: 'This man whose sexual life deviates so strangely from the norm can also be expected to deviate from other social norms in any other respect.' However, here again the overestimation of personality unity has probably misled their interpretative reaction" (pp. 50-51).

The Flow of Biography. How does biography flow? Two things might be meant by *flow.* One refers to how people's lives develop over time so that they become what they are presently. The second refers to how people's past lives change, from moment to moment and from place to place, as others consider them. We are mainly concerned with the second sense of *flow,* although we shall also speak of the first. It might be useful to consider an analogy in answering this question. Let us turn to the same question of flow from an historiographer's point of view. Why this analogy? There are at least two reasons for looking at the general problematic of writing history (historiography) as useful in answering the question of biographic flow: one is substantive and the other is analytic.

Substantively, there are a number of affinities between history and life history. First, both are considered to be substantively a collection of events. Second, both historians and biographers consider these events in a temporal frame; they concern themselves with order and sequence among events. Third, the time frame they principally deal with is past time, although they certainly do engage, on occasion, in any number of prognostications.

Analytically, it seems to us that historians have eclipsed human scientific biographers in their comparative awareness of the influence of their *own* work on what they produce. This, perhaps, has an ideological explanation and may stem from the urgent desire of human scientists to divorce themselves from the "mere" speculations of philosophy in order to establish an intellectual respectability in its own right. In any event, this eclipse may be useful to explore in that we might learn from historiography about what human biographers do.

With this in mind, let us turn to the question of how biography flows. We shall lean heavily on Collingwood's (1959) essay, "The Historical Imagination."

Collingwood distinguishes between what he calls the commonsense theory of history and constructive history. He describes the commonsense theory this way: "According to this theory, the essential things in history are memory and authority. If an event or a state of things is to be historically known, first of all someone must be acquainted with it; then he must remember it; then he must state his recollection of it in terms intelligible to another; and finally that other must accept the statement as true. History is thus the believing someone else when he says that he remembers something. The believer is the historian; the person believed is called his authority" (p. 69). The commonsense historian believes that the meaning of history lies buried in the statements of authorities and that the historian's work as a writer of history is to locate and report on this as precisely as possible. He must, above all, minimize his own involvement in the process. When his work is done well, the commonsense historian presumably can claim to have obtained *the* historical truth.

The commonsense historian assumes history to have actually flowed; his task is to accurately depict the flow as it happened, as objectively as possible. Likewise, conventional biographers (both lay and professional) assume that the biographies of those with whom they are concerned—be they children or elders, normal persons or schizophrenics—lie in the past flow of events in their subjects' lives. Like the commonsense historian, their job is dependent on the "memory" (charts, files, testimony, vitae, patient histories, and so on) of a variety of "authorities" (such as nurses, aides, parents, children, friends, and counselors). They consider their job to be the accurate description and explanation of how the flow of biography has led to some current state of living. As we mentioned above, this is a search for the "conventional past." Collingwood's commonsense past is analogous to what we have called people's "conventional past."

Collingwood challenges the commonsense theory because it is "bankrupt." It has outlived its credibility. Why is this so? First of all, according to Collingwood, authority is not a matter of objective fact but, rather, "authorities abide a verdict which only he [the historian] can give" (p. 73). As for memory, Collingwood states that the historian, in practice, does not depend on simple recollective memory, as such, as the commonsense theory would suggest. Rather, the historian, himself, is embedded in his own creative craft of discovering and rediscovering various documents and artifacts that have no deliberate or unwitting traditional flow toward the present, selecting and reselecting among them.

In contrast to the commonsense theory, Collingwood depicts what he calls a "constructive theory" of history. The constructive theory implies that, ironically, the past essentially emerges in the present (compare G. H. Mead, 1932). The past is the work of the practicing historian who uses "facts" and studiously invokes authority to argue the developmental meaning of the present. The past is what the practicing historian produces by reflecting on "facts" and speaking or writing of them in such a way that "facts" are made intelligible. As Collingwood states: "No historian, not even the worst, merely copies out his authorities; even if he puts in nothing of his own (which is never really possible), he is always leaving out things [glossing] which, for one reason or another, he decides that his own work does not need or cannot use. It is he, therefore, and not his authority, that is responsible for what goes in. On that question he is his own master: his thought is to that extent autonomous" (p. 71).

When the historian is viewed as actively involved in the construction of history (so that history becomes practical historiography), the question of how history flows leads to a radically different answer than the one provided by the commonsense theory. From a constructive point of view, history (or the past) flows with the contingencies of the present. Every present has its past so that as the present changes, so does history. "Any imaginative reconstruction of the past aims at reconstructing the past of this present, the present in which the act of imagination is going on, as here and now perceived" (Collingwood, p. 83). There is the constructed past of this present, the constructed past of that present, and so on without end as long as the past remains a historical task for the present.

The commonsense historian, in principle, considers his work finished when he has discovered the objective flow of history. To him, there is meaning *in* history and his task is to discover it. For this, he depends on the precision of his technology. To the constructive historian, on the contrary, history has no final meaning. It flows and will continue to flow as do the vicissitudes of the present. As Collingwood describes the constructive answer to the question of finality: "Because of these changes which never cease, however slow they may appear to observers who take a short view, every new generation must rewrite history in its own way; every new historian, not content with giving new answers to old questions, must revise the questions themselves; and—since historical thought is a river into which none can step twice—even a single historian, working at a single subject for a certain length of time, finds when he tries to reopen an old question that the question has changed" (p. 84).

Our own view of the flow of biography is analogous to Collingwood's depiction of constructed history. All biographers, whether professionals or laypersons, are actively involved in the practice of making individual pasts. They usually do *not* see their work in this way, at least not seriously. However, when we set aside concern with the objects of their work, biography becomes a dialectical affair between those lives that people have reconstructed and the same people's deliberations over the lives.

Lest we push our analogy too far, let us note one important difference between Collingwood's depiction of the constructive historian and constructive biographers in relation to the flow of history as compared with biography. Except for debate over the authenticity of documents and dissent from living figures of the recent past, historians' constructs of the past remain unchallenged by their subjects and the events that surrounded them. Debates over the meaning of history largely center on exchanges between present and future historians. For historians, subjects of the past do not arise, *in vivo*, to challenge and negotiate the meaning of events. Historiography is safe from this, for the most part.

This is not so for biographers. Certainly, some amount of biographical work is done on people of the distant or recent past. For example, some of their work falls within the realm of what might be called historical biography, such as psychoanalytic studies of major historical figures (for example, E. Erikson, 1958, 1969). However, it is probably safe to say that most biographical work is practiced on the pasts of living individuals. Such work happens in clinics, employment agencies, admissions offices, recruitment meetings, life-history interviews, record-keeping, on "strange" occasions, and in any number of other places where some people consider it to be their momentary casual or formal business to make sense of the past life of other people, or even themselves.

The living presence, whether actual or potential, of associates in biographical work, who are its subjects, makes for a difference in the constructive practices of biographers as compared with historians. Besides imaginatively constructing a past life, biographers (whether lay or professional, casual or formal) may negotiate an individual's biography with him. Perhaps the best-known example is the psychoanalytic session, where patient and analyst talk and exchange questions, answers, or interpretations of the patient's past and its assumed relation to the present. Through the work they do together in trying to understand and make sense of the patient's past, a biography develops.

Whether lay or professional, casual or formal, biographers tacitly assume that the business in which they engage when they do biographical work is real business. The reality of things and

events past, which are being recollected or reconstructed, motivates conventional biographers to act as if, at some perhaps
indefinite but yet imminently final point, they will "know" the
past life of some individual or collection of individuals. The
final reality of the object of their work is one feature of the
task that makes it meaningful. How absurd the world would
appear to them should they suddenly take seriously the idea
that what they search for in the past is a kind of fantasy, changing with developments of the very work they do to discover it.

There is an implicit theory of motivation underlying our
distinction between the conventional past and the constructed
past of people's lives. As long as people tacitly assume that what
they search for is real and that their work, at some indefinite but
yet real point in time, will come to completion, they carry on.
Although they encounter things which they define as "ridicu-
lous" along the way, the basic reality of the objects of their
labor makes what they do meaningful. Should this tacit assumption be shaken, people would begin feeling—if not speaking of
it—a sense of the absurd. At this point, serious everyday life
activity would cease (compare Sartre, 1964).

For most people, reality (and in the present case, biography) is too obviously real and too familiar to become seriously questioned. On occasion, when gathered together, some
people may raise questions about the "absurdity" of their work
or what they might speak of as the "implications or reality of
what we are really doing." However, conventional business
usually glosses over such questions, as those who object are impatiently reminded that they "are just philosophizing" or that
no one has "all day to just speculate about the meaning of existence, you know," and so on. Objections are often glibly dismissed, but when pushed "too far," people become angry about
those who are making "things" so difficult. Whether flippant or
angry, reactions are not presented as fear for the implications of
taking questions of tacit meaning seriously. Rather, reactions
revolve around the "real" business that is being unduly disrupted. When people are together, their conversation tacitly
urges them—sometimes glibly, sometimes impatiently—to accept

the reality of the moment since doing so is a basic feature of their ability to get on to the next meaningful episode in their common lives.[1]

Professional Versus Lay Biographers. In Chapter Three, we distinguished between professional and lay people in their deliberations over varied "strange" and "not-so-strange" events. We stated that the professional claim to expertise in making sense of events had more definitive implications for the course of people's everyday lives than laypersons' deliberations. The features that distinguish professional and lay typifications of "strange" events apply to biographical work. A variety of professionals claim to have special expertise in discovering individual biographies. Some are clinical, such as psychoanalysts, social workers, and pastoral counselors. Others are less so, such as psychologists, sociologists, and anthropologists.

Not having a publicly codified technology for doing biographical work suggests that the latitude and tolerance of typifications among laypersons are wider and higher, respectively, than among professionals. A biography generated by a professional is more likely to have a stylized patterning than one generated by a layperson. Patterning and stylization aside, however, all people engage in the practical work that categorizes behavior displays as one type of conduct or another. The difference between lay and professional biographers lies not in their practice but in the stock of knowledge by which each interprets past lives.

Biographical Work

Biographical work refers to the negotiations in which people engage when the topic at hand is the past lives of individual persons. People may claim to be professional at this work, or

---

[1]What urges *us* on, of course, is that we *deliberately* accept the social phenomenological task as real. It is important to keep the *deliberateness* of this in mind and be continually aware of it. When it is forgotten, our own task and its routines are likely to become cultlike. When it is remembered as we encounter other ways of approaching the world, we are, in effect, able to control our thinking and appreciate that of others.

they may not so claim. The subject of biographical work may be directly involved in its construction, or he may not be involved. Biographical work may be a formal activity of professionals or laypersons, or it may be a rather casual affair.

Certainly, there are other contingencies to biographical work. Among these are: the believed or claimed prestige or power of the subject; the social and personal claims of biographers; the presence or absence of documents; whether or not a record is to be made of a biography; the time people have in which to do their work; the cost or profit claimed by biographers in producing one kind of biography rather than another; the presence or absence of audiences in biographical work situations; the amount and/or claimed quality of "evidence" that biographers have at hand in the work they do; and the available "theories" of past lives that people invoke to order "evidence." Each of these contingencies, as well as others not listed, is likely to be part of the process of biographical work.

It is important to note that we are not concerned with such conventional questions as the relations among these contingencies or combinations of them—as real things separate from biographers—as they affect the production of biography, although this may be an important concern for some. Rather, we treat these so-called variables as "parts of speech," as it were. They are categories of meaning that may enter people's conversations and which they *use* in their practical work, in this case, biographical work.

File Biographies. It is characteristic of formal organizations that they maintain files on their personnel and clientele. Let us concentrate on what commonly are called personnel files. This section has been inspired, in part, by Stanton Wheeler's (1969) edited collection of essays on files and dossiers in American life. Our discussion is suggestive rather than being a set of generalizations based on actual filing practices in specific work settings.

Personnel files may provide an important resource for biographical work for the following reasons. First, they are ordered around individuals. Second, they contain a variety of documents and information about the past life (or portions thereof) of an individual. Third, such files are periodically consulted in order to obtain biographical information.

The social organization of personnel files, in some ways, illustrates the difference between what Collingwood has called the commonsense theory as opposed to the constructive theory of history. Let us speculate about the social organization by focusing on what may be seen as two relatively separate processes: how files are built up and how the content of files is interpreted.

When someone is of concern to certain members of a work organization because that individual may be employed there, a file is born. Somewhere in some office, a folder of some sort is labeled with his name and placed in a location that indicates his present, formal status as an employee of the organization.

The groundwork for a biography exists even before its subject has gained formal entry into the organization. Indeed, an individual may never become an employee and still have some sort of institutional biography in the organization, which may even remain "active" after his death.

The establishment of a potential personnel file, despite lack of formal employment, means that one exists in the organization and one's biography is available for interpretation. Biographical work, by anyone or any group who looks up the file, can be done—and, of course, redone. Emerging from the work of certain members of an organization, a biography is constructed by them as they peruse the content of a file. It may be reconstructed any number of times as they reconsult the file. The reconstruction is dependent on the occasioned needs, moods, felt constraints, accounts, and other practical affairs of biographers.

Ironically, such personnel biographical work may be strangely divorced from the current or even future life of its subject as he sees it. A once-potential member of an organization may continue to have a periodic biography in it despite having totally dismissed and practically forgotten that at some time in his past he had applied for employment. This is not uncommon; institutional biographies are constructed from the contents of potential personnel files whenever employers, or whoever serves in that capacity, for example, consult "old files" for possible candidates for positions now available.

How is a file built up? Building-up is the process by which the contents of a file come to be located in it. These contents include documents ranging from academic transcripts, letters of reference, vitae, résumés, and samples of the written work of the file's subject to memos related to the work performance of the subject, statements about him that have come to someone's attention and "must be" deposited somewhere after they are read, evaluations of the subject, and formal or informal notes of complaint about his work activity. These are certainly not exhaustive of the content of personnel files. Moreover, we have limited the content of files to written documents. With the increased mechanization and breadth of information storage and retrieval systems, files may come to contain mostly unwritten contents such as video tapes, taped products of a variety of surveillance techniques, the taped verbal statements of persons describing or evaluating the subject of a file, and statistical information stored on computer tape and programmed for individual retrieval in order to "get the dump" of someone's file when needed.

Compared with consulting of a file, the process of building up a file is relatively casual. Those who file something in a subject's file—filers—do not usually plan what the content of someone's file shall be. We say "usually," for, on occasion, a filer may in fact conspire to plant some document or other in someone's file in the hope that, upon consultation, consultants (that is, those who consult files) will take such a document or documents into account in their interpretation of the file's contents.

Although documents or other information may be planted in someone's file, this alone is no guarantee that consultants will interpret the content of a file in a way desired by planters. Whether or not the plans of planters go awry depends on a number of situated contingencies; for example, the extent to which the content of a file is known to planters; who the consultants are; whether or not planters eventually become consultants; consultants' situated needs, accounts, and/or claimed constraints in perusing the contents of files; and the like. Let us limit our discussion to the social organization of files that are built up without calculated conspiracy.

We have suggested that the process of file generation is usually casual. This tells us a number of things about filers. First, it tells us that there is no overall reason for *why* documents are placed in someone's file save the fact that the documents presumably relate to its subject in some way or other. The cut-off point for what is considered to relate and what is not is a practical affair for both filers and file consultants. What relates and what does not may be negotiated while a file is being built up, which filers consider to be a matter of filing something "properly." What relates may be opened or reopened to negotiation upon consulting the contents of a file, whereupon a document may be questioned as to whether it was "filed properly" or is "relevant." Being misfiled is not simply a product of not having properly filed a document—although, as in what Collingwood calls the common-sense theory of history, file biographers (in this case, filers and file consultants) would speak of that which is claimed to have been misfiled to be an outcome of not having originally done one's work properly. There is no finality to the conventional office problem of misfiling with respect to specific documents. The same applies to the so-called "authenticity" of file documents. What comes to be a file at any point in its existence is a product of the rationales that filers provide on each of the, more or less, unconnected occasions when filing is done. Out of unconnected situations of filing, a file (in retrospect) is built up.

This brings us to the second thing that a casual build-up tells us. There is no overall patterning to the times *when* documents are placed in someone's file, although there certainly may be regular periods when specific types of documents are filed. When some document is placed[2] in a file, the occasion at that

---

[2] We are limiting our discussion here and elsewhere to building up as a matter of putting something *on* file. The process of building up a file also includes excising documents from a file, although there are organizational reasons to believe that deletion is a less common means of building up a file than adding to it. See Lemert's (1969) discussion of the difficulty involved in expunging juvenile court records, for example.

point is not necessarily meaningful in any way other than what it is momentarily contingent upon, which may be said to be any number of things, the simplest being that there is something at hand that relates to an organizational someone and for the time being must be stored since it has no immediate importance. The meaningful chronology of all documents together that are contained in a file is constituted and reconstituted only when and each time a file is consulted, not before. It is the work of file consultants that makes the overall documented events of a person's biography meaningful.

The fact that documents often have some type of date attached (when sent or when received) does not prevent the possible reconstruction of chronology on each occasion a file is consulted. Dates have no set or objective meaning for those who construct or reconstruct file-related biographies, save those "objective" meanings that they invoke and come to accept: for example, the "fact" that someone "must have" backdated such-and-such or that something "really" got delayed in the mail or something he or she "must" have meant to write earlier but never got around to it until later because of all the pressing business he has, "you know," may all serve as accounts for altering the "objectivity" of dates.

A third thing that a casual build-up tells us about filers is that *who* filers are is not well defined. This contrasts with the usual rather explicit category of persons who may consult a file.

Let us briefly turn to the process of consulting and interpreting file contents. It has greater formality than the generation of a file in that building it up is more a product of the need to deposit and store somewhere existing information on someone in the form of documents, while those who consult a file are probably more explicitly oriented to its overall content and meaning. Filers mostly file, while the work of consultants is likely to be more than mere retrieval. Consulting is often organized into periodic, formal occasions, such as quarterly personnel reviews, annual promotion or dismissal hearings, recruitment conferences, and the like.

File consultants as biographers produce a "sense" of the meaning of documents in a file. There are two perspectives on what might be meant by the production of a "sense" of meaning. First, there is what might be called, analogous to Collingwood, the commonsense perspective. This is the operating perspective claimed by file consultants. Commonsense consultants treat file documents as documentary evidence of organizationally relevant events in the subject's life. There is an "objective" sense to the meaning of documents in a subject's file and consultation centers on the business of interpreting, as accurately as possible, what "really happened" in the subject's past organizational life.

A second perspective on what is meant by the production of a "sense" of the meaning of documents in someone's file is analogous to Collingwood's constructive perspective. The "sense" of the meaning of documents lies in the practice of consultation, the point of view we take.

Consultants are an essential aspect of the very things they consult. For example, when file consultation is considered to be for purposes of termination, the product of such work is founded on consultant negotiations. Consultants produce the very thing that they "objectively" terminate.

One might object that, surely, consultants do consider the very documents before them in their deliberations over file contents. Although it may be granted that contextual contingencies affect the outcome of file deliberations, "objective" documents and their contents are still being evaluated and, thereby, prevent the products of such deliberation from being the "mere fictions" of consultants' practices. On the contrary, even the apparently "certain" reality of the documents themselves is a matter of construction. The language of "misfiling," "document authenticity," and "relevancy," for example, which consultants use, makes this possible. Such language serves as a body of accounts for the reasonable dismissal, reinterpretation, or addition of documents and their contents from or to someone's file. Any document, in practice, may be judged inauthentic or irrelevant for one reason or another, and thereby may be dismissed. Everything that consultants do and consult when they practice the interpretation of personnel files is generated out of the contingencies of their talk together in the "obvious" business at hand.

The final irony (and existential absurdity) of file biographies grows out of direct comparison of the process of how files are built up with the process of their interpretation. In the first place, documents are largely deposited casually with little or no connection between any two filing occasions except that documents are judged to be chiefly related to the subject of a file. In the second place, all these unconnected documents are connected periodically into a meaningful whole, representing the biography of its subject for whatever purpose is at hand (for example, evidence of the *development* of mature judgment, the subject thus "clearly" being due for promotion). As Peter Berger (1963) once described it, everyday life (and in this case biography) is much like a tacit conspiracy in which people unwittingly convince themselves that what they do, they do in good faith and seriousness.

Patient Records. Like personnel files, information on patients' charts is considered to be a record of patient institutional activity. Chart information, however, is more frequently and regularly entered than information deposited in personnel files. As with personnel files, charts or records are consulted when business necessitates obtaining someone's organizational biography.

Personnel files are open to subjects only insofar as subjects are allowed to deposit documents in them. For example, the subject of a file may hand a document to someone who has official consultory access to it, requesting that the document be deposited in his file. Personnel files, however, are usually closed to their subjects as far as consultation is concerned.[3] Patients' charts, however, are closed to their subjects at both ends; patients are not considered to be competent enough to record information on their charts (although they certainly do so

---

[3]There are at least three official exceptions to this. One occurs upon someone's promotion, in which case he now may have access to files closed to him before promotion. Knowledge of this may play no small part in who is elected to promotion in formally democratic institutions. The second exception exists in those organizations (especially civil services) where an employee is asked to sign the evaluation that his supervisor eventually places in the former's file. The third occurs as a result of the Buckley Amendment, which legally allows students access to their files.

indirectly by providing requested information to care personnel), nor is it considered "their business" what their charts say.

Let us consider a brief example of biographical work on
patient charts documented by Suchar (1975). The example is
drawn from work of an institutional staff in a state mental
health clinic for emotionally disturbed children. Although
Suchar speaks of his data as "deviant labeling practices," the
data may also be described as biographical work.

Suchar analyses an in-service psychotherapy training program for social workers who are involved in child psychotherapy. The program is directed by a psychiatric social worker and
a small staff of coordinators. Analysis focuses on the in-service
training seminars supervised by a consultant child therapist, a
Mr. K., who was hired as a trainer-supervisor.

Like other patients in other institutions, the children who
are patients at this mental health clinic have records. Staff enter
a "selected" variety of information on the records which, in
turn, becomes grist for the patient's official institutional biography.

Periodically, records are consulted by the same staff that
built them up in order to check on the reliability of their current diagnostic assessments. Staff are urged to consult and
check with the record in making diagnostic assessments. As
Suchar suggests, this is a rather curious process, since the staff
who check the reliability of their assessments of children in
their charge with the "facts" in the record, on earlier occasions,
selectively built these "facts" up. Subsequently, what is said to
be a way of checking on the reliability of assessments becomes a
process of *making* current biographical data (diagnostic assessments) consistent with the "facts" in the child's record. Staff,
in practice, work to construct a consistent biography of the
child from beginning to end, although to staff members, varied
aspects of the work are assumed to be independent of each
other (for example, recorded data and diagnostic assessments).
Take the following statement by Mr. K.: "It is important to be
informed about diagnostic information about [the] child before
we interact with him; we must develop a picture in our mind
before we go into the session. As soon as things click, that you

realize that what is happening related to previous information about the child, you're on the right track" (Suchar, 1975, p. 14).

Throughout what Suchar calls the institutional career of the patient, a biography is built up by members of the staff. This is closed to patients. To members of the staff, however, their work with the children is a multifaceted affair, the patient's record "merely" being a passive document of what has occurred as a product of the rational application of therapeutic procedures. Suchar puts it this way: "Thus, the influence of the recording system and the norms that develop concerning it, upon the biographical conceptions that the clinical staff have of these cases, is quite significant. The early typifications or characterizations of the case help to structure the accounts that are made later in the career of the patients and 'co-patients.' In this way, the call for consistency essentially becomes a call for the fulfillment of the diagnostic prophecies made in the pre-patient phase of the institutional career" (p. 15).

The biography that is generated in the patient's record may be described in two ways: (1) the way staff members see it and (2) the way it is portrayed when seen as a negotiated product of collective, staff-only practices. In the first instance, a patient's record is simply a record. It is a reflection—subject to inaccuracies, of course—but still a reflection of "real" events in the patient's institutional life. In the second instance—seen by the staff, but not noticed by them—the record is a tacit conspiracy. Mr. K., co-members of the staff, and his social work trainees, together, construct "perfect" biographies of the children, through varied nuances of what we, in Chapter Three, called a "purification process."

Public Biography. Files, records, and charts contain relatively private information about an individual. As a matter of fact, filers and especially consultants often remind each other of this by urging the maintenance of confidentiality in inspecting their contents. Public biographies are different. First of all, their audiences are not as restricted, by definition. File and chart biographies tend to be contained within institutional boundaries. Public biographies are not. Second, the generation of public biographies is often the subject of moment-to-moment, public documentation. Media of various kinds, especially daily newspapers, document the process of construction. Such media are not simply vehicles, for they contribute substantively to the content of news by the way they "report" it (compare McLuhan and Fiore, 1967).

Lofland (1969) describes the part that the process of biographical reconstruction plays in what he calls "escalating" someone to a deviant identity. His examples are taken from newspaper (*Detroit Free Press*) accounts of the personalities and personal histories of two mass murderers, Richard Speck and Charles Whitman.

Lofland argues that biographies are subject to the ongoing practical theories of those who generate them. Not only do biographers make the past lives of individuals meaningful by placing the "facts" of such lives into some kind of interpretive frame, but also they utilize a variety of explanations (for example, misreports) to make or dismiss "facts" as really or not really factual.

Lofland suggests that, for reasonable men, it is imperative to be consistent in description and explanation. This, of course, also applies to biographers. Lofland describes the generation of a deviant biography this way: "Whatever may have been the preexisting selection of facts from the Actor's life line that supported a view by Others of him as a pivotal normal, there now begins a reexamination of that life line to discover if these selected biographical events are consistent with the prospective reclassification. Efforts are made to render the known facts consistent, either through discounting (or redefining the significance of) what is known or through undertaking to discover additional facts that support the new *imputation*" (Lofland, 1969, pp. 149-150).

Newspapers strive for consistency in the generation of public biographies, among other means, by manipulating the immediate visibility of "facts" about someone's past life. For example, when a now public figure has committed some highly commendable or gravely repugnant act, speaking of it necessitates "making" sense of it. This means that it may be put into historical perspective. Lofland argues that one technique of managing the visibility of inconsistent facts is to place such facts on back pages of the newspaper. When a public figure is highly newsworthy and the "facts" are consistent with what he has typically and publicly come to be, "facts" become part of front page news. Now, newspapers, being what they are, claim to report the news. This, it seems, at least formally prevents the complete omission of new "facts" from being a way to manage inconsistency in the construction of biography. However, this does not prevent newspapers from managing the consistency problem by varying visibility.

Consider the case of Richard Speck. In July 1966, he was charged with the murder of eight student nurses in Chicago. As Lofland puts it, "Wire services and local newspapers went into a frenzy of research to find out about Richard Speck" (p. 150). At first, the results of interviews with people who knew Speck found him to be "an intelligent, gentle and sensitive young man." Lofland found this buried in the back pages of the *Detroit Free Press.*

These "facts" about Speck's behavior seemed inconsistent with the "fact" that he stood accused of murdering eight women in cold blood. A few days after Speck's apprehension, however, "facts" seemingly consistent with the murder became more visible. As Lofland continues:

> Under the headline "Richard Speck's Twisted Path," the rite of consistency could begin:
>> Charged with the brutal slaying of eight student nurses, Richard Speck was trapped by the tattoo that bore his credo: Born to Raise Hell. Here is a special report on the man accused of mass murder, a report on the twisted path that led to tragedy (*Detroit Free Press,* July 24, 1966).
> And, of course, the facts were consistent. He was a "murder suspect" in another case who "had been hating for a long time," and "had been arrested 36 times." In his youth he was already "a reckless tough . . . with the leather jacket crowd" who "would drink anything." "A high school dropout" who was "divorced," he had served three years for burglary and was "woman crazy" [pp. 150-151].

Now consider the newspaper account of Charles Whitman's shooting of fourteen people from atop a tower at the University of Texas. This took place about a month after the Speck murders. Lofland describes the consistency effort as "more strenuous" in this case since the facts on Whitman's biography "were less amenable to reconstruction than were Speck's." Whitman had been an Eagle Scout in his youth; he had a record of exceptional service in the Marines; and he had excelled academically in college. This All-American image did not square, in the public mind, with the fact of mass murder.

According to Lofland, it took a whole week to generate a biography even slightly consistent with the image of a mass murderer. As Lofland reports:

> Buried in the third section of the *Detroit Free Press*, a *New York Times* story headlined: "Friends and the Record Dispute Sniper's All-American Image."
> Charles J. Whitman . . . has been described as an all-American boy. But according to his friends, he has gambled with criminals, poached deer, written bad checks, kept illegal guns and tried to sell pornography (*Detroit Free Press*, August 19, 1966).
> Interestingly enough, the concrete acts that are then spelled out in the story seem less malevolent than the abstract characterization of them given above. This is perhaps why the *Detroit Free Press* felt the story merited only page three of section three for that day [p. 151].

The difficulties of building even these allegedly consistent facts into a "reasonable" biography of a mass murderer might explain the later popular acceptance of a brain tumor as explanation for Whitman's acts, according to Lofland. Thus, the seeming lack of a proper (factual) social or psychological account for Whitman's shootings led the search for a reasonable biography to Whitman's physiology.

The "Cult of Expertise." The benefits of expertise are widely celebrated. It is said that with specialization, work performance on specific tasks becomes more efficient. The specialized worker becomes intimately acquainted with the nuances of his work and, thereby, becomes skilled at expediting a number of work contingencies that a lesser expert would need to ponder.

With professionalization, expertise takes on public visibility and legitimation. The man or woman who has grown to be intimately acquainted with some claimed area of work now is said to be *one* who is so acquainted. Being *one* who is so acquainted suggests that expertise is recognized and spoken of as an entity in its own right, separate from, but yet part of, the person who is its claimant.

Although not all sociologists describe it as we do, let us speak of expertise and professionalization as part of the ordinary talk that makes people recognizable. Expertise and professionalism are also a kind of rhetoric. They convince those who formally or informally adhere to the same language that work done by a claimed expert or professional is somehow more creditable than that done by others. In this view, of course, the widely celebrated benefits of expertise take on a different meaning; the benefit now seems more rhetorical than "real." Experts and professionals benefit from such a language in that it provides them greater merit for what they do than is accorded to nonexperts or nonprofessionals who are engaged in the same or similar practices.

This is related to the matter of biography. We suggest that the difference between professional biographers and nonprofessional ones is, to some extent, a matter of rhetoric. What people do when they practice biographical work is basically fairly homogeneous: at the very least, all are engaged in trying to understand and make sense of some *thing* that they assume real; they all try to *reasonably* make sense of it; and they test or *check* their considerations in what they believe to be the real biographical world. In short, all biographers are practical scientists. The difference between professional or officially expert biographers and other biographers is that the language by which they describe what they do differs. This is an invidious difference, for being expert or professional invokes merit.

As far as the construction of biography is concerned, what we have gained with the professionalization of the process involved is a new body of accounts. These accounts are better known as personality theories, developmental schemas, and the like, and accountants as psychologists, psychiatrists, counselors, therapists, and so on. In their attempt to develop a "fully social theory of deviance," Taylor, Walton and Young (1973) suggest something similar: "We have, however, attempted to open out the criminological debate by pointing to certain *formal* and *substantive* requirements of a fully social theory of deviance, a theory that can explain the forms assumed by social control and deviant action in 'developed' societies (characterized—we have argued—by the domination of a capitalist mode of production, by a division of labor involving the growth of armies of 'experts,' social workers, psychiatrists and others who have been assigned a crucial role in the tasks of social definition and social control, and, currently, by the necessity of segregating out—in mental hospitals, prisons and in juvenile institutions—an increasing variety of its members as being in need of control)" (p. 269).

Let us turn to the work of Suchar (1975) again for two illustrations of the "use" of expertise by a psychiatrist in the mental health clinic for emotionally disturbed children. These are excerpts from conversations between a child psychiatrist and staff counselor-trainees at psychiatric staffings. Staffings are, in Suchar's words, "clinical meetings attended by the staff of the clinic where the cases of several children would be reviewed and evaluated by the child psychiatrist."

[A male, nine-year-old child who had been diagnosed as having "childhood psychosis of a chronic nature" is being discussed by the psychiatrist and the child's counselor, Mrs. Star. The child has been in the program for about one year and they are evaluating his progress. The psychiatrist seems hopeful while the counselor seems to be pessimistic about the child's future.]

Dr. J.:   I see something in him. I can smell it, something hopeful. Since he's rejected all avenues of pleasure, I don't think you should give him tasks to do. I think you're [*counselor*] doing all right with him . . . [*To the program directress:*] I suggest we also begin seeing this mother and child together for a few visits for diagnosis.

Mrs. Star: The father's a jerk—he's too rigid. I don't know if he'd like that. Anyways, I don't know, he's [*child*] still twiddling [*major symptom* *of child*]. It's so sad . . . There's this kid in my neighborhood who's 20 and still does that. I don't know if [*child*] will ever change. It's so sad . . .

Dr. J.: He [*child*] may do that at 20 also. He should have physical contact with someone. Mrs. Star, you're too pessimistic . . . The hopeful thing with this type of kid is their opposition, I know. It takes experience with these kids to understand this. [*Note: expertise invoked.*] Once they give in and "yes" you all the time—they're cooked. Why don't you talk to him about his not talking. In time, he'll begin responding in a variety of ways, you'll see.

Mrs. Star: He *is* a great listener. I guess you're right. He knows what I'm saying. You can tell he knows [Suchar, 1975, pp. 19-20].

In negotiating what to do next with this child, Dr. J. and Mrs. Star seem to be momentarily at odds. Mrs. Star suggests avoiding a family session with the child and his parents. Then, on the basis of what Mrs. Star knows of and feels to be the biography of someone in her neighborhood that is similar to that of the child, she expresses her pessimism about the child's future. In opposition to this, Dr. J. speaks of the typical biography of "this type of kid," which "in time" "really" will begin responding if her suggestions are followed. Dr. J.'s suggested biography, of course, tacitly is claimed to have greater merit than Mrs. Star's because "it takes experience" to understand such matters, which Dr. J. implies she has. Her invocation of expertise appears in two other phrases that she uses in speaking with Mrs. Star: "I know" and "you'll see."

In another staffing, a twelve-year-old boy, who has been diagnosed as borderline schizophrenic, is being discussed. As in the preceding case, this boy has been in the program for about one year. Again, in negotiating the typical biography of "such cases," Dr. J. invokes her expertise, which apparently brings the conversation, but not competing sentiments, to an end.

Dr. J.: I'll tell you what he is, he's pervasively anxious, he's absolutely driven by his anxiety. [*Addressing the boy's counselor, Mr. E.:*] If you really want to know what a hyperactive child looks like, you've got him . . . Yeah, O.K., he's begun to build controls for himself, but it was all built around his anxiety; all his activity is frenzy . . . I think with him there is a vast split between what he says and what he feels. Most of what he says is garbage.

Mr. E.:   [*Visibly angered by the psychiatrist's last statement:*] But sometimes he does mean what he says!

Dr. J.:   But look, even from your material [*progress notes written on a
daily basis by counselors and submitted to the psychiatrist before the
staffing*] I get the feeling that what he verbalizes means nothing.

Mr. E.:   But one time for example, he told me "I miss you" and he meant
it.

Dr. J.:   But that's different. Some things like that may touch him, but
I'm still very ˜dubious that words mean anything to him. I do not think
words reach him at˸ all. [*The psychiatrist's tone of voice becomes more
insistent and the counselor is still angered by the evaluation.*] Look . . .
Mr. E., I know what I'm talking about. I've seen cases like this before. It
takes time to understand this. You must not kid yourself that what he says
means anything. There's a lack of integration between his feelings and his
words. [*After this last statement the counselor did not again verbally respond to the evaluation made by the psychiatrist but remained visibly
angered for the remainder of the meeting.*] [pp. 20-21]

Suchar then goes on to describe how Mr. E. expressed himself after the meeting was over.

> When the meeting was over I asked him how he felt
> about the evaluation. Mr. E. said, "She really pisses me off.
> She doesn't give me credit for knowing my own kid. That stuff
> about his use of language, words is bullshit. He does communi-
> cate and he means what he says." It is also important to note
> that in the official transcript or report of the meeting the
> counselor's objections to the evaluation were not recorded at
> all and the psychiatrist's evaluations became the official eval-
> uation of the "clinical team" [p. 21].

Thus, we see that the invocation of expertise by Dr. J. and its
public acceptance by Mr. E. at the appropriate moment sus-
tains a particular biography and typification of the child involved in this case. As Suchar describes it, the counselor-trainee
has run up against the "cult of expertise."

At this point, it is important to make a slight digression
before we go on to another form of biographical work. In the
foregoing conversational data (between Dr. J., Mr. E., and Mrs.
Star) one gets a fairly clear impression that something we conventionally call "power" may be influencing what members of

the conversation are saying and what the official outcome of the case will be. This poses an interesting theoretical problem for us as social phenomenologists of human biography (and, of course, for social phenomenology in general). Since social phenomenology considers the reality of everyday life to be located in conversation, its negotiation, and flow, what sense can it make of a condition that seems to suggest that there is something extraconversational that structures the flow of talk and that, once known, would enable us to predict the outcome of negotiation?

The sense that a social phenomenological point of view makes of social structure is tied to a crucial distinction, one which we have alluded to throughout this book. Although we have chosen to suspend belief in "conventional" social structure, among other extrasubjective entities, this *does not* mean that our subjects do likewise. People (as our subjects) have a sense of social (or power) structure that is often "only too real." It is people's sense of the "objective" reality of social structure that makes social structure "work" for them and, by the way, for social scientists who deal objectively with social structure as well. "Objective" social structure tends to do what it did for Dr. J., Mr. E., and Mrs. Star above; namely, it allowed Dr. J.'s invoked biography to predominate both in conversation and on record. For example, Mrs. Star concludes with, "I guess you're right," and Mr. E. remains silent.

Admittedly, the theoretical problem we are introducing here is a very complex one. We introduce it only as a way of suggesting that a social phenomenological position is not necessarily incompatible with one that gives primacy to the dialectics of social interests. Let us briefly mention one way the two are actually quite compatible.

We treat social structure as people's *sense* of it. Of course, that we do this does not mean that we cannot use the term *social structure* and others like it as convenient shorthand in our work. The use of types of shorthand, however, as with other linguistic devices, sometimes involves the hazard that the shorthand may assume more "reality" than the reality it was considered to conveniently reference. The danger of such a convenience is that it may unwittingly "talk us into," as it were, the dismissal of people as conscious, rational, and practical entities who are in the business of making sense of their lives.

Karl Marx knew this problem well. His was not a simple theory of social structure and its impact on people. Hardly that, although there are interpreters of his writing who see it that way. Rather, for Marx, in some times and in some places people's sense of social structure becomes so "real" that they come to believe, privately or publicly, in its effect on their lives. Through the complexities of their exchanges, people's beliefs become bound up with all sorts of material and immaterial things. Material things, to people, are the most visible and visceral reminders[4] of where their own (or someone else's) beliefs have led them. Thus, in a seemingly strange, contradictory sort of way, people's talk and deeds come to be "alienated" from them through the varied contingencies of their exchanges—what we and others have described at a face-to-face level of human activity as conversing oneself into the reality of social life.

Now, although there is a measure of compatibility between the dialectics of social interest, on the one hand, and the social phenomenology of power and influence, on the other, there is a sense in which the two have been said to lead to different sorts of politics. For Marx, the problem of consciousness is a crucial one, for only by "seeing through" social structure can it be changed. By becoming aware of the human roots of social arrangements, men and women gain control, once again, of what was once a product of their very existence. For Marx, the political task is the generation of consciousness and the subsequent human control of social life. This is a radical task. For Marx, it had a historical endpoint, but this final utopian vision does not necessarily follow from his dialectical thinking. What could and what for some Marxists does follow is a political

---

[4] For Marx, the "consciousness" of these reminders is a critical factor in social change. When reminders are, in effect, only visceral, people feel but do not know social structure. When they are seriously conscious, people are wide-awake to the essential artificiality of social structure. Being wide-awake, although most critical in social change, by itself is not adequate to the task, however.

vision of ongoing, radical awareness that serves to continually reaffirm the human essence of social arrangements.

The social phenomenological view of human life that we have been developing and illustrating in this book does not portray the practice of change as having an endpoint. In fact, there is a sense in which we have said that there is no "real," final change in everyday life in that everyday life is under continual negotiation, albeit people may feel and/or admit to a sense of finality. Therein lies a possible conclusion that a social phenomenological view of human life is politically conservative.

We take issue with this kind of conclusion. First and foremost, we conceive of people as essentially political and practical in that they continually work to make the events in their lives meaningful so as to get on with them. What social arrangements come to be settled upon, however, are people's affair. For us, the basic reality of political life lies in neither the maintenance nor the change of social arrangements as substantive things. Our vision of politics focuses on its social practice, which necessitates never taking politics for granted. The anarchistic consciousness of social phenomenology is substantively divorced from the politics of both the left and the right and, at the same time, is basic to both. For example, whether maturity is an ideology of elders or a coming of age, it is still an idea spoken to by all; its meaningful existence, in practice, is generated out of its collective negotiation on the varied occasions in which it is a topic for consideration.

"Scientific" Biography.   Let us conclude our short survey of biographical work by turning to a recent textbook on human development, Douglas Kimmel's (1974) *Adulthood and Aging.* [4] Unlike many writers on this topic of human behavior, Kimmel conceives of development as a lifelong process. The book's chapters trace life changes through young adulthood, marriage, family life, retirement, and dying and bereavement. However, like most writers on human development, Kimmel conceives of

[4] Excerpts from D. C. Kimmel, *Adulthood and Aging,* on the following pages are reprinted by permission of John Wiley & Sons, Inc. Copyright © 1974 by John Wiley & Sons, Inc.

human biography as "real," stagelike, and understandable
through the use of conventional modes of study. He describes
his approach to human development this way:

> Our approach will be to underplay individual variation
> and to emphasize the developmental theme. We argue that
> when the developmental theme is understood, one may then
> bring in the individual variations and examine a specific indi-
> vidual in a specific place at a specific time in life; however, if
> we do not understand the theme clearly, individual variations
> may be a confusing "noise" of idiosyncratic differences that
> make little sense [Kimmel, 1974, p. 4].

Kimmel then goes on to indicate how he will illustrate the
developmental theme across the space of human biography:

> There will be several "interludes" of individual case his-
> tories interspersed between some of the chapters in this book.
> We see these interludes as examples of individual variation in
> which both the general developmental theme as well as the
> interaction of this theme with idiosyncratic differences stand
> out. The interludes (and other persons we see around us) chal-
> lenge our ability to understand the developmental theme in
> the midst of its variations; yet if we can understand the theme,
> the variations can be better understood [p. 4].

Six interludes are presented as illustrations of the variations in
and about an underlying developmental reality that structures
persons' biographies. Their format is comprised of transcriptions of interviews that Kimmel conducted with persons of various ages. Thus, they provide data about both sides of the data-
collection process—namely, conversation that occurred between
Kimmel and his respondents in the interview situation.

These interludes may be read in two ways. They may be
read as Kimmel suggests. This focuses attention on *the* data that
are collected from respondents. Presumably, what respondents
say, and its nuances, are suggestive of a developmental logic
operating in their lives as they grow older. From this point of
view, Kimmel's side of the conversation is glossed over and
tacitly understood to be, at best, a passive instrument for the
collection of individual data on a real, but only partially visible,

common theme. This would be a conventional reading of the interludes. Kimmel suggests that this kind of reading is the only way to make general sense of them. This viewpoint is apparent above when he states that ignoring the reality of the developmental theme leads virtually to nonsense—"noise," as he puts it.

However, there is indeed another way to make sense of these interludes. This alternative operates when we set aside belief in the reality of development, its stages, and conventional understanding as a way of knowing it. From this point of view, Kimmel's side of the conversations in the interludes is taken to be as active and as essential a part of the data as the respondents' side. Reading the interludes from this point of view shows how situated, constructed, and, indeed, conversational the business of development is "in reality." In the following excerpts from three interludes, note how Kimmel and his respondents negotiate and converse themselves into developmental biographies. While Kimmel interviews, both he and his respondents take for granted the former's scientific work of gathering data "about" the developmental nuances of past lives.

The first excerpt is from an interview with George, a twenty-seven-year-old man. Kimmel's own questions and answers are italicized. These excerpts are selected not so much to illustrate what was substantively reported by respondents as to focus on the conversations *between* the interviewer and his respondent.

> *As you look back over your life, what are some of the milestones that stand out?* [*Note initial typifying of respondent's biography in developmental language.*] In terms of just profession, in terms of personal life? Do you want specifics? *Yes.* What made me choose my profession? *Was that a milestone?* It certainly was . . . *and that was the turning point* [*note interviewer's suggestion of stage transition*] *for you?* I look back and that's what I remember, so that's a milestone for me, what one would have to call a milestone. . . .
>
> Anyway, other milestones. Oh, I'm sure I have some. Oh! Telling my folks I was gay was a milestone. Partly because of the way they responded [*laughs*]. *When did that happen?* [*Note chronicling of a transition.*] . . .
>
> Okay. More milestones. Can you think of some other areas maybe that would interest you? Or that would help me

remember? [*Note that respondent now, ironically, asks the interviewer to help him construct stages.*] *What about more recent milestones? Like coming to New York?* Well, coming to New York wasn't really a milestone for me because that was so planned, so matter-of-fact that I was going to do it that it wasn't really a milestone. . . . *It sounds like in a very real sense, once you made the decision to become a dancer, then somehow the rest of it is kind of an unfolding and fairly continuous.* [*Note developmental typification.*] Oh, yes; very much. . . .

We've been talking about milestones. What about crisis points? Have there been any crisis points that stand out? Yes, I've had a lot of crises. Do you want some of them? *Yes. . . .*

Have there been any crisis points in your relationship with your family? Not really. Some childish things. Nothing really recently. I've never run away from my family or anything like that as a child. *You said at one point when we didn't have the recorder on that your mother was in the hospital.* Yeah, she is. *Is this a serious matter?* It's not, now, as it's turned out, thank goodness. Oh, I see what you mean, a crisis in those terms [Kimmel, 1974, pp. 116-120].

Conversation between Kimmel and his respondent in a second interlude shows how life stages in a person's biography unfold at the behest of the interviewer. The following excerpts are from an interview with Theresa, a thirty-four-year-old woman.

[*After asking about milestones that stand out in Theresa's memory:*] *Are there any other milestones that stand out to you?* I guess another milestone was moving to New York because I met my husband. *You met him in New York?* Right. . . . Another milestone? It's hard, you know, when you think back for milestones you can't think. *Anything more recently?* More recently. Not really. I guess my husband's business probably is a milestone. . . . *Are there milestones in terms of your career? Your occupation?* I guess so. . . .

Would you say that being married or the birth of your child was a milestone? Oh, yes. It was. Getting married for me was especially a milestone. . . .

No real crisis points in your marriage? No, no, we have a pretty good life. . . .

What about in terms of your job? Any crisis points there? There was a crisis with Jan [pp. 177-178].

Finally, let us look at excerpts from a third interlude. This is an interview with Murray, the forty-eight-year-old vice-president of a large organization who also teaches at a university. Note the problem that Murray has thinking of his life as a unilinear series of developing events, which, on the other hand, is the way that Kimmel's questions are typifying them, thereby constructing developmental "data."

> *What are some of the milestones in your life? As you look back over it, what are some of the events that stand out?* . . . There are pockets. The third pocket of my life is my academic life, which I find probably the most rewarding of all my pockets. . . .
> Another milestone was deciding that I didn't want to be an accountant and starting a career in my present field. So these are the milestones; I never put them together. . . .
> Let me tell you something that just, you know, popped in and out of my head. I never had this feeling of desire for security until in the midst of my career there was a milestone. . . . [*Murray describes certain events he experienced during the Depression.*] So, I don't know how you put it together. I haven't thought about it enough. . . .
> *You fought in the second war?* Yeah, I was in the Navy. It wasn't really that bad. *But you indicated that it was one of the milestones for you.* Oh, yes . . . it was a milestone, being away from the protected environment very young, naive, traveling around the world for better or worse. That's certainly a milestone. And, wondering if your ship is going to get hit or not by a submarine. That's a milestone. Getting by it was a milestone also. [*At this point, Murray begins to define all events in his life as milestones.*] [pp. 275-278]

Biographical construction and reconstruction occur on many occasions, indeed, on every occasion in which biography is a topic of consideration and conversation. This, of course, includes those occasions when human scientists, such as Kimmel, speak of or inquire about people's past lives. Like many people, Kimmel converses with his subjects about events in order to make sense of them. But in the process of conversation, he as well as his subjects unwittingly generates—on that very occasion—developmental sense and reality in subjects' biographies.

Chapter Seven

Disciplinary
Implications

In this concluding chapter, we will briefly address three general issues that deal not so much with the consequences for research of looking at life change from a social phenomenological point of view as they do with the disciplinary implications of doing so. First, what is the general aim of a social phenomenological science of life change? Second, what is its "benefit"? Third, what sort of intellectual relation can exist between conventional and phenomenological sciences and other disciplines of man?

The Aim of a Social Phenomenological
Science of Life Change

Throughout the history of the social and behavioral sciences, there has been persistent agonizing over what a science of life and life change can and should be. This agony, it seems, results from a penchant for two things. On the one hand, there is the aim of trying to make sense of the often erratic actions of people, whether individually or collectively; on the other hand, there is the hope of making this effort as classically rational and technically rigorous as possible. The agony emerges whenever the seemingly nonrational, sloppy, and vague recalcitrance of people's actions confronts rigorous procedures to know and consider it.

Given the source of this agony, there are two ways to avoid it. One is to adjust our thinking and technology so as to make them compatible with what, in practice, is encountered as the nebulous chaos of life and life change. The other is to enhance the rigor of our working technology in the hope of capturing the "real" meaning of action, meaning that is believed obtainable but for the witting and unwitting efforts of human beings to keep scientists from knowing it in all its presumed well-organized and reasonable splendor.

The choice, though, is not a simple one, for it has been, and continues to be, bound with historical sentiment. The social and behavioral sciences were by no means the first disciplines to be concerned with the actions of man. However, they were first in the attempt to construct disciplines of man that emulated the efforts of natural scientists to understand, predict, and in some respects to control the physical world, efforts that presented social and behavioral scientists with grand possibilities. The ensuing infatuation with the natural-science model did give, and continues to give, direction to the sciences of human behavior. None of them ceases to be captured by the passion of this romance in one way or another.

The choice also is bound by its social organization. Knowledge, like anything else, is a practical and value-laden thing. In any discipline, knowledge emerges out of the ongoing, ordinary languages that its members speak. To speak in a discipline, as elsewhere, implies speaking with others—known and unknown, directly and indirectly—others who have both sentimental and material investments in speaking in certain ways. To speak differently, and be tolerated, slows down others' material accumulation, among other things. Such tolerance, then, is a costly thing. If it is permitted to exist, it is likely to be token and, if that, well-contained.

Of course, to speak differently is, essentially, a matter of human choice, a kind of choice that cuts across the social organization of our lives as well as history, not existing "beneath" or "above" either, as some social theorists might order them. It seems to us that it is time to reconsider this choice face-to-face and entertain what sense a science of action would have were we to adjust our thinking and technology to make them compatible with what we described earlier as the nebulous chaos of life and life change. In this book, we have attempted to describe what this kind of science might look like, both in theory and in method, as it specifically applies to life change. What is the more general aim of the approach we have taken?

First of all, its aim is to be a radically empirical science. This may appear ironic in view of the fact that it is sometimes described by conventional (and especially, highly positivistic) human scientists as "philosophical," implying that to be philosophical is somehow to be concerned with realities other than those existing in what is presumed to be *the* real world. It is radical in that it deliberately suspends belief in a priori behavioral constructs so as to see to and through the practical side of "things" in the real world as they are realized by, and exist for, people. What could be more objective than this? Indeed, is there not something strange about feeling, and possibly knowing, that people are sometimes vague—fleeting in their thoughts and deeds—and yet deliberately assuming that these are really technical or personal aberrations?

Second, because it is radically concerned with, and takes seriously, the practice (praxis) of people's lives, its ultimate aim, as a science, is adjusted to this. If the very basic stuff of human living is that terribly precarious thing we call "meaning"—something that is a continual task for people as they launch on each mundane or dramatic project of everyday life—then meaning and its constitutive practices must be *understood*. It certainly cannot be our aim to predict it, for it is in the nature of prediction that there is some "thing" meaningful to predict from one moment in time to another. Thus, a phenomenological science of man must abandon the predictive/explanatory goal of the natural sciences. Its task is to explicate and, by doing so, understand the process by which things come to be meaningful for people, how they become meaningless, and the way that people make sense of apparent contradictions. The task, for example, is to understand the process by which tacit circumstance and ordinary language make sensible, to people, the maturity of one moment and the immaturity of the next, how one's life in some places is a progressive liberal's delight with a straight and rising course, while in other places it is cynically said to be headed for hopeless decay.

Third, a human science of the sort we have described in this book has a sense and awareness of its own history. To say that man makes his world and that his projects in it are essentially bound up with their meaningful constitution is to make no exceptions. A human science, itself, is a meaningful artifact in the strict sense; it is artificial. There is a good measure of humility in this sense of a human science. Such a science is critically self-aware that in its deliberation over people's lives, their actions and problems are, in a fundamental sense, what *it* makes of them from beginning to end.

The "Benefit" of a Social Phenomenology of Life Change

In recent years, social and behavioral science has experienced a tremendous increase in the attention given to and the importance assigned to the applied aspects of its various disciplines. Piagetian and behavioral psychology, for example, have been used to design new curriculum materials for children and training programs for teachers. Sociologists are working to develop a policy-oriented branch of their discipline and are placing their students in various governmental and community agencies, with the justification that their sociological skills can be put to work to solve social problems. Economists are in increasing demand from governmental advisory boards, regulatory agencies, and planning commissions. There appears to be a growing attitude, both in these sciences and in the public at large, that scientific knowledge is useful in matters of public policy and decision making.

The notion of "useful" knowledge is grounded in a faith in a real, objective world. If the variables specified as existing in such a world influence one another in complex but identifiable and consistent ways, it makes some sense to attempt to manipulate them to produce social realities more in line with desired values or ideals. Such manipulation, presumably, is the domain of applied social science.

If one suspends belief in the positive status of variables, however, the argument for applied social science no longer appears to be obvious. "Real" social forces become man-made, emergent social constructions, engendered by negotiation and definitional change in the everyday lives of the people who both make and experience them. Even the specification of problems to study and do something about takes on a different meaning. Rather than self-evident social ills, they are now seen as certain people's theories of social malaise, subject to the interpretations and political machinations of any number of "interests."

Social phenomenology does not tout the promise of ameliorative utility. The utility of a phenomenological vision, rather, lies in insight, namely a recognition of the contribution that action itself makes to the constitution of the objects of its acts. As an illustration of this argument, consider one research problem that we are currently investigating, the problem of professional decision making on matters of life-course transition (for example, promotions, discharges, and tracking).

Professional literature exists on the rationale for, and techniques of, specialists' (scientific, clinical, managerial, or technical) decision making on life-course transitions. It ranges from that which outlines criteria for decision making in the psychiatric assessment, diagnosis, and treatment of patient problems to school counselors' and school psychologists' rationales for tracking students, and promotion or tenure criteria for employees in various organizations.

Such literature and the specialists for, or by, whom it is written take for granted the real status of the object of decision making, be it mental illness, maturity, intelligence, or competence. Conventional wisdom assumes that whatever it is that professionals do in considering life-course transitions, the decision-making process is, at its best, a successful attempt to understand and decide on how to deal with what are, after all, the "real" transitions of "real" people as they develop along some course of living. This wisdom knows of, and admits to, the influence that working professionals have on the decision-making process, including the errors they make in attempting to understand and deal with life-course transitions, but decision making is never treated as a constructive process in its own right. Professionalism as such is incapable of such an insight.

The conventional notion of the professional suggests, first, that such a person has a service to offer to those who are in need of it. Second, it suggests that the professional has the expert training and skills with which to deal with needs. Ideally, the expert application of skills should lead to proper life-course decisions. Thus, for example, when the business at hand is whether or not a student should be placed on a remedial school track or remain on a regular track, school counselors or school psychologists describe and report on their work as being a matter of using their training and skills to decide on what they take for granted to be assessable educational needs of the student. Or, for instance, when the decision to be made is whether or not to grant a discharge or leave of absence to a mental patient or to change his mode of treatment or to reclassify his state of health, psychiatric personnel assume that the basic problematic of their task stands before them among patients under review, not essentially in the process of consideration and review itself.

What we have been describing is the conventional view of professional life-course decision making. An alternative view, the one we propose, does not prejudge the matter of who the subjects of decisions "really" are, or their life-course transition problems. Rather, belief in such subjects, the life course, transition, and their presumed developmental problems as real, to-be-studied entities is set aside. This shifts the focus of our attention from a concern with such tacitly real people as students, mental patients, aspiring academics, and the like and how specialists who claim to be able to deal with transitions apply their skills, to the practice of professional decision making. To focus on practice is to document the process by which psychiatrists, school counselors, tenure reviewers, members of promotion committees, and other such people-processing agents come to have a sense of their subjects as due for, or not due for, life-course transition, and how this is meaningfully accomplished.

Implicit in a focus on the practical accomplishment of decision making is the claim that professionals are an integral part of the very phenomena that they assume to be realities separate from themselves. The negotiating by decision makers as they go about what they assume to be serious, to-be-dealt-with business is, in practice, reality-constructing and reality-accomplishing work. It is not simply and obviously just the "out there" business of professionals. This suggests that professional decision makers, who consider and/or deal with life-course transitions, engage in a wide range of nonprofessional activities as they enter and accomplish their tasks. Indeed, it implies that in order for the tasks to be meaningful to those who engage in them, such influences must of necessity be part and parcel of the work involved.

Interdisciplinary Relations

When we introduced the concern of this chapter as the disciplinary implications of looking at life change from a social phenomenological point of view, we took for granted the meaning of *discipline*. Most would define it as something akin to a fairly well bounded set of intellectual concerns that a group of academicians professes to think about and work at, knowledge of which they claim to generate and document. Presumably, what distinguishes one discipline from another is some "real" stuff that its members feel needs thinking about and investigating, be it minds, minerals, or metaphysics. A discipline is organized to deal with whatever it claims this "real" stuff to be.

Leaving aside the organizational underpinnings of disciplines for the moment, we might ask what belief supports the idea of discipline and, of course, the actions that the idea justifies. This is an important and rather timely question because the social and behavioral sciences, if not all the sciences, are currently being faced with the question of the interrelationship of their disciplines and how to establish interdisciplinary dialogue in dealing with publicly defined problems that seem to cut across them.

The distinction we have made between conventional and social phenomenological views of the world suggests something very basic about the possibility of having disciplines. The idea of discipline simply makes more sense if there is something, "out there," real and hard, to be disciplined about. Needless to say, it is a positive view of the reality of things that supports this. By the conventional acceptance of, and tacit faith in, the positive features of human action, whether individual or collective, the social and behavioral sciences establish an objective empirical ground for themselves as disciplines and subdisciplines.

The distinction suggests something else about disciplines. Not only does the concept of positive worlds provide a rationale for disciplines, it also divides them. The "things" of a positive world are not necessarily homogeneous. Indeed, conventional human scientists take for granted essential qualitative distinctions among varied categories of human action. Thus, for example, they speak of categories such as individual as opposed to collective behaviors. These are said to be the concerns of separate human disciplines.

Now, in view of the positive rationale for scientific disciplines and the very basic divisions among them, how is it possible for serious, analytic dialogue to exist between them, let alone dialogue with other disciplines of man conventionally labeled the humanities? We maintain that, in view of what might be called an unreflective faith in positivism, it is *not* possible for serious dialogue to occur. How could it when the analytic languages that members of each discipline speak are grounded in incompatible beliefs about what the "real," essential stuff of the world of human action is?

Positivistic human scientists—especially those committed to or engaged in what is called "interdisciplinary" research or programs—do not realize how deep their divisions are. All the interpersonal attraction and openness in the world would not overcome their analytic differences. The rub is not basically a matter of incompatible personnel (although, to be sure, they are annoyances in their own right) nor is it a matter of incompatible technology or the need for substantive theoretical integration. The rub is a matter of values, for example, values about the reality, concreteness, and objectiveness of worlds considered to be individual or collective.

When interdisciplinary research or programs do exist, they are technically or organizationally integrated. Everyone's sentiment may favor teamwork and each may appreciate the elegance of everyone else's technology, but no one can *seriously* entertain an appreciation of another discipline's positive view of the world. At one extreme, positivism divides disciplines into schools; at another, it generates intellectual imperialism.

Serious interdisciplinary dialogue, in contrast to this, can occur only when the "disciplines" involved are wide-awake to the assumptions made about the stuff of human action, when there is continuous awareness in "disciplines" that the human stuff that their members profess to think of and learn about is, first and foremost, a matter of faith. This immediately locates the essential problems of life change, for example, in the accounts of human scientists. It establishes a basis for serious dialogue, founded on the humanistic constructs of practicing scientists. Each discipline comes to be in the business of gaining insight into human lives. Each, as it were, tells its story, knowing full well that the stuff of lives is as much a matter of what is taken to be its presumed subjects as the constitutive practices of those who think about and investigate them. As we noted in Chapter Six, for example, lives develop and change as much by way of the actions of those whose lives we describe as by way of human scientists' serious and careful efforts to understand their development. The very language of human scientists creates developing "things." How much different is such creation from the alleged unique creativity of humanists?

The idea of a reflective human science blurs the boundary between what conventionally are called the "humanities" and the "sciences." It makes possible serious dialogue between them, dialogue founded on a wide-awake awareness of the value-work in which all practitioners of human disciplines engage. It makes meaningless the search for *the* objective course of subjects' lives. Rather, it focuses attention on the constitutive practices of our own working lives as well as those of our so-called subjects, who together negotiate and accomplish the latter's worlds. Our common criterion of work well done becomes its intelligibility.

Relationships between scientific disciplines or subdisciplines that make fundamentally different assumptions about the essential features of the empirical world, thus, inevitably evidence a degree of conflict. Certainly some conflict exists between conventional and phenomenological sociologies.

Conventional sociologists often accuse social phenomenologists either of attending to trivial sociological problems or of simply repeating accusations about well-known limitations of conventional research methods (see Coser, 1975). Social phenomenologists respond that what may appear trivial in conventional eyes is extremely important to understanding the very constitution of social realities of central concern to conventional sociologists (for example, Zimmerman, 1976; Mehan and Wood, 1976). Talk, gesture, and their contextual interpretation are not trivial, nuisance happenings, but rather the very stuff of day-to-day living. Further, the continuing critique of conventional methods is necessary because conventional methodologists insist on treating such nuisances as technically remediable.

The dramatic divergence in perspective between conventional and phenomenological sociologies is also evident in the social organization of sociological knowledge, as we spoke of it above. Conventional sociologists accuse social phenomenologists of being cultlike, of rigidly following the directives of a few leaders, of publishing in relatively obscure places, of not publishing but rather informally sharing papers with one another, and of cutting themselves off both intellectually and organizationally from the traditions and mainstream of sociology. While it is clear to social phenomenologists that many of their theoretical and methodological leads have come from such classical sociologists as Karl Marx, Georg Simmel, Max Weber, and perhaps Emile Durkheim, they are not the same insights or methods that have prominence in modern-day sociology. One result is that recently some social phenomenologists have concluded that indeed they are not sociologists by current standards but rather members of a different order of social scientific enterprise (Mehan and Wood, 1975).

While intellectual relations between mainstream and phenomenological sociology are strained, this is probably as it should be. Strain and conflict, however, need not imply dissociation. Sociology as a scientific discipline has a strong tradition of passionate intellectual debate on fundamental issues. The discipline has never been totally dominated by a single paradigm, whose followers succeeded in laying claim to the "true" theory about the nature of the social world, notwithstanding such seemingly prevalent fashions as the functionalism of the 1950s. Rather, there have been, and continue to be, multiple paradigms, each with its own claims on what the social world is really like and how it can best be studied. The criticisms and antagonisms that result from their divergences are, in our view, basic to the health of sociology. They force continual reflection on and examination of the procedural assumptions on which any social scientist operates. Without this continual contest and challenge, sociology would become a normative science, with technical journeymen endlessly applying accepted methods to obvious ideas.

Social phenomenology, then, is important to other brands of sociology and vice versa. Their reciprocal importance to one another lies not so much in a liberal toleration of letting each man "do his own thing" or even in the substantive contribution one makes to another, but rather in the fundamental antagonism and reflection that arises when intellectual problems are attacked with quite different theoretical perspectives and methodologies. Underlying this is a dialectic of mutual encouragement to pursue the very serious and exciting game of discovering where one arrives when he begins with assumptions radically different from those of others.

As far as studies of life change are concerned, the debate will likely be mostly with psychologists and social psychologists who take a developmental perspective and with sociologists who speak of socialization, more or less, as internalization. For the former, while the social environment influences development, the person is the locus of maturity, competence, stability, and similar "real" attributes. These presumed attributes are also important for the latter, but primary attention is focused instead on the cultural mechanisms for transmitting these attributes and on the positive roles they play in expanding or limiting life changes.

The social phenomenological notion that a person can assume, or be negotiated into, one combination of attributes in one context and a different combination in another denies, wholesale, the conventional notion of a more or less stable set of personal characteristics. It highlights the ad hoc, contextually bound dynamics of decision making about people's lives and undermines faith in the order and predictability that stand above or outside of human experience. In short, social phenomenology eclipses the most basic assumptions of conventional human development. It is incompatible with them.

Alas, again, there is a dialectical sort of accommodation that stems from the acknowledged awareness of such incompatibility, an awareness that we alluded to above. When disciplines that claim human scientific status become sufficiently reflective to realize their own basic artificiality in the values that support their empirical worlds, the possibility of wide-awake humanistic accommodation arises. This is a different order of accommodation than an analytic one. It centers on, and admits to, the constructed and accomplished quality of all the human sciences.

References

Ariès, P. *Centuries of Childhood: A Social History of Family Life.* Translated by R. Baldick. New York: Vintage Books, 1962.

Ariès, P. *Western Attitudes Toward Death: From the Middle Ages to the Present.* Translated by P. Ranum. Baltimore: Johns Hopkins University Press, 1974.

Averch, H. A., and others. *How Effective Is Schooling?* Englewood Cliffs, N.J.: Educational Technological Publishers, 1974.

Ayllon, T., and Kelly, K. "Effects of Reinforcement on Standardized Test Performance." *Journal of Applied Behavior Analysis,* 1972, *5,* 477-484.

Bandura, A. *Principles of Behavior Modification.* New York: Holt, Rinehart and Winston, 1969.

Baratz, S. S., and Baratz, J. C. "Early Childhood Intervention: The Social Science Base of Institutional Racism." *Harvard Educational Review,* 1970, *40,* 29-50.

Becker, H. S. "Notes on the Concept of Commitment." *American Journal of Sociology,* 1960, *66,* 32-40.

205

Becker, H. S. *Outsiders*. New York: Free Press, 1963.

Becker, H. S. "Personal Change in Adult Life." *Sociometry*, 1964, *27*, 40-53.

Becker, H. S., Geer, B., and Hughes, E. C. *Making the Grade: The Academic Side of College Life*. New York: Wiley, 1968.

Becker, H. S., and Strauss, A. L. "Careers, Personality, and Adult Socialization." *American Journal of Sociology*, 1956, *62*, 253-263.

Benedict, R. *Patterns of Culture*. Boston: Houghton Mifflin, 1934.

Benedict, R. "Continuities and Discontinuities in Cultural Conditioning." *Psychiatry*, 1938, *1*, 161-167.

Berg, I. *Education and Jobs*. Boston: Beacon Press, 1971.

Berger, M. B. "On The Youthfulness of Youth Culture." *Social Research*, 1963, *30*, 319-342.

Berger, P. L. *Invitation to Sociology*. Garden City, N.Y.: Doubleday, 1963.

Berger, P. L. "Sociology and Freedom." *The American Sociologist*, 1971, *6*, 1-5.

Berger, P. L., and Kellner, H. "Arnold Gehlen and the Theory of Institutions." *Social Research*, 1965, *32*, 110-115.

Berger, P. L., and Kellner, H. "Marriage and the Construction of Reality." In H. P. Dreitzel (Ed.), *Recent Sociology No. 2*. New York: Macmillan, 1970.

Berger, P. L., and Luckmann, T. *The Social Construction of Reality*. Garden City, N.Y.: Doubleday, 1966.

Bittner, E. "Police Discretion in Emergency Apprehension of Mentally Ill Persons." *Social Problems*, 1967a, *14*, 278-292.

Bittner, E. "The Police on Skid Row: A Study of Peace-Keeping." *American Sociological Review*, 1967b, *32*, 699-715.

Bittner, E. "Objectivity and Realism in Sociology." In G. Psathas (Ed.), *Phenomenological Sociology*. New York: Wiley, 1973.

Blumer, H. *Symbolic Interactionism: Perspective and Method*. New York: Prentice-Hall, 1969.

Boocock, S. S. *An Introduction to the Sociology of Learning*. Boston: Houghton Mifflin, 1972.

Brim, O. G., and Wheeler, S. *Socialization After Childhood: Two Essays.* New York: Wiley, 1966.

Carlson, R. "Stability and Change in the Adolescent Self-Image." *Child Development,* 1965, *36,* 659-666.

Castaneda, C. *The Teachings of Don Juan: A Yaqui Way of Knowledge.* Berkeley: University of California Press, 1968.

Castaneda, C. *A Separate Reality: Further Conversations with Don Juan.* New York: Simon & Schuster, 1971.

Castaneda, C. *Journey to Ixtlan: The Lessons of Don Juan.* New York: Simon & Schuster, 1972.

Cazden, C. B. "The Neglected Situation in Child Language Research and Education." In F. Williams (Ed.), *Language and Poverty.* Chicago: Markham, 1970.

Cicourel, A. V. *The Social Organization of Juvenile Justice.* New York: Wiley, 1968.

Cicourel, A. V. "The Acquisition of Social Structure: Toward A Developmental Sociology of Language and Meaning." In J. D. Douglas (Ed.), *Understanding Everyday Life.* Chicago: Aldine, 1970a.

Cicourel, A. V. "Basic and Normative Rules in the Negotiation of Status and Role." In H. P. Dreitzel (Ed.), *Recent Sociology No. 2.* New York: Collier-Macmillan, 1970b.

Cicourel, A. V. "Delinquency and the Attribution of Responsibility." In R. A. Scott and J. D. Douglas (Eds.), *Theoretical Perspectives on Deviance.* New York: Basic Books, 1972.

Cicourel, A. V. "Some Basic Theoretical Issues in the Assessment of the Child's Performance in Testing and Classroom Settings." In A. V. Cicourel and others, *Language Use and School Performance.* New York: Academic Press, 1974.

Cicourel, A. V., and Kitsuse, J. *The Educational Decision Makers.* Indianapolis: Bobbs-Merrill, 1963.

Clausen, J. A. (Ed.) *Socialization and Society.* Boston: Little, Brown, 1967.

Coleman, J. S. *The Adolescent Society.* New York: Free Press, 1962.

Coleman, J. S., Campbell, E. Q., and others. *Equality of Educational Opportunity.* U.S. Department of Health, Education, and Welfare, Office of Education. Washington, D.C.: U.S. Government Printing Office, 1966.

Coleman, J. S., and others. *Youth: Transition to Adulthood.* Report of Panel on Youth, President's Science Advisory Committee. Chicago: University of Chicago Press, 1974.

Collingwood, R. G. "The Historical Imagination." In H. Meyerhoff (Ed.), *The Philosophy of History in Our Time.* Garden City, N.Y.: Doubleday, 1959.

Collins, R. "Functional and Conflict Theories of Educational Stratification." *American Sociological Review,* 1971, *36,* 1002-1019.

Comenius, J. A. *The Great Didactic.* Translated and edited by M. W. Keating. London: A. & C. Black, 1923.

Coser, L. A. "Two Methods in Search of a Substance." *American Sociological Review,* 1975, *40,* 691-700.

Cox, R. D. *Youth into Maturity.* New York: Mental Health Materials Center, 1970.

Cumming, E. "Further Thoughts on the Theory of Disengagement." *International Social Science Journal,* 1963, *15,* 377-393.

Cumming, E., and Henry, W. E. *Growing Old.* New York: Basic Books, 1961.

Dahrendorf, R. *Class and Class Conflict in Industrial Society.* Stanford, Calif.: Stanford University Press, 1959.

Dale, R. *The Culture of the School.* London: Open University Press, 1972.

Davis, K. "The Sociology of Parent-Youth Conflict." *American Sociological Review,* 1940, *5,* 523-535.

Davis, N. J. *Sociological Constructions of Deviance.* Dubuque, Iowa: William C. Brown, 1975.

Denzin, N. K. "Symbolic Interactionism and Ethnomethodology: A Proposed Synthesis." *American Sociological Review,* 1969, *34,* 922-934.

Douglas, J. D. *The Social Meanings of Suicide.* Princeton, N.J.: Princeton University Press, 1967.

Douglas, J. D. (Ed.) *Understanding Everyday Life.* Chicago: Aldine, 1970.

DuBois, C. *The People of Alor.* Minneapolis: University of Minnesota Press, 1944.

Durkheim, E. *The Rules of the Sociological Method.* New York: Free Press, 1950.

Edgerton, R. B. *The Cloak of Competence.* Berkeley: University of California Press, 1967.

Eisenstadt, S. N. *From Generation to Generation.* New York: Free Press, 1956.

Elkin, F. *The Child and Society.* New York: Random House, 1960.

Elkind, D. "Egocentrism in Adolescence." *Child Development,* 1967, *38,* 1025-1034.

Ennis, B. J., and Litwack, T. R. "Psychiatry and the Presumption of Expertise: Flipping Coins in the Courtroom." *California Law Review,* 1974, *62,* 693-752.

Entwisle, D. R., and Webster, M. J. "Expectations in Mixed Racial Groups." *Sociology of Education,* 1974, *47,* 301-318.

Erikson, E. H. *Childhood and Society.* New York: Norton, 1950.

Erikson, E. H. *Young Man Luther: A Study in Psychoanalysis and History.* New York: Norton, 1958.

Erikson, E. H. *Gandhi's Truth: On the Origins of Militant Nonviolence.* New York: Norton, 1969.

Erikson, K. T. "Notes on the Sociology of Deviance." *Social Problems,* 1962, *9,* 307-314.

Esland, G. *The Construction of Reality.* London: Open University Press, 1972.

Filmer, P., Phillipson, M., Silverman, D., and Walsh, D. *New Directions in Sociological Theory.* Cambridge, Mass.: MIT Press, 1972.

Flacks, R. "Social and Cultural Meanings of Student Revolt: Some Informal Comparative Observations." *Social Problems,* 1970, *17,* 340-357.

Flude, M., and Ahier, J. (Eds.) *Educability, Schools, and Ideology.* New York: Halsted Press, 1974.

Freud, S. *New Introductory Lectures on Psycho-analysis.* New York: Norton, 1933.

Friedenberg, E. Z. *The Vanishing Adolescent.* New York: Dell, 1962.

Friedman, N. *The Social Nature of Psychological Research.* New York: Basic Books, 1968.

Friedrichs, R. W. *A Sociology of Sociology.* New York: Free Press, 1970.

Gallagher, J. J. "The Special Education Contract for Mildly Handicapped Children." *Exceptional Children,* 1972, *38,* 527-535.

Garfinkel, H. "Conditions of Successful Degradation Ceremonies." *American Journal of Sociology,* 1956, *61,* 420-424.

Garfinkel, H. *Studies in Ethnomethodology.* Englewood Cliffs, N.J.: Prentice-Hall, 1967.

Goffman, E. *Stigma.* Englewood Cliffs, N.J.: Prentice-Hall, 1963.

Goldberg, M. L., Passow, A. H., and Justman, J. *The Effects of Ability Grouping.* New York: Teachers College Press, 1966.

Goldstein, H., and others. "Schools." In N. Hobbs (Ed.), *Issues in the Classification of Children,* Vol. 2. San Francisco: Jossey-Bass, 1975.

Gouldner, A. W. "Organizational Analysis." In R. K. Merton, L. S. Cottrell, Jr., and L. Broom (Eds.), *Sociology Today.* New York: Basic Books, 1959a.

Gouldner, A. W. "Reciprocity and Autonomy in Functional Theory." In L. Gross (Ed.), *Symposium on Sociological Theory.* New York: Harper & Row, 1959b.

Gouldner, A. W. *The Coming Crisis of Western Sociology.* New York: Basic Books, 1970.

Gubrium, J. F. *Living and Dying at Murray Manor.* New York: St. Martin's Press, 1975.

Gubrium, J. F. "Practical Survey Research and Therapy: An Analogy." *Annals of Phenomenological Sociology,* 1976, *1,* 127-147.

Gutmann, D. L. "Aging Among the Highland Maya: A Comparative Study." *Journal of Personality and Social Psychology,* 1967, *7,* 28-35.

Gutmann, D. L. "Alternatives to Disengagement: The Old Men of the Highland Druze." In J. F. Gubrium (Ed.), *Time, Roles, and Self in Old Age.* New York: Human Sciences Press, 1976.

Hall, G. S. *Adolescence*. New York: Appleton-Century-Crofts, 1916.

Hamblin, R., Buckholdt, D., Ferritor, D., and Kozloff, M. *The Humanization Processes*. New York: Wiley, 1971.

Hargreaves, D. *Sorting Them Out: Two Essays on Social Differentiation*. London: Open University Press, 1972.

Havighurst, R. J. *Developmental Tasks and Education*. London: Longmans, 1951.

Havighurst, R. J., and Dreyer, P. H. *Youth: The Seventy-Fourth Yearbook of the National Society for the Study of Education*. Chicago: University of Chicago Press, 1975.

Haydon, D. F. *Competition for Self in a Therapeutic Setting*. Unpublished master's thesis. Department of Sociology, Marquette University, Milwaukee, Wisc., 1974.

Heath, D. H. *Explorations of Maturity*. New York: Appleton-Century-Crofts, 1965.

Hewitt, J. P., and Hall, P. M. "Social Problems, Problematic Situations, and Quasi-Theories." *American Sociological Review*, 1973, *38*, 367-374.

Hewitt, J. P., and Stokes, R. "Disclaimers." *American Sociological Review*, 1975, *40*, 1-11.

Holt, J. *How Children Fail*. New York: Dell, 1964.

Humphreys, L. *Tearoom Trade*. Chicago: Aldine, 1970.

Hunt, J. McV. *Intelligence and Experience*. New York: Ronald Press, 1961.

Hurn, C. "Recent Trends in the Sociology of Education in Britain." *Harvard Educational Review*, 1976, *46*, 105-114.

Ichheiser, G. *Appearances and Realities*. San Francisco: Jossey-Bass, 1970.

Inkeles, A. "Social Structure and Socialization of Competence." *Harvard Educational Review*, 1966, *36*, 265-283.

Inkeles, A., and Levinson, D. J. "National Character: The Study of Modal Personality and Sociocultural Systems." In G. Lindzey (Ed.), *Handbook of Social Psychology*, Vol. 2. Cambridge, Mass.: Addison-Wesley, 1954.

Jackson, P. W. "After Apple-Picking." *Harvard Educational Review*, 1973, *43*, 51-60.

Jackson, P. *Life in Classrooms.* New York: Holt, Rinehart and Winston, 1968.

Jefferson, G. "Side Sequences." In David Sudnow (Ed.), *Studies in Social Interaction.* New York: Free Press, 1972.

Jencks, C. "The Coleman Report and the Conventional Wisdom." In F. Mosteller and D. P. Moynihan (Eds.), *On Equality of Educational Opportunity.* New York: Random House, 1972.

Jencks, C., and others. *Inequality.* New York: Basic Books, 1972.

Jennings, K. H., and Jennings, S. H. M. "Tests and Experiments with Children." In A. V. Cicourel, and others, *Language Use and School Performance.* New York: Academic Press, 1974.

Kagan, J., and others. *Change and Continuity in Infancy.* New York: Wiley, 1971.

Kaplan, D. H., Dirlam, J. B., and Lanzillotti, R. *Pricing in Big Business: A Case Approach.* Washington: Brookings Institution, 1958.

Kardiner, A. *The Individual and His Society.* New York: Columbia University Press, 1939.

Kardiner, A. *Psychological Frontiers of Society.* New York: Columbia University Press, 1945.

Keniston, K. *Youth as a Stage of Life.* New Haven, Conn.: Yale University Press, 1968.

Kiefer, C. W. *Changing Cultures, Changing Lives.* San Francisco: Jossey-Bass, 1974.

Kimmel, D. C. *Adulthood and Aging: An Interdisciplinary, Developmental View.* New York: Wiley, 1974.

Kluckhohn, C., and Murray, H. A. (Eds.) *Personality in Nature, Society, and Culture.* New York: Knopf, 1948.

Kohl, H. *36 Children.* New York: New American Library, 1968.

Kohlberg, L. "Stage and Sequence: The Cognitive-Developmental Approach to Socialization." In D. A. Goslin (Ed.), *Handbook of Socialization Theory and Research.* Chicago: Rand McNally, 1969.

Kohlberg, L. "Continuities in Childhood and Adult Moral Judgement." In P. B. Baltes and K. W. Schaie (Eds.), *Life-*

span Developmental Psychology: Personality and Socialization. New York: Academic Press, 1973.

Kozol, J. *Death at an Early Age*. Boston: Houghton Mifflin, 1967.

Kuhn, T. S. *The Structure of Scientific Revolutions*. Chicago: University of Chicago Press, 1962.

Kutner, L. "The Illusion of Due Process in Commitment Proceedings." *Northwestern University Law Review*, 1962, *57*, 383-399.

Labov, W. "The Logic of Nonstandard English." In F. Williams (Ed.), *Language and Poverty*. Chicago: Markham, 1970.

Leiter, K. "Ad Hocing in the Schools: A Study of Placement Practices in the Kindergartens of Two Schools." In A. V. Cicourel and others, *Language Use and School Performance*. New York: Academic Press, 1974.

Lemert, E. M. "Paranoia and the Dynamics of Exclusion." *Sociometry*, 1962, *25*, 2-20.

Lemert, E. M. "Records in the Juvenile Court." In S. Wheeler (Ed.), *On Record*. New York: Russell Sage Foundation, 1969.

LeVine, R. A. *Culture, Behavior, and Personality*. Chicago: Aldine, 1973.

Linton, R. *The Study of Man*. New York: Appleton-Century-Crofts, 1936.

Linton, R. *The Cultural Background of Personality*. New York: Appleton-Century-Crofts, 1945.

Lockwood, D. "Some Remarks in 'The Social System.'" In N. J. Demerath III and R. A. Peterson (Eds.), *System, Change, and Conflict*. New York: Free Press, 1967.

Loevinger, J., and Wessler, R. *Measuring Ego Development*. San Francisco: Jossey-Bass, 1970.

Lofland, J. "The New Segregation: A Perspective on Age Categories in America." *Journal of Higher Education*, 1968, *39*, 121-143.

Lofland, J. *Deviance and Identity*. Englewood Cliffs, N.J.: Prentice-Hall, 1969.

Lyman, S. M., and Scott, M. B. *The Sociology of the Absurd*. New York: Appleton-Century-Crofts, 1970.

MacKay, R. "Conceptions of Children and Models of Socialization." In H. P. Dreitzel (Ed.), *Childhood and Socialization.* New York: Macmillan, 1973.

McKinney, J. P. "The Development of Choice Stability in Children and Adolescents." *Journal of Genetic Psychology,* 1968, *113,* 79-83.

McLuhan, M., and Fiore, Q. *The Medium Is the Massage.* New York: Random House, 1967.

Manning, P. K. "Existential Sociology." *Sociological Quarterly,* 1973, *14,* 200-225.

Mead, G. H. *The Philosophy of the Present.* Chicago: Open Court Publishing Co., 1932.

Mead, M. *Coming of Age in Samoa.* New York: William Morrow, 1928.

Mead, M. *Growing Up in New Guinea.* New York: William Morrow, 1930.

Mead, M. *Sex and Temperament in Three Primitive Societies.* New York: William Morrow, 1935.

Mead, M. "The Swaddling Hypothesis: Its Reception." *American Anthropologist,* 1954, *56,* 395-409.

Mead, M., and Metraux, R. *The Study of Culture at a Distance.* Chicago: University of Chicago Press, 1953.

Mehan, H. "Assessing Children's School Performance." In H. P. Dreitzel (Ed.), *Childhood and Socialization: Recent Sociology No. 5.* New York: Macmillan, 1973.

Mehan, H. "Accomplishing Classroom Lessons." In A. V. Cicourel and others, *Language Use and School Performance.* New York: Academic Press, 1974.

Mehan, H., and Wood, H. *The Reality of Ethnomethodology.* New York: Wiley, 1975.

Mehan, H., and Wood, H. "De-Secting Ethnomethodology." *The American Sociologist,* 1976, *11,* 13-21.

Mercer, J. R. "Labels and Reality: Diagnosing Mental Retardation." In L. Rainwater (Ed.), *Social Problems and Public Policy: Deviance and Liberty.* Chicago: Aldine, 1974.

Meyerhoff, H. (Ed.) *The Philosophy of History in Our Time.* Garden City, N.Y.: Doubleday, 1959.

Mills, C. W. "Situated Actions and Vocabularies of Motive." *American Sociological Review,* 1940, *5,* 904-913.

Mills, C. W. *The Sociological Imagination.* New York: Oxford University Press, 1959.

Moller, H. "Youth as a Force in the Modern World." *Comparative Studies in Society and History,* 1968, *10,* 237-260.

Neugarten, B. L. (Ed.) *Middle Age and Aging.* Chicago: University of Chicago Press, 1968.

Parsons, T. "Age and Sex in the Social Structure of the United States." *American Sociological Review,* 1942, *7,* 604-616.

Parsons, T. *The Social System.* New York: Free Press, 1951.

Parsons, T., and Bales, R. F. *Family, Socialization and Interaction Process.* New York: Free Press, 1955.

Perrucci, R. *Circle of Madness.* Englewood Cliffs, N.J.: Prentice-Hall, 1974.

Phillips, D. L. *Abandoning Method.* San Francisco: Jossey-Bass, 1973.

Piaget, J. *The Psychology of Intelligence.* New York: Harcourt Brace Jovanovich, 1947.

Piaget, J. *The Origins of Intelligence in Children.* New York: Norton, 1952.

Piaget, J. *The Language and Thought of the Child.* New York: Meridian Books, 1957.

Piliavin, I., and Briar, S. "Police Encounters With Juveniles." *American Journal of Sociology,* 1964, *70,* 206-214.

Polanyi, M. *Personal Knowledge.* Chicago: University of Chicago Press, 1958.

President's Committee on Mental Retardation. *The Six-hour Retarded Child.* Washington, D.C.: U.S. Government Printing Office, 1970.

Psathas, G. (Ed.) *Phenomenological Sociology.* New York: Wiley, 1973.

Riley, M. W., and Foner, A. *Aging and Society,* Vol. 1. New York: Russell Sage Foundation, 1968.

Rist, R. C. *The Urban School: A Factory for Failure.* Cambridge, Mass.: The MIT Press, 1973.

Rogers, C. "Toward a Modern Approach to Values: The Valuing Process in the Mature Person." *Journal of Abnormal and Social Psychology,* 1964, *68,* 160-167.

Roheim, G. *Psychoanalysis and Anthropology.* New York: International Universities Press, 1950.

Rose, A. M. "Group Consciousness Among the Aging." In A. M. Rose and W. A. Peterson (Eds.), *Older People and Their Social World*. Philadelphia: Davis, 1965a.

Rose, A. M. "The Subculture of the Aging: A Framework for Research in Social Gerontology." In A. M. Rose and W. A. Peterson (Eds.), *Older People and Their Social World*. Philadelphia: Davis, 1965b.

Ross, H. A. "Commitment of the Mentally Ill: Problems of Law and Policy." *Michigan Law Review*, 1959, *57*, 945-1018.

Roszak, T. *The Making of a Counter Culture*. New York: Doubleday, 1969.

Sartre, J. *Nausea*. New York: New Directions, 1964.

Scheff, T. J. "Social Conditions for Rationality: How Urban and Rural Courts Deal with the Mentally Ill." *American Behavioral Scientist*, 1964, *7*, 21-27.

Scheff, T. J. *Being Mentally Ill: A Sociological Theory*. Chicago: Aldine, 1966.

Schultz, T. W. "Reflections on Investment in Man." *Journal of Political Economy*, 1962, *70*, 1-8.

Schutz, A. "Common-Sense and Scientific Interpretation of Human Action." *Philosophy and Phenomenological Research*, 1953, *14*, 1-37.

Schutz, A. *Collected Papers*. Vol. 1: *The Problem of Social Reality*. The Hague: Martinus Nijhoff, 1962.

Schutz, A. *Collected Papers*. Vol. 2: *Studies in Social Theory*. The Hague: Martinus Nijhoff, 1964.

Schutz, A. *The Phenomenology of the Social World*. Translated by F. Lehnert. Evanston, Ill.: Northwestern University Press, 1967.

Schutz, A. *On Phenomenology and Social Relations*. Edited with an introduction by H. R. Wagner. Chicago: University of Chicago Press, 1970a.

Schutz, A. *Reflections on the Problem of Relevance*. New Haven, Conn.: Yale University Press, 1970b.

Scott, M., and Lyman, S. "Accounts." *American Sociological Review*, 1968, *33*, 46-62.

Singer, M. "A Survey of Culture and Personality Theory and Research." In B. Kaplan (Ed.), *Studying Personality Cross-Culturally*. New York: Harper & Row, 1961.

Smith, L. M., and Geoffrey, W. *The Complexities of an Urban Classroom.* New York: Holt, Rinehart and Winston, 1968.

Smith, M. "Equality of Educational Opportunity: The Basic Findings Reconsidered." In F. Mosteller and D. Moynihan (Eds.), *On Equality of Educational Opportunity.* New York: Random House, 1972.

Speier, M. "The Everyday World of the Child." In J. D. Douglas (Ed.), *Understanding Everyday Life.* Chicago: Aldine, 1970.

Spiro, M. E. "Social Systems, Personality and Functional Analysis." In B. Kaplan (Ed.), *Studying Personality Cross-culturally.* New York: Harper & Row, 1961.

Strauss, A. L. *Mirrors and Masks.* New York: Free Press, 1959.

Suchar, C. S. " 'Doing Therapy': Notes on the Training of Psychiatric Personnel." Paper presented at the Annual Meeting of the Midwest Sociological Society, Chicago, Illinois, April 1975.

Sudnow, D. "Normal Crimes: Sociological Features of the Penal Code in a Public Defender Office." *Social Problems,* 1965, *12,* 255-276.

Sudnow, D. *Studies in Social Interaction.* New York: Free Press, 1972.

Symonds, P. *From Adolescent to Adult.* New York: Columbia University Press, 1961.

Taylor, I., Walton, P., and Young, J. *The New Criminology.* New York: Harper & Row, 1973.

Trice, H. M., and Roman, P. M. "Delabeling, Relabeling, and Alcoholics Anonymous." *Social Problems,* 1970, *17,* 538-546.

Turner, R. (Ed.) *Ethnomethodology.* Middlesex, England: Penguin Books, 1974.

Warren, C. A. B., and Johnson, J. M. "A Critique of Labeling Theory from the Phenomenological Perspective." In J. D. Douglas and R. Scott (Eds.), *Theoretical Perspectives on Deviance.* New York: Basic Books, 1973.

Weber, M. *Theory of Social and Economic Organization.* New York: Free Press, 1947.

Weber, M. *From Max Weber: Essays in Sociology.* Edited by H.

Gerth and C. W. Mills. New York: Oxford University Press, 1958.

Wheeler, S. *On Record: Files and Dossiers in American Life.* New York: Russell Sage Foundation, 1969.

White, L. *The Science of Culture.* New York: Farrar, Strauss, 1949.

Whiting, J. W. M., and Child, I. L. *Child Training and Personality: A Cross-Cultural Study.* New Haven, Conn.: Yale University Press, 1953.

Yarrow, M. R., Schwartz, C. G., Murphy, H. S., and Deasy, L. C. "The Psychological Meaning of Mental Illness in the Family." *The Journal of Social Issues,* 1955, *11,* 12-24.

Young, M. F. D. (Ed.) *Knowledge and Control: New Directions for the Sociology of Education.* London: Collier-Macmillan, 1971.

Zigler, E. "The Environmental Mystique: Training the Intellect Versus Development of the Child." *Childhood Education,* 1970, *46,* 402-412.

Zimmerman, D. H. "A Reply to Professor Coser." *The American Sociologist,* 1976, *11,* 4-13.

Zimmerman, D. H., and Pollner, M. "The Everyday World as Phenomenon." In J. D. Douglas (Ed.), *Understanding Everyday Life.* Chicago: Aldine, 1970.

Index

219